Pilgrimage to Anywhere

T0164301

Pilgrimage
to Anywhere

Rijumati Wallis

BOOKS

Winchester, UK
Washington, USA

First published by O-Books, 2011
O-Books is an imprint of John Hunt Publishing Ltd., Laurel House, Station Approach,
Alresford, Hants, SO24 9JH, UK
office1@o-books.net
www.o-books.com

For distributor details and how to order please visit the 'Ordering' section on our website.

Text copyright: Rijumati Wallis 2010

ISBN: 978 1 84694 675 2

A CIP catalogue record for this book is available from the British Library.

Design: Stuart Davies

Printed in the UK by CPI Antony Rowe
Printed in the USA by Offset Paperback Mfrs, Inc

We operate a distinctive and ethical publishing philosophy in all
areas of our business, from our global network of authors to
production and worldwide distribution.

CONTENTS

To my parents, my teachers and the strangers
who helped me

Acknowledgements

With thanks to: the many friends who have helped with the manuscript; VG for the maps; the Museo Carillo Gil, Mexico City, for the image of Orozco's *Christ cuts down his Cross*.

Contact Details

rijumati.wallis@gmail.com

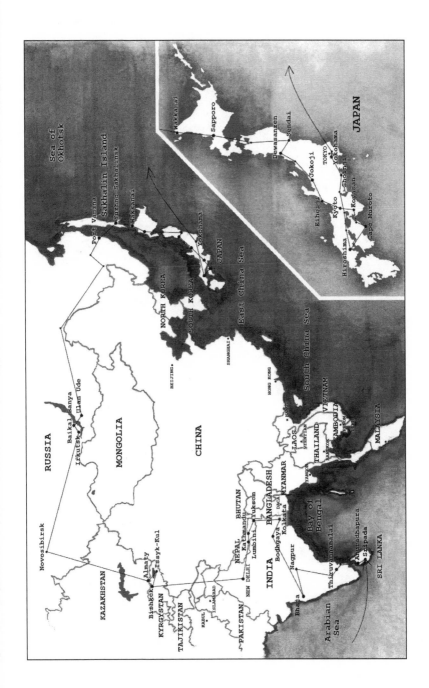

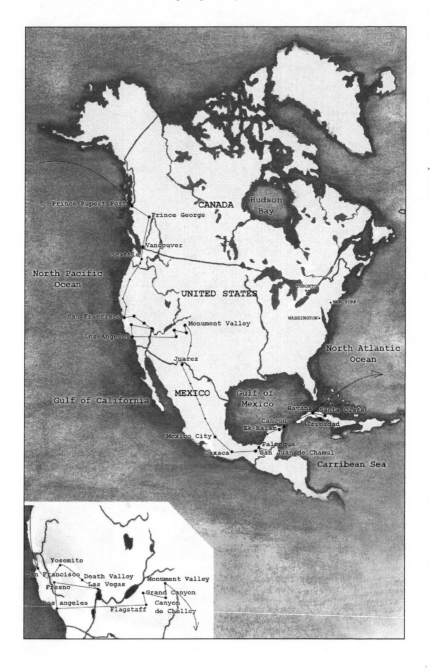

Why I Set Out

What is the difference between travel and pilgrimage? In an age of mass transit to ever more distant and exotic destinations, more often than not travelling involves a short visit, via the ubiquitous airport shopping mall, to a pre-booked hotel at the perfect beach or city of culture. The holiday, now divorced from its original significance as a *holy day*, has value as a way of refreshing and relaxing us, but few would suggest it bears any resemblance to pilgrimage. Yet all travel contains an inescapable element of uncertainty and confusion; whether it is the layout of a new town, a foreign language, alien food, or just the local vagaries of immigration and baggage handling. It is the way we respond to these confusions and uncertainties that reveals the different modes of travelling: are they a hassle to be endured so we can get on with enjoying ourselves, or are they a reminder of the assumptions we brought with us? If we are open to having our assumptions challenged then travelling is one of the most enriching and transformative activities a human being can undertake, and it starts to shade into pilgrimage.

In May 2007, aged 42, I left my job as a director after nearly twenty years working in an ethical trading company, and I prepared to head for the Open Road. It was a wonderful company and a wonderful job: meaningful work with like-minded people, stimulating and demanding. I also lived with close friends in a beautiful 17th century house in Cambridge, England, and had a very nice girlfriend. What was it that led me to leave all of this behind, box up my possessions into a few crates and set off around the world for what turned out to be fifteen months? Despite all the wonderful things in my life I felt trapped, as if I were in a cage: a golden cage. I knew I had to do something before I lost touch with the feeling of freedom and *joie de vivre*. A few years previously, having already been a Buddhist for many years, a spiritual friend said that she saw for me the image of a Buddhist monk sitting alone on a dusty road with nothing but his begging bowl. At the time I was shocked by the implications of this image. Instinctively I recognized its truth but I also knew what it meant giving up. This thread stands out from the rich tapestry of conditions that led to me abandon my nice life in Cambridge. I realized that I should never turn away from what my deepest self knows to be true, no matter how hard it seems, for I would spend the rest of my life regretting it.

As in Walt Whitman's iconic poem, the Open Road sang to me of freedom, a new beginning, opportunity, exploration and transformation. I wanted to travel without a clear destination in mind, travel for a touch of mystery, danger and the unexpected. Who had I become after so many years of life, work and Buddhist practice? I wanted to travel as a way of seeking illumination: in traditional terms as a *pilgrim*. As I fathomed the nature of this journey more deeply it became clear that I would have to avoid air travel as much as possible. There were two reasons for this: firstly, I didn't want the carbon footprint of repeated long-haul flights on my conscience. Secondly, the only affordable option by air was the classic round the world ticket that requires you to book each stage before setting out. Though there was some flexibility in re-arranging the itinerary, I knew I couldn't let my journey be dictated by airline schedules planned over a year in advance. The prime mover on this journey must be the unfolding of the heart and the response to the unexpected. So it would have to be ship, train, bus, jeep, bike, camel, foot and whatever else came my way. I never did find a camel.

You could say that I undertook three journeys: an outer journey, an inner journey and a secret journey. The outer journey was the geography and the various destinations through which I passed. Since I conceived of this journey as a pilgrimage I intended to visit various holy sites, spiritual friends and places of inspiring natural beauty. In fact I had three principal destinations in mind: I wanted to travel again to India, that land of ancient spiritual genius, both to revisit some of the holy sites and also to see the Buddhist teacher who ordained me in 1993 and was now living there. I also had a strong wish to visit Japan, with its spectacular beauty and ancient Buddhist culture, a land utterly different from my European home. Lastly I wanted to visit one of my close friends who lived in Seattle with his family. Thus I sketched a route by land and sea, always going east, connecting these three places. In the course of the next fifteen months I travelled throughout South Asia, Central Asia, Siberia, Japan, North America, Latin America, arriving back in Europe via Spain. The magic of allowing the journey to mould itself was that at the outset I didn't even envisage many of the most significant destinations. In my heart there is both a pilgrim and an independent budget traveler. So whenever I had an equal choice between routes I always thought "I'll take the road less travelled, that's bound to be interesting".

Pilgrimage, however, is not purely about visiting holy sites and spiritual teachers. You can visit the holiest of holies and be left completely untransformed by the experience. Real pilgrimage can only occur when the motivation and state of mind of the pilgrim in some sense resonates with the people and places visited. This is not to say that you don the hair shirt and go shoeless through the dirt. Rather, you go confidently bringing the best of yourself but with a profound sense of what you don't know, and ready to learn. Then the holy places and the spiritual teachers can be benevolent with their gifts. Yet there is more to it than this, since the attitude of awe and reverence for the unfathomable in life is not only restricted to those people and places that are conventionally regarded as holy, special though these may be. Essentially, *all* life is unfathomable, *all* people and places

3

can offer you the fruits of their wisdom, and sometimes the greatest gifts come from the least expected quarters. I discovered that with the attitude of reverence in my heart, anywhere could be a place of pilgrimage. The outer journey was really a *Pilgrimage to Anywhere*.

What of the inner journey? Was I simply having a classic mid-life crisis? Well, I didn't know what to do next with my life and I intuited that a journey of this sort would at least open up the possibilities. I began to realize that to ask "What next" was too ambitious. I no longer knew who I was in the face of bewildering choices and life's potential. Again and again whilst I travelled questions of identity, meaning and purpose arose, resounding at ever deeper levels of my being, at times even shattering parts of my being. Rather than try to answer "What next?" I just needed to take a small step towards finding out *how to discover what next.* That felt a more attainable goal. It has been said that the soul travels at the speed of a camel. Mine seemed to travel at the speed of a snail. Yet slowly, inexorably these questions began to recast themselves into the question, "What is it that I most deeply believe in?" And as the variety of experiences associated with a long journey stirred up all sorts of feelings and emotions, thoughts and intuitions, from time to time I would catch a glimpse of an answer. And the secret journey? I hope that will emerge obliquely as the story unfolds.

What follows is not a systematic and complete description of the journey. Instead, here are thirty-one pieces in roughly geographical order that illuminate the outer, inner or secret dimensions of the journey. I hope that they will find some resonances with your own journey, in whatever dimension this is taking place, and that they will make you laugh from time to time.

Life on Board

No landlubberly musings can adequately prepare one for a great sea voyage; it had long been my dream to undertake one. On a freezing December morning, ice winds blowing off *La Manche*, I arrived in Le Havre, France's largest container port, seeking my berth on the freight ship Hanjin Chicago. We were bound for Colombo and the voyage would take 15 days.

Entering the world of container freight is like entering a zoo of giants and ants. Huge cranes slung over leviathan vessels load hoards of seemingly tiny lorries, each scuttling away with a single container. Hour after hour the cranes delve into the ship's belly, slowly building towers of containers lashed together by steel poles. The operation's efficiency is staggering, having completely supplanted the gangs of stevedores who once ruled the docks. Without these monstrous machines the global economy would not exist.

Though not the biggest of container ships, Hanjin Chicago's vital statistics are impressive: length 280m, width 40m, draught 14m, height 58m. She holds 6,000 containers up to a weight of 68,000 tons and carries 10,000 tons of fuel, a low-grade diesel known as bunker that has to be cleaned in the ship's centrifuges to extract the grit. The engines that power these immense freighters are the largest in the world. Each of the ten pistons is nearly twice the height of a man. The combined torque generated by these exploding chambers is so great that no gears can withstand it, and the direct drive propeller shaft is a solid pillar of steel a meter in diameter. This drives a propeller eight-and-a-half-meters across and generates a maximum speed of 24 knots, the fastest a ship like this can travel without generating uselessly dissipative bow waves. On the Hanjin Line the officers are predominantly German and the crew are Filipino: an advantageous arrangement that allows the owners of the shipping line to pay the crew significantly less. The official language is English, however. The usual crew is 23 plus a few supernumeraries: passengers like myself.

Captain Ziems welcomed me on board warmly. He assured me that I could go anywhere I liked on the ship, apart from the engine room. He also informed me that the ship's *slop chest* was available for the purchase of spirits, snacks and cigarettes: the legacy of maritime terms that the British have bequeathed the world is not particularly elegant. The Captain was a stout, warm and jovial character with a partiality for drink. He ran the ship with an easy rule, such that officers rarely had to be uniformed on duty, and liked to foster an air of informality and bonhomie. But when it came to discipline his word was law. "You are sitting in Mr. Helmut's seat" he reprimanded me as I arrived for dinner on my first night. The three paying passengers Mr. Helmut, Mr. Dove and myself were accorded the status of officers as far as the ship's hierarchy went and as such we were required to eat in the officers' mess where everyone was allotted a place. Changes in the seating arrangements were not permitted.

Life on board revolves around the ritual and liturgy of the seaman's world: duties, eating, drinking and sleeping. The meals offer a regular social context, for much of the work is either solitary or anti-social, like working on the deafening engine decks where everyone is required to wear ear mufflers. With the fixed seating plan there is never any change of mealtime company and after hearing the chief engineer holding forth a few times on identical topics, it seemed as if we were doomed to endless repetition. When not working, eating or sleeping most of the crew seemed to spend their time drinking and watching poor quality DVDs.

Since I had no duties, much as I would have welcomed the opportunity to work my passage, for much of the day I was free to amuse myself. With no casino, no cinema, no heated swimming pool (the small pool could only be filled with chilly sea water) and no ballroom this might seem like the pinnacle of dullness. For me, however, it was perfect: a time to relax, turn inwards, contemplate the journey ahead and spend time getting to know the sea and its moods. Whilst watching from the bridge was always fascinating, seeing how one navigates a ship of this enormity, my favorite spot was on the bow. As the ship thundered through the surf, virtually unmoved by the oncoming swells, just behind the prow was a spot where the air remained completely still, an envelope of calm amidst the gales. Here there lingered a haunting silence, disturbed only by the shrieking of air over steel cables holding the foremast; or was it perhaps the wailing of passing sirens? Here I would watch the sea's changing hues: from grey, to green, to aquamarine, to blue. And here I would marvel at the hardy seabirds far from shore, flying fish capable of darting above the water for 30 meters, dolphins leaping and plunging in the bow wave, and occasionally a solitary turtle or shark. The miraculous views from the prow seemed to be a well-kept secret, for few other people ever stopped there.

In this oceanic realm the elements are strong: sun, wind, water are all raw and visceral in their power. The moods of the sea can turn from benign to menacing in a matter of hours, and it feels as if we aboard are aliens intruding upon another universe. Between the vastnesses of the horizon our world was comprised purely of iron and steel, and suddenly the ship seemed tiny in contrast to the watery immensity. To fall out of this little world would be tantamount to death, in the freezing Atlantic waters hypothermia would set in before you could be rescued. In a sense we were thus prisoners of the sea. This was confirmed to me by chatting with the crew, many of whom dwelt often on how much they missed their families. The bosun, a youthful 51-year-old Filipino, confided that when his time came he longed to retire to the mountains and never to go to sea again. The cook, known affectionately as *Cooky*, told me that modern telecommunications have dramatically changed relationships with those back home, since now it is possible to have a real-time involvement in the lives of one's family. Perhaps this has only made the longing greater. And perhaps this in part explains the hard-drinking culture of seamen, and their love of rum-induced forgetfulness.

For me, however, each stage of the journey filled me with boyish anticipation. Our first sight of Africa was as we approached Tarifa and the Gibraltar Strait. Only a few nautical miles wide, the mouth to the Mediterranean teems with a chaos of vessels moving at all speeds and in all directions. Captain Ziems, contrary to his afternoon routine, remained on the bridge as the second mate made the navigation. The radar was awash with blips, and from a respectful distance I wondered how on earth – or water – we were going to avoid all the potential collisions. Changing the course of 80,000 tons of steel is not done quickly. However, we calmly threaded our way through the Strait and set course for Egypt and the entrance to the Suez Canal.

Every member of the crew has his specialty and, broadly, there are two teams: above deck navigating and maintaining, below deck servicing the engines. The chief engineer, unsurprisingly known as *Chief*, was a man who loved his work. And rightly so since he was responsible for one of the biggest machines ever built. With a team of oilers he monitored and maintained thousands of controls and systems that did everything from driving the engine to creating electricity, heating the cabins and purifying water. He invited the passengers on a tour and as I asked him more probing questions about how the ship worked his eyes lit up and he became more and more animated. It was as if he were playing with the biggest toy ever made. The second mate was a stereotypical young German: quick-tempered, liked everything to be neatly ordered, had strong opinions (he hated India for its lack of punctuality), and said what he thought of you without qualms ("Your drink smells like a toilet"). In a naïve way he was quite likeable: helpful, honest and one day he would probably make a good captain. On his shoulder he sported an intricate tattoo of the grim reaper of which he was rather proud, but then in a candid moment he asked me whether I thought it looked good. Early on during our voyage he started to quiz me about vegetarianism. More or less his opening gambit was "You know that vegetarians live shorter!" However, the Captain quickly diverted this line of conversation by calling him to the radar, obviously wanting to avoid any quarrels with the passengers. The third mate was a Filipino who was rostered on the first night shift, where I would sometimes join him on the bridge, darkened for night vision. We would spend time studying the radar, looking at maritime charts and identifying star constellations. He was a quiet and thoughtful man and, unusually for a seaman, wasn't a drinker, saying that it affected his work too much.

The Christmas Eve Party was no place for a vegetarian Buddhist. Officers and crew gathered in the mess, which had been scantily decorated with unopened packets of tinsel taped to the wall. Clearly we were in desperate need of a woman's touch. The celebrations commenced with the Captain dutifully reading out a worthy and exceedingly dull message from head office in Buxtehude assuring everyone of the Company's goodwill and exhorting all to greater efforts in the year ahead. The crew looked on with bored forbearance. However, when the food and drink arrived their faces lit up. Huge platters of meat, fish and chicken weighed down the tables (still segregated between officers and crew), and large plastic dustbins full to the brim with ice and cans of beer were distributed for easy access. Amid the boozy swilling and the carnivorous masticating there was an air of abundant enjoyment. I managed to find a bit of rice and some vegetable spring rolls to satisfy my hunger, and placated my companions by sampling a fine Tiger beer. When Cooky got out his guitar and started singing Filipino songs it threatened to drown the proceedings in waves of homesickness. The bosun rushed off to the bridge to try and make a satellite call to his family. Others graduated from beer to rum and as the insistence that I participate increased eventually I excused myself and headed for the calm of the bridge. Here the third mate and I watched the stars rising over the Mediterranean and I mused on the voyages of Odysseus, Aeneas, Jason and other ancient heroes who had set sail on these waters.

It was a balmy night as we anchored off Port Said and took on board our Egyptian pilot. He was a corpulent man of middle years who now had command of the ship's course as we navigated the Suez Canal. The cost of taking a merchant vessel through the canal is on average $250,000, and annual revenues exceed $5 billion. No wonder President Nasser was keen to oust the British in 1956. By day our convoy made its way slowly to the mooring at El Ballah where we would wait for the Northern Convoy to pass. The sight of these huge ships passing through the desert must be one of the most incongruous imaginable. The rope handlers from the pilot boat, having finished attaching the

huge hawsers to the mooring posts, took the opportunity to make a little extra baksheesh by setting up a bazaar on the ship's deck. "Come down!" called a portly man with a wonderful Arab moustache. He touted a selection of Egyptian look-alike tat, mostly made in China, and a few dubious-looking digital watches. There wasn't much trading going on. Later at dinner the Captain bemoaned the baksheesh culture of these transits and how it affected his accounting. He'd already given out eight boxes of cigarettes, he complained, he'd offered the pilot one but the man had demanded three, and he feared there would be more to come. German accounting and Egyptian backhanders don't make happy bedfellows.

We passed the Bitter Lake at night and by morning were steaming through the Gulf of Suez at a rate of knots, between deserts and mountains. Perhaps one of the busiest shipping lanes in the world, the Gulf is peppered with oilrigs spewing forth black plumes of carbon before the distant backdrop of ancient peaks. To the west is Egypt, land of the Pharaohs, to the east the mountains of Sinai, land of the Prophets. Once again I mused on the power of ancient myths, for it was here that the old

lawmakers went into the wilderness seeking inspiration and theophany. What a shaping force this rugged geography has exerted on the human race.

Apart from a small scheduled deviation of our course to avoid Somalian pirates as we exited the Red Sea, there were few further diversions to the routine of life on board. As I settled into a mostly solitary existence I began to feel that I was more deeply adrift. Having cast away the anchors of my old life in England, my sense of self was dissolving into the deep blue. Why was I undertaking this journey, what was I doing with my life, who was I now apart from all I had left behind? The questions would take hold of me with a compelling intensity, whirling round my mind, leaving me dizzy and confused. Sometimes the sense of emptiness was very painful and a sort of panic would begin to arise: would I just grow into a lonely old man who had done nothing of worth with his life? Frantically, I would try to find a solution, work out my deeper purpose and identity, but it seemed like a hopeless problem. At last, in a lucid surrendering moment I stumbled into the eye of the maelstrom, and it dawned on me that the very attempt to calculate and grasp an answer was the main problem: the more desperate the calculations, the more empty I felt. I began to sense the great poverty of the calculating mind as it tries to grasp hold of life. My voyage into the Unknown had inadvertently called into consciousness mighty untamed creatures of the Deep. The feelings of emptiness and panic were a by-product of my quest for freedom and had to be forborne patiently. There was no simple answer to the big questions of my meaning and purpose. I had to just find a small step forward. And this was why I was travelling: I was on a pilgrimage to find myself.

Heaven and Hell in Anuradhapura

Walking down a long tree-lined avenue (now road-blocked for security reasons) I entered a high-walled rectangular enclosure, the Buddhist temple of the sacred Sri Bodhi Tree. It is said to be a cutting of the original tree under which the Buddha gained

Enlightenment and was brought to Sri Lanka by Sanghamitta, daughter the of great Mauryan emperor Ashoka whose son, Mihinda, converted the King of Sri Lankan to Buddhism in the 3rd century BCE. All around this fortification grow large scions of the ancient *ficus religiosa*, each in their own right mighty trees. The centerpiece, however, is a raised platform enclosing the majestic tree whose branches shimmer with thousands of Bodhi leaves. The raised platform is tiled in white marble, ideal for circumambulating barefoot and sitting in prayer or meditation. The tree itself is embedded within the platform and guarded by railings leafed with gold and fluttering Buddhist flags. It is a beautiful and peaceful place where nature and devotion come together. I'd arrived in Anuradhapura, the ancient northern capital of Sri Lanka also famous for its ancient parks and lakes, somewhat heedless of being on the edge of a war zone.

As the sun began to set, many white-clad devotees were arriving for prayer. The prevailing mood was of joy; even the ubiquitous soldiers sporting machine guns seemed friendly. Lay worshippers and the occasional monk surrounded the sacred tree in small groups, undertaking their holy observances. The warm evening air was filled with drifting chants, wafting incense and flickering candles. Sitting quietly and observing for a while from a discreet corner I felt moved to chant my own worship and intoned the ancient Pali Buddhist verses of the *Tiratnavandana*, salutation to the Buddha, Dharma and Sangha. Though my eyes were closed I gradually became aware that people had started to congregate around me. Chanting with a sense of joy at being part of the river of devotion to the sacred tree, I felt utterly different from a tourist. When I opened my eyes, a young man next to me simply said "Hello" and then walked away smiling. There were many smiles from the white clothed worshippers at the temple. I left feeling uplifted, looking heavenwards where the sky teemed brilliantly with stars. A meteorite flared into glorious homage and was gone. What an auspicious and beautiful night for meeting the Buddha. I felt the kiss of heaven on my forehead.

With the sense of human connection strong I got chatting to a well-attired gentleman and his wife as we walked back down the long avenue through the balmy night air. Emboldened by the peacefulness I decided to ask him for help in finding a place to eat. He and his wife recommended the Tissawewa restaurant, a short ride away, but already at this time of night there were very few auto-rickshaws to be seen. He found and arranged one with a rough-looking boy of about 18, who was so offhand that I nearly got out before we started. Eventually, we got going and the boy, bringing his old mother along for the ride, set off in the opposite direction to that which my friend had indicated. We started to get further and further away from the city, though I couldn't be sure since perhaps we were just traversing one of the large parks. We were racing at full speed into the deep blue-black night and surrounded by the thick impenetrable darkness of the jungle. Did they plan to take me somewhere secluded and rob me or worse? I tapped the boy's shoulder but he ignored me. I considered jumping out and making an escape, but at this speed a twisted ankle was likely to be the least I would get away with. Soon, to my relief, we reversed direction and began to head towards town by a back road. Suddenly we met a checkpoint and two soldiers pulled us over shouting loudly and angrily, something was clearly wrong. They demanded papers from the boy, he and his mother became fearful and conciliatory. Were they suspected of being Tamil sympathizers, was it forbidden for them to travel after dark? The soldiers swaggered, brandishing their machine guns. The younger soldier, perhaps only 18, had hyped-up, bulging eyes, and giggled erratically as he poked his head into the auto-rickshaw and asked me where I was from in broken English. Was it my imagination or was he on amphetamines? The older soldier, perhaps in his late 30s but looking over 50, had a hard, tired look in his eyes, without a smile or softness: just a cold deadening stare. I knew I had to be very careful not to alarm these men with their mood of restrained aggression. Occasional bursts of angry questioning were followed by long menacing silences, lasting for minutes at a time. The boy and his mother had all their papers out, there was a kind of pathetic pleading in their voices and she was almost bent double in fear. It seemed ludicrous to imagine these soldiers would attempt any violence with a foreign tourist involved, but in a sudden shock it flashed before me that were there to be violence they would have to kill all three of us and dispose of the bodies. The impact of this intuition ricocheted through my consciousness, a hot flush shot through my body, an intimation of rising panic. And then, as if receiving a blessing, the mantra of Green Tara, Buddhist goddess of compassion who protects from fear, arose in the depths of my mind and something in me relaxed. Perhaps the moment of death was approaching, here in the dark Sri Lankan jungle. Some part of me accepted this, I felt incredibly aware and alive. The mantra continued to sound without any conscious effort on my part. Time slowed to moments of prolonged intensity.

As the minutes languished and the mood dulled from intensity to indifference, it seemed less and less likely that anything violent would take place. The mood of fear and aggression seemed to subside. It only 8.00 p.m. and occasionally, other vehicles passed by unchecked. We were caught at the checkpoint for nearly 20 minutes, though it seemed like eternity; but in the end relief came. For no apparent reason the older soldier came to a decision and suddenly moved us on with a brash and careless wave of the hand. The boy raced us away and into a built-up part of the city once more. We drove onwards for another few kilometers before he tried to deposit me at the wrong hotel. Here a friendly lady gave him clear directions and eventually we got to the Tissawewa Grand. The boy and his mother disappeared quickly, barely waiting for payment, all three of us were still in shock. I wondered how they would get across town again safely, perhaps they wouldn't bother but just sit out the night somewhere nearby.

Situated in the old royal pleasure gardens the Tissawewa certainly lived up to the name *Grand*. However the food arrived cold and I sent it back, and then it was too spicy to eat. In any case, after such a brush with death my appetite was severely curtailed. I still had the problem of returning to my own hotel a few kilometers across town and I was decidedly jumpy about another night trip in an auto-rickshaw, especially as it was now much later, and the city was utterly silent. A friendly waiter said all would be fine in a typically superficial South Asian way, but as the hotel receptionist phoned around he had difficulty in finding any sort of taxi. Eventually an auto-rickshaw arrived driven by a smartly attired middle-aged man, he seemed reluctant to be there, but nonetheless accommodating. I shared the taxi with a couple of friendly Milanese women who were going in the same direction. The roads were totally deserted apart from packs of dogs that seemed to run wild as if they alone were the true night-time denizens of Anuradhapura. After passing another checkpoint uneventfully we were chased by a pack of snarling hounds, acting as if they were hunting our taxi like a large prey. All three of us were silent and kept our hands and feet well away from the open doorway of the auto-rickshaw and those vicious muzzles. When humans are absent from the city streets the dogs become kings. The frisson of fear was once again present and we were relieved to arrive at our respective hotels. And thus in Anuradhapura I had a taste of both heaven and hell in the same evening.

Dawn on Sripada

I had been in war-torn Sri Lanka for a month. After visiting the Buddhist caves of Dambulla, the ancient cities of Polonnaruwa, Sigiriya and Anuradhapura, the temples of Kandy, the luscious jungle, the beaches of Galle and the chaos of Colombo (complete with daily bombings), I felt culturally full-up, and my stay was rapidly nearing its end. However, the image of Sripada, Sri Lanka's most holy mountain, kept coming into my mind. Rising dramatically from the Sri Lankan highlands like a natural pyramid above the vast Ceylonese tea plantations, it is considered sacred to no less than four great religions. On its

summit is a boulder with a footprint-like indentation that has sparked many myths. To Hindus it is the footprint of Shiva, to Buddhists it is where the Buddha stepped down from heaven after teaching the Dharma to his deceased mother, to Muslims and Christians it is Adam's footprint as he stepped into this world after the Fall and thus the mountain is also known as Adam's Peak. As an aspiring pilgrim I realized that I needed to answer the mountain's call. So in the last few days I hurriedly booked a train, made a few enquiries, received a few recommendations and flung myself into the unknown yet again.

The railway from Colombo into the highlands is a masterful feat of engineering, one of the happier consequences of the British colonial period. The train snakes its way along precipitous ridges through the jungle towards the plateau at Kandy. The views are stunning and the landscape forbidding, it is no wonder that it took over 200 years for European invaders to capture Kandy: few colonial armies were willing to take on such a broken and buckled topography. My companion for the journey to the *Up Country* was Tom Sutherland, a veteran American traveler. He

regaled me with stories of his adventures in Asia and South America and we met as kindred spirits. As the hours passed with our train halting occasionally at idyllic hill stations like Watawalla, our conversations became richer, more personal and more meaningful in a magical way that is sometimes possible between newly-met travelers. We touched on deeply held values and beliefs and both became inspired and uplifted. Tom later wrote to me of spiritual insights and saying "The simplest things are the hardest, and it helps to be reminded of them by conversing with a kindred spirit". We both knew that it was unlikely we would ever meet again. How wonderful that complete strangers can make a heartfelt connection like this.

At Hatton the usual South Asian chaos ensued at the bus stand. It seemed as if a great many people were headed for Sripada that evening, and there was much uncertainty about the availability of buses. Eventually, a direct bus to Dalhousie turned up and we all crammed on. I was left seat-less until two bright-eyed Sri Lanka boys doubled up to make space for me. They

were going to climb Sripada for the first time, were very excited and plied me with the usual questions: "Where are you from?" "Are you married?" A festival atmosphere enthused the bus and it began to dawn on me that these great throngs of pilgrims were heading to Sripada because tonight was the full moon. The tradition of pilgrimage to Sripada is old. It is most propitious to climb the mountain on full moon night and arrive in time to see the daybreak on the summit. At 2,200m and with over 5,000 steps the climb is not for the faint-hearted. By pure chance I was undertaking this labor on the holiest day.

Arriving in Dalhousie after fourteen hours of travel and making my way to the guesthouse recommended by a friend, I fortuitously obtained the last available room and found myself just in time to join a large communal supper for Western travelers all intent on making the night climb of Sripada. Amongst them were three French doctors who had been working in the war zone and told distressing stories about the civil war and the plight of the Tamils. The contrast between our traveler's camaraderie and the stories of the war was very stark.

At 2.00 a.m. I rose along with other bleary-eyed aspirants and prepared to depart into the jungle's engulfing darkness and silence. I made my way alone past shut-up stalls and shops along the pilgrim's road. Few people stirred and I hoped the route would be obvious. Trees loomed like giants out of the shadows; occasionally a creature would start somewhere in the jungle and my senses were alert, on tenterhooks. Who, or what, was watching me? There is always a frisson of fear when alone in the jungle at night. After being accosted by some drunken Sri Lankan teenage boys I teamed up with three young friends from the guesthouse, Kate, Steve and Stefan. As the four of us climbed higher the path got steeper and the canopy thinned permitting the silver radiance of the full moon to illuminate our way. We chatted a little. The three were all students in their early twenties doing voluntary service overseas. Kate was intelligent, idealistic and beautiful; I couldn't help slightly falling in love with her. The stream of pilgrims increased and we passed whole families including even grandparents slowly making their way upwards. The determination of these old people to make the climb moved me greatly. From time to time the sound of a generator emerged from the night and we found ourselves approaching a makeshift café with flickering fluorescent tubes, offering tea and other refreshments. At the final stage the stone steps became metal ladders and we had to queue to ascend. At last, around 4.30 a.m. we made the summit. It was two hours before dawn and already there were hundreds of people milling around the small patio that encircles the Temple of the Footprint. It was cold and our clothes were damp with sweat. In several places small braziers were burning, surrounded by shivering individuals; most had climbed without jumpers or coats. We huddled together sharing my raincoat for warmth and talked about our lives and our hopes. Kate had done other voluntary work in Ecuador and wanted to be a doctor. Aged 23 she was daunted by the choices that immediately lay ahead of her, knowing they would irrevocably shape her future. It was as if she were afraid to make the first independent brushstroke on the canvas of her life. She was fascinated by my descriptions of meditation and my having given up a good life in Cambridge to set out on this journey. She said she wanted to meet me again somewhere on my travels.

Around 6.00 a.m., the sky started to brighten in the east, Sripada temple was now thronging with people. Some were here out of devotion, some for the festival atmosphere, but all were rapt in silent admiration at the glory of the sunrise. The subtle, ever shifting dawn canvas etched itself unforgettably on my inner eye. The temple guardians started their drumming, as if calling forth the sun. The uniqueness of Sripada is that it allows the dogmatic differences between Hindu, Buddhist, Muslim and Christian to fall away as we all share a sense of wonder and delight. The crescendo came as the sun licked over the eastern horizon, great cheers rising from the crowd, and then we turned to the western rim to see the famous shadow. Despite the skewedness of Sripada's physical form, its dawn shadow presents a near perfect isosceles triangle which hovers momentarily above the blanket of cloud and then shoots towards the western base of the mountain. The waxing light revealed a vista of jungle-covered granite peaks floating like a miraculous archipelago in a sea of clouds. To the east were spectacular glimpses of the waters of the sprawling Maskeliya reservoir. The warmth of the rising sun, the vistas and the companionship left me joyful and lost for words.

The descent was rapid and crowded. Solemnity broke into festivity, the mountain was soon heaving with people talking, buying and selling. By the time we reached our guesthouse my legs were quivering from the strain of 10,000 steps. We were inspired by a sense of achievement, but really the greatest achievement was that of the old men and women who had struggled to the peak out of devotion. Our generous hosts had provided a delicious slap-up breakfast and then most of the travelers retired for a nap before departing. I decided to stay an extra night to explore the Up Country a little more and reflect on the mysterious synchronicity of this pilgrimage to Sripada. Kate and I parted warmly with promises to keep in touch. I never heard from her again.

Fawlty Keys

Though I had arrived in Sri Lanka by ship, my attempts to secure a departure by sea had come to naught. After three weeks of trying, it became clear that the intensifying civil war had debarred all sea transits to India and the only way to keep my no-fly principle would involve bribery or risk-taking, probably both. With some regret at compromising so early in the journey I realized that my principles had to adapt when I faced political roadblocks. So I booked on the shortest possible flight over the Palk Strait, to Trichy in Tamil Nadu, a mere 40 minutes away. Thus I arrived in the town of Seeduwa, really just a nondescript sprawl of shops, hotels and office buildings along five kilometers of the busy Negombo highway. My destination was the Copper Lamp Hotel, a few kilometers from the airport, where next morning I had an early flight.

Ostensibly the Copper Lamp Hotel is a reputable modern establishment, a generously built four-storey building with nicely tiled rooms. However the up market veneer is very thin indeed. On being shown my room I queried whether the sheets on the bed were clean, was assured that they were, but could see they were covered in hair and even the odd nail clipping. Being a good-natured Buddhist on a tight budget I shook the sheet out, but also demanded a fresh one. The hairy pillowcases I covered in a shawl. The staff were friendly and ever helpful, it's just that the hotel was rather shambolic. The old man known as *Uncle* brought me a bowl of hot water for washing, he had a genuinely warm glint in his eye. On discovering that I was English he made small talk about Lady Diana, and at my request even swept the floor, which was also covered in hair. So far so good, the room was shaping up. The only missing ingredient was a mosquito net and although I had my own there was no hook on which to attach it. I went down to see the reception and was assured of receiving some help, but on returning to my room couldn't get back in. I recalled that the manager had had problems with the lock when he gave me the key, but since the door had been already open took no further action. The key definitely didn't fit, and looking more closely I saw that it had the number 101 in small hand written ballpoint scrawled across the bottom, whereas my room was 102. I pointed this out to the manager as he accompanied me back to the room but he seemed uninterested and persisted in trying to force the key in the lock. After several exasperating minutes of key waggling, he demanded "Was this the key I gave you?" as if I'd somehow switched a false key into his hands.

Eventually he gave up and went to find the spare keys, none of which of course were numbered. One of them did indeed open the door. He seemed to express a great deal of satisfaction at his foresight as he said to me "there is a small problem with this key", pointing to my original, something that had been patently obvious from the start. At this point, the door now open he seemed ready to depart, but he didn't offer me the spare key. He said that as long I locked the room from the inside no one could get in. "Well that's great" I thought, I'd figured that out about 20 minutes earlier. "What if I want to go out?" I demanded, "Ah yes, if you want to go out" he echoed thoughtfully as if this was a novel idea. I once again pointed out that the number on the key was for a different room to mine. At this point he decided to try the key for a third and completely different room, 103. This key actually worked, it was numbered 103 and it opened the door to room 103. Perhaps we were getting somewhere, or perhaps not since 103 was a room that had no guest. Finally I decided to force the logic of the impasse and asked him to try the key he'd originally given me in the door for room 101. He sent his obliging young man who had arrived with a beaming smile and an air of helpfulness. Surprisingly it worked. There was no "small problem" with the key when taken to the right door. At this point a penny seemed to drop and in a short time a new key marked 102 was procured and, to our mutual relief, it opened my door. There were smiles all round, and some mutterings about the lady at the front desk giving the wrong key.

As he was about to depart I once again asked for a hook to be put up on which I could hang my mosquito net, the very reason the whole key saga had happened. He said "Ah yes I have the same problem with mosquitoes, I can give you a mosquito coil" clearly evading the difficulty of hanging the net from the wall. I explained that with nearly 30 bites currently on my body I seemed to qualify as the main dinner course for most local blood-sucking creatures and would feel much happier sleeping under a net, either one belonging to the hotel or my own. He pointed to a rusty protrusion from the ceiling that wasn't above the bed and clearly any net hanging from it would get entangled in the fan. Summoning what deep reserves of patience I could find I pointed out the impossibility of this option to him. At this point his increased assurances of his desire to be of assistance, sounded utterly hollow and left no room for confidence. When I asked pointedly whether his assistance would be now or later, he started asking what time I would like to go to sleep. Since it was currently 3.30 p.m. he seemed to be envisaging a time scale way beyond that which I normally allow for simply attaching a hook to the wall. In a moment of sheer desperation I offered to do it myself if he could provide me with a hammer and nail, at which he smiled, perhaps sensing that he was winning this duel between Western directness and Eastern inscrutability. "There is an Uncle here, he will come to your assistance" seemed to be his final word on the matter, and I was left wondering how I had been so convincingly out-maneuvered. I decided to give it up as a bad job and visit the famous beach at Negombo to see the sunset.

Negombo bus stand was thronging with people, in fact there seemed to be a public event happening in the middle of the intersection between the two main highways. A canopy and array of plastic chairs had been arranged on the tarmac and the little old ladies had arrived in their best saris. I stared on in disbelief at the

incongruity of the venue. After a gorgeous orange sunset looking out across the Indian Ocean and a delicious thali I caught the bus back to my hotel in Seeduwa. The only problem was that it was now pitch dark, there being almost no street lights, and I had no idea where along the sprawling highway conurbation I should alight. I explained this to the bus conductor as he took my money and in confident English he assured me he knew the stop for my hotel and would set me down there, I relaxed. When some 20 minutes later he dropped me in front of a completely different hotel, I knew I was stranded. Was Copper Lamp Hotel north or south of here, how far away? Asking within this new hotel I received blank stares, no one seemed to have ever heard of Copper Lamp Hotel, I even began to wonder whether perhaps it was just a figment of my deranged imagination. Then I remembered that I had their business card in my pocket and could ring them for directions. "I am sorry I cannot help you" was all I could get out of the receptionist as I explained my predicament and gave him details of where I was, "but are you north or south of this hotel?" I pleaded not knowing what else to do. "I am sorry I cannot help you" came the inevitable liturgy. Finally guessing from my own horse-sense of direction that I needed to go north I decided to risk life and limb by trying to flag down a rickshaw on the busy two lane highway in the dark. A game of cat and mouse ensued in which I would block the carriageway waving my hands wildly until just before the moment of impact the taxi driver would swerve as I jumped out of the way. At last one of these taxi men got the message and screeched to a halt a little way down the tarmac. I got him to drive me north slowly for a few kilometers until eventually I recognized the dimly lit hoarding of Copper Lamp, I had never imagined that this would fill me with so much joy.

Back in the room, things were just as I'd left them, and the local blood-suckers were squaring up for a banquet. In a peak of stubbornness I decided to mount a vigil at the reception desk until the manager did something to help. But after what seemed like stalemate, it was after all too late for me to check out for the night and try somewhere else, I gave up and went back to the room resigned to an itchy and uncomfortable fate. So when there was a knock on the door 20 minutes later I was most surprised. Uncle and a helper had arrived with a long stretch of nylon rope. He proceeded to string this between the door closer and the curtain rail, allowing me to hang my net above the bed. Good-naturedly he explained that the walls were solid concrete and that trying to hammer in a nail wouldn't work. In a flash it dawned on me that the whole charade had a crazy South Asian logic to it. I just hadn't understood what I was asking of them. In the end I had a good night's sleep and the mosquitoes, disgusted, left for a feed elsewhere. The next morning I got to the airport in good time but nearly missed my flight because it never appeared on the information displays, yet another story of Western expectations meeting Asian realities.

A visit to the Cave

An unforeseen and uplifting consequence of my journey was the inexorable call of holy mountains. Whenever I heard about a sacred peak my ears would prick up, and I would feel a thrill of interest. That is how I came to be travelling across Tamil Nadu along suffocatingly dusty roads in a furnace-like bus whose blaring Bollywood music was so loud that I could only bear it by putting in earplugs. I was on my way to Thiruvannamalai at the base of Arunachala, the sacred Mountain of the Dawn. I had just left a restful but spiritually disappointing visit to the Aurobindo ashram in Pondicherry, and a fascinating but equally unmoving visit to the famous temple of Nataraja in Chidambaram. Both places have a great spiritual reputation but had left me rather cold. At the Aurobindo ashram it was unfriendliness and the air of *trying too hard* spirituality around Aurobindo's grave, whilst at Chidambaram it was my sheer incomprehension at the arcane liturgy. Nataraja, the form of Shiva that dances the creation and destruction of the world, stands dancing in a halo of flames with tremendous grace and power. He had moved me strongly since I first encountered him in my late teens and I hoped to find a deeper connection with this archetypal figure by visiting one of the most important temples of his cult. Although the Brahmins at Chidambaram were friendly enough there seemed to be nothing in their complex and exclusive rituals with which a non-Hindu could connect. Sadly I had to admit that I felt a deeper resonance with the principle of Nataraja by simply spending ten minutes gazing at the fine Chola dynasty statue in the British Museum. At Srirangam temple in Trichy it had been a rather different story. This vast and impressive temple certainly had a powerful atmosphere, but most of the shrines I visited (almost every Hindu deity is represented in some form in the 150 acre complex) emanated an ancient chthonic air. In Srirangam I felt more susceptible to being possessed by a primeval force than being inspired by a spiritual muse.

Arunachala is also sacred to Shiva, though in this case because of the cult of the lingam, Shiva's penis. Apparently Arunachala is the point in space and time where the blazing lingam first manifested in the universe. As such the mountain hosts an annual festival in which, as I was to discover firsthand, the summit is doused in ghee and set alight, burning in homage to the apparition of the sacred member. What I love about Hinduism is the unashamedness with which a huge blazing penis can be an object of devotion. Thiruvannamalai has long been a place of pilgrimage for yogis and sadhus, and in the early 20th century the great yogi Ramana Maharshi lived in a cave on the mountain for many years, later founding an ashram. His fame as a meditator drew many disciples to him and my own Buddhist teacher, Sangharakshita, came here in the late 1940s to seek guidance in meditation from him. Sangharakshita and a friend had spent a number of months living in the said cave, and one night he had a significant and pivotal vision of the Buddha Amitabha, the red Buddha of compassion. For me therefore the holy mountain was doubly a place of pilgrimage.

Arriving in Thiruvannamalai I was immediately struck by the friendliness of the people as compared to Trichy, Chidambaram and Pondicherry. The town offered a bright and helpful welcome. At the first hotel I tried the receptionist could only offer me one night, but he went to some lengths to help me find alternative accommodation. At the Ramana Maharshi ashram, where you usually have to book months in advance, I spoke to the director explaining that I was a disciple of Sangharakshita who had learnt from the Maharshi 50 years ago. He listened sympathetically, recommended that I apply to the ashram next door and come to see him again in a couple of days. He promised also that should I need it he would find someone to show me the way to the *Virupaksa Cave* where Sangharakshita had his vision all those decades ago. I was very grateful for these small acts of helpfulness and was fast warming to Thiruvannamalai.

From the rear of the ashram a paved path climbs gently. Leaving the town behind you slip between the mountain and a large hill adorned by tall and graceful trees. Shielded by these ancient rocks suddenly all the din of India is silenced and a beautiful tranquility pervades the forest. Amidst the butterflies and flowers, lizards and tiny squirrels nature is astonishingly peaceful. In a continent so populous and polluted with noises of every sort, this haven of silence comes as a delightful surprise, a blessed place. Further along you descend rapidly down roughly-hewn steps to the Virupaksa Cave. Snaking around a huge boulder you suddenly emerge onto a small secluded platform, with a *kuti* (hut) butting onto the rock, the entrance to the sacred cave. A vine of crimson flowers grows along the wall and a few young trees offer shade from the searing Tamil Nadu sun. Great mud-colored boulders enclose the platform on three sides, giving it an air of seclusion and harmony with nature. Below is a clear

vista of the large and colorful Arunachaleswar temple, its four great gateways adorned with hundreds of gods. This lovely spot is only slightly marred by the din of horns, engines and Bollywood music echoing up from the town below. The rise of industrial India hasn't benefited the mountain's peacefulness.

I entered the cave and was instantly disorientated by the pitch-blackness and the hot, stuffy, airless atmosphere. It felt oppressive. The cave had been heavily molded in concrete with a central cube surmounted by a solid Hindu *lump* decorated by an orange cloth. Only the sharply descending roof indicated that this was once a natural rock formation, and even this had been

sealed in paint. Slowly I became aware that there were two motionless figures meditating in the dark. Signs asked for silence so I restrained my natural impulse to chant devotional verses. Instead I sat for some time silently intoning the mantra of Amitabha. After a while the two unknown figures departed and I chanted out loud admiring the resonant echo. With further arrivals I began to feel the soporific effect of the airless heat. I left and lay down on the bulwarks feeling disappointed. After so long a journey to this cave my expectations had built up and I longed for some significant spiritual experience here. But I felt no special joy or inspiration. Virupaksa Cave was no longer an abode of yogis and hermits, but a museum piece for spiritual tourists, and I had become one of them. By grasping at spiritual experiences I was learning once again the foremost lesson of a pilgrim: *the expectation of realization is what hinders realization most.* I consoled myself that perhaps another visit with less loaded expectations would be more fruitful. The following afternoon I came again. As before the airless and oppressive atmosphere in the cave was most unsuitable for meditation, so instead I meditated outside on the shaded platform. This time the gentle breeze, the rocks and flowers and the spirit of the place lifted me into a still, effortless, radiant state of mind. I felt refreshed and that in some way I had found what I sought. Returning to the Ramana Maharshi ashram I got chatting to one of the many colorful westerners who abound in Thiruvannamalai, a Dutch-gone-native swami with a long, matted grey locks and his young, silent Japanese girlfriend. He declared that he had been in India for twenty years, was a painter, played the flute, and spent his time travelling the length and breadth of the subcontinent. He ranted a little about the government, though it didn't seem to be any particular government, and extolled the beauties of Tamil Nadu's rural landscape. I didn't risk asking him *what* or *where* he painted lest I seem too incredulous.

At 6.00 a.m. next morning I headed for Arunachala's summit rising 800m above the plain. The peak was shrouded in mist, or was it perhaps smoke from the burning lingam? Within minutes a man was following me asking where I was going. "To the top" I replied, at which he seemed amazed and perplexed. He spoke rapidly to another man, and I sensed that I was being seen as a baksheesh opportunity. There followed a bizarre quarrel between the two of them as both suggested they knew the path to the summit and pointed in opposite directions, a typically Indian dilemma. I followed the lower path for a little way, but my own judgment told me it was wrong. Doubling back I found the two of them still bickering over me and the way to the top. In the end I just strode off along the upper path, to the evident satisfaction of the one and the crest-fallen disappointment of the other. Still following me he obviously wanted to act as my paid guide. I avoided his overtures saying forcefully "I don't want a guide!" He said that he worked on the mountain for the forestry board, though he had no uniform. He walked ahead of me some way, we weren't really climbing together, but when I stopped he waited for me.

To start with the climb was straightforward; there were even a few barefoot western devotees already making their way to the holy caves. The sky was grey with haze and cloud, a good day for climbing in fiery Tamil Nadu. We left the main path following roughly daubed marks *To the Mountain*. My self-appointed guide, who called himself *Thorai*, waited for me to catch up and we started to ascend rapidly. Soon I was sweating heavily. Thorai lithe, fit and without any baggage climbed effortlessly. He said that he'd been working on the mountain for many years. The path was evident but rough, with many small boulders jammed into a makeshift uneven stairway. Though high above Thiruvannamalai, the din of the town resounded as if we were standing in the bazaar. The vegetation thinned as we climbed. Drenched in sweat I twice rested on large boulders, gazing out across the haze to the plains. I felt light-headed and wondered if I would have to turn back. Thorai led me by an easier route and although his guidance was given without my consent, I appreciated it. I decided I would give him 50 rupees.

As we came close to the top, nearly two hours later, the mountain became one solid mass of granite. The refuse also became ubiquitous: plastic bags and wrappers strewn as if

marking the path to the holy summit. Finally emerging out of the lazy mists we saw two makeshift shacks thrown together with plastic, bits of string and wooden poles. Thorai entered one and, amazingly, there appeared a young sadhu called Jodi, ready with a filthy coconut cup brimming with hot chai, a most welcome apparition. We sat there sipping the tea, enjoying a sense of achievement. Thorai lifted his cup high intoning "OM Arunachala". Also in attendance were a couple of healthy-looking dogs, a rare sight in India, and a few very cheeky monkeys who kept trying their luck, especially when I peeled an orange and offered it around. Jodi said that he often slept here at the summit and that he spent his time either collecting food or doing *puja*, devotional practice. I said that I also wanted to do puja and he gave me a little mat saying "the top is covered in ghee". Sure enough, as we climbed onto the highest rock we found it so black and greasy as to be almost impassable. This was the aftermath of the annual Shiva festival. Thorai cautioned me to be careful and took me to a nice spot, free of ghee, where I could meditate and recite a puja. At this point, catching me by surprise, he asked for payment. I gave him 50 rupees, but he was very unhappy, protesting "I've climbed 3,000ft, I am a poor man". In the end I made it 100 rupees and he left rather disgruntled.

Sitting on the mountain top drenched in sweat in the drifting mists I was appreciably chilled. I wrapped myself in a shawl and begin to chant a puja. The verses rolled out mechanically, but whether it was the strain of the climb or an incipient headache, there was little feeling in them. After an equally bland meditation I was rejuvenated by playing a tune on my tin whistle. "Stairway to Heaven" by Led Zeppelin seemed like an appropriate ode for a sacred mountain. On the way down I returned the mat to Jodi and offered him a donation of 10 rupees. He didn't want to accept, but I couldn't tell if he really wanted nothing, or just felt 10 rupees was too small. The combination of money, Westerners and Indians is often incomprehensible.

No description of Thiruvannamalai could be complete without mentioning the large international community of spiritual seekers who ranged from young adventurers to aged devotees. In the room adjacent to mine at the ashram an old Western lady, deeply wrinkled and wearing a long flowing white Indian dress, chanted her pujas every few hours with a halting, breathless voice, yet with a deep look of sincerity on her face. But many of the Westerners I met seemed distant and unfriendly, as if absorbed in the world of their own spirituality. For the most part they participated in various *satsangs* or truth meetings where it was claimed you could gain almost any spiritual attainment. I noticed a course emphasizing that it was teaching traditional Advaita Vedanta, another boasting to teach neo-Advaita Vedanta. Both had a hefty price tag coming in at several hundred dollars. There were courses on obscure energy-healing methods, most of which I'd never heard of, all types of yoga and meditation, and courses where you simply met an Awakened person (also costing hundreds of dollars). Most of the teachers being advertised were Westerners. Many of them claimed to be

Awakened or *awakened* (it wasn't clear what the capitalization of this overused word was meant to signify).

According to one elderly, yet lively lady from Kent, Thiruvannamalai was a bit of a spiritual supermarket, rather like transplanting Glastonbury to South India. "But", she added "it makes me feel so much younger being here", and from her face I could see that this was true. I made one good friend, an Israeli yoga teacher in her late 50s called *Aytana*. We practiced yoga each day and talked about life, the path of spiritual practice and Israeli politics. Although we found common ground on the first two issues, politics was a different story: as a rule it is best to avoid talking about Middle Eastern politics with Israelis. I liked Aytana for her no-nonsense and devoted practice and her youthfulness of spirit.

One day over a huge and tasty 25 rupee thali from the ashram kitchen, I met an English woman in her early forties. Or rather she met me by sitting opposite and starting conversation. She seemed like a hardened Advaita seeker and, though attractive, there was little innocence in her eyes. With her was a silent German with a somewhat boorish appearance to whom she paid almost no attention. The only time they spoke to each other was when he grunted a request for the rice from her plate. She kept it back for a while, as if holding out for something in return, but then gave it to him. I couldn't mistake the feeling that she wanted something from me, which left me intrigued but wary. Having stayed a few days, seen the cave, climbed the mountain and tasted the Advaita scene, I began to feel that I didn't belong in Thiruvannamalai. It was time to head north and to find Buddhist India.

From Bhaja to Bodhgaya

Bodhgaya is the site of the sacred Bodhi Tree beneath which the Buddha gained Enlightenment over 2,500 years ago. Here all the rivers of Buddhism find their source, and now all those rivers flow back to modern Bodhgaya as Buddhist pilgrims from around the world renew the teaching of the Buddha in India

where it has been silent for 1,000 years. The Mahabodhi temple has been lovingly restored after centuries of neglect, work that took many decades. Especially onerous was wresting control of the site from the local Hindu priests who were hostile to Buddhism. This was largely achieved in the early 20th century through the efforts of the vigorous Sri Lankan Buddhist missionary Anagarika Dharmapala. All who come to Bodhgaya and bask in its uplifting atmosphere owe a great debt of gratitude to Dharmapala.

I was in Bodhgaya to gaze upon and practice the teachings of the Buddha at the seat of Enlightenment. Bihar's hot, dry climate means that worship at the temple usually takes place outdoors in the lovely park surrounding the Bodhi Tree and monumental tower. Fittingly, the tree's current incarnation was grown from a cutting brought back from the Anuradhapura Bodhi Tree in Sri Lanka. Here you listen to the collected voices of Thai, Burmese, Tibetan, Sri Lankan, Korean, Japanese, Western and others singing praises. You see many circumambulating the Holy Tree and watch those meditating on what the Buddha attained. At all times of day visitors and devotees come and go in a sea of colors: maroon, orange, white, denim blue. Joining in with this ebb and flow of devotion and inspiration, you let go of your national and cultural identity for a while, and submerge yourself in the waters of faith. A beautiful atmosphere of sharing and respect pervades the temple, and it is usual for complete strangers to support each other in various ways.

Most fervent of all are the hundreds of prostrating Tibetans with their springboards arrayed around the sacred Tree. Hour after hour, they throw themselves to the ground clocking up their quota of 100,000 prostrations required by the lamas as a preparation to further teaching. Bihar in April can be punishingly hot at midday and since most of the Tibetans wisely go off for a break, it is a relatively quiet time to visit the temple. As with most Asian temples you are required to remove your shoes and getting across the burning marble slabs to a patch of shade becomes a grueling hot coals walk, an impromptu test of faith.

Arrayed around the Mahabodhi complex are the temples of many of the great Buddhist traditions of the world: elegant Thai roofs, colorful Tibetan paintings, immaculate Japanese gardens. Their splendor and magnificence is breath taking, though you wonder about the appropriateness of such expense in a state like Bihar that is wracked with poverty and corruption. The evening is especially alive in the Mahabodhi temple. Loudspeakers blare out pujas around the town, and the mullahs of the local mosque are especially vocal: is there a touch of religious competition in their call to prayer? Large numbers of devotees light candles and circumambulate the outer and inner screened walkways. Soon the warm evening air is filled with chanting and the gentle flicker of flames.

The Journey to Bodhgaya

The journey to Bodhgaya was as significant as arriving there. Having slowly made my way north from Tamil Nadu by train, I had started from another important Buddhist site. Bhaja, in the Western Ghats between Pune and Mumbai, is home to ancient and beautiful Buddhist caves as well as a modern Buddhist retreat centre. The Western Ghats, running the length of the

Malabar Coast, relieve the monotony of the great plain that covers so much of the sub-continent. Their gnarled weathered profiles give the land an ancient aboriginal atmosphere. The shapes of the mesas are at times utterly improbable, looking more like abstract architecture than rock formations. The broken peaks and tables tower above old strategic trading routes, and it was here over 2,000 years ago that some of the oldest cave architecture in India was hewn. Wealthy the merchants who traded along these corridors sponsored the magnificent cave dwellings and temples for the new religion of the Buddha that was sweeping through India in the 2nd and 3rd centuries BCE. In March the landscape of the Ghats is dry, hot, orange and dusty, punctuated only by hardy evergreen shrubs and trees and the occasional man-made lake. The caves are a cool relief from the intense heat.

It was here that I had been invited by my Buddhist teacher to give talks and lead workshops on a retreat for men about to join the Triratna Buddhist Order. For two weeks about fifty of us meditated, studied, discussed and lived in harmony as the postulants prepared for their ordinations. I enjoyed the teaching very much, and it elevated me to something like celebrity status, but what moved me most was the powerful feeling of inspiration and brotherhood between us. When the public ordination ceremony came nearly a thousand people from all over Maharashtra descended on the retreat, transforming it into a huge festival. Having delayed my departure for these spectacular celebrations, I began the long journey to Bodhgaya. My train left late that night from one of the busiest railway stations in India, *Kalyan Junction*, and as luck would have it I was offered a lift by some of the visiting Buddhists. It was a long hot drive through the parched mountain terrain, and as we descended from the Ghats into the Kalyan valley the heat and the dust became more intense.

Celebrity status is a double-edged sword. I was invited into Mr. Jadhav's house and fed a delicious meal by his wife and assorted aunties. Along with two other ordained Buddhists I was invited to lead a small puja and give a talk. Since my train was still a few hours away I accepted and before I knew what was happening a dozen other people had arrived, flower garlands had been sent for and a program was developing at alarming speed. As was the case so often in India all this was totally out of my control. I spoke about Dr Ambedkar, the great hero of Buddhists and the impoverished in Indian society, and the significance of conversion in the spiritual life. Dr Ambedkar's deep grasp of the interaction between politics and religion led him to convert to Buddhism in 1956, along with hundreds of thousands and later millions of his *dalit* followers, inaugurating the return of Buddhism to India on a mass scale.

As the impromptu program slowly came to an end, some of the bright young men were keen to discuss Buddhism and social action. I was very aware of time ticking away to my departure, so it was with some unease that I discovered I was supposed to lead a second program at someone else's house before going to the railway station. I hadn't even been consulted. I expressed my disquiet but the decision seemed to have a life of its own, I was assured we would reach Kalyan Junction station in plenty of time for the train. I decided to assert my independence, to the point of rudeness, and flatly refused to go, insisting instead that the auto-rickshaw just take me to the railway station.

Kalyan Junction is the epitome of Indian travelling chaos. As the primary junction serving Mumbai, thousands of trains pass here every day. With no central display from which to ascertain particulars, you are reliant on loudspeaker announcements. Although these were in English and Hindi, the terseness of expression, vagaries of Indian English and crackle of the PA system left me none the wiser. Fortunately I was accompanied by Mr. Jadhav's son, Santosh, without whom I would have been utterly lost. The platform of an Indian railway station is so much more than a point for alighting from a train. It is a microcosm of much human and non-human existence. Every corner of the platform is filled with life or the detritus left over from life. And every life on the platform fights for its space. So the man in the little kiosk in front of which Santosh and I sat down was constantly battling to make a pathway to his shop through the unrelenting piles of families and possessions that tried to park there. Each train prompted a huge movement of beings, but somehow the platform never became less crowded, no matter how many people crammed on. Perhaps the Indian railways have a quantum field that creates new people, like strange particles, from an uncertain foaming void. The non-human life was pretty mangy, but obviously making a living. Scavengers from dogs to rats to lizards to birds and every form of insect were recycling the detritus. Each day some twenty million people travel on the Indian railways.

Having left Maharashtra and my friends in the Buddhist community, I was once again cast adrift in the anonymous sea of the budget traveler. As the train shunted and jolted its way across India, I felt my celebrity status dissolving mile-by-mile, and with it the sense that I was anybody in particular. This seemed to call into question more than just a passing identification as a Dharma teacher; it touched something visceral. "Who am I? What am I doing with my life? Why am I on this journey?" At the same time I felt the freedom of being nobody, not subject to expectations, ties or demands. The contrast between being somebody and being nobody took me into a very uncomfortable but fruitful series of reflections. Often we desire status or kudos, and yet seeking such an ephemeral quality brings a degree of bondage. We all laugh at the comical plea "Do you know who I am?" but such outbursts mask just how deeply important it is for us to feel that we are somebody. Not for the first time, nor would it be the last, I felt my sense of identity dissolving.

A Visit to Uruvela

"Are you Rijumati?" said a rather elegant Western woman in a blue Indian suit as I looked up from my walking and chanting around the Mahabodhi temple. "You must be Siddhisvari", I said since I had heard that she was staying with the Triratna community in Bodhgaya. I spent some time with the young men of the community and with Siddhisvari, whom I was to meet again on my journey in very different circumstances. We studied together, did yoga and I had another brush with stardom when I led a program for about 200 boys at a hostel adjacent to the grim looking Gaya prison. This venue has to rate as the most decrepit to ever host the improbable combination of a Buddhist talk and Scottish folk dancing led by an irrepressible Glaswegian woman called Anne. Anne, somewhere in her fifties, had transplanted her life from Glasgow to Bihar and now lived with a handsome young Indian man in a well-appointed bungalow on the edge of Bodhgaya. She seemed to specialize in doing spontaneous altruistic works.

Towards the end of my stay Sachin, Siddhisvari and I went to Uruvela Hill (also known as Pragbodhi), famous for the cave where the Buddha-to-be practiced fearsome austerities in his quest for freedom. Uruvela is one of the large rocky hills that punctuate the great plain like a sand-locked archipelago. To reach there from Bodhgaya, though only a few kilometers as the crow flies, requires a long detour via Gaya where one can cross the dusty riverbed of the dried up Niranjana. The sprawling monsoon river is over a kilometer wide and there are few bridges. Our rickshaw rocked and jumped as we ran over the rough village tracks that led to the hill. Uruvela village could have been unchanged for a thousand years apart from the new tarmac road built through the middle. It was a timeless scene of water buffalo indifferently chewing, children running and screaming, men sitting around idly, women busily working.

The climb to the cave was especially demanding. Apart from the heat, an unusually persistent selection of beggars awaited us. I gave a few coins to some of the more desperate ones. Then we had to face the touts selling biscuits, and finally the monkeys ready to snatch anything easily graspable. As we got to the

temple halfway up the cliff I heard several shouts and suddenly glimpsed a large female monkey escaping with a packet of biscuits. The cave itself was small, smoky, sweaty and airless. On the main altar was a statue of the austerity Buddha, all bone and sinew, seated in meditation posture. Despite its roughness the image had a certain power, gilded and gazing from sunken socket eyes, telling of terrible struggle and hardship. To the side, covered in orange cloth, were two Hindu images probably Vishnu and Ganesh, but it was hard to tell. We started doing a Buddhist puja, chanting the ancient words of worship to the Buddha, Dhamma and Sangha. As we chanted a number of Indian people came into the cave, they seemed happy just to sit and listen, and then to our astonishment they joined in. We finished the puja all together. It was a beautiful moment of spontaneous fellowship. Four generations of the family were on Buddhist pilgrimage together from Maharashtra. Afterwards we exchanged photos and asked each other questions, parting warmly with the classic Buddhist greeting of *Jai Bhim!* (Victory to Dr Ambedkar). On the way down the beggars were very vocal I

even thought one rather crazy woman might strike me as she started shouting and pursuing us. Such are the extremes in India, from fellowship to harassment in the blink of an eye.

I spent many days drifting in and out of the Mahabodhi Temple, undertaking various spiritual practices, eating in the cafés and making new friends. In the end I felt that there was an almost seductive air to Bodhgaya. One could stay there indefinitely, basking in the atmosphere and experiencing a kind of vicarious spiritual attainment, but with no real purpose. When it came time to leave I felt sad, but I knew that my own inner journey needed to get moving again.

Sublime Sikkim

The Road to Khacheodpalri

A three-day trek around the great monasteries of Sikkim became a precious episode on my journey: precious for the abundance of the Sikkimese jungle, for the sublimity of the sacred sites and, above all, for the companionship of my old friend Janaka. He had accepted my invitation to rendezvous in Asia. We met in Kolkata and through several bizarre twists now found ourselves high in the Sikkimese hills. On a beautiful sundrenched morning, we took the first steps into a world of precipitous gorges, fecund jungle and mountain hermitages.

Down, down, down. Sikkim takes you through precipitous hillsides carved by fast flowing Himalayan Rivers, remote temples and unnamed villages. The 600m descent from Pelling to the rickety old footbridge over the Ranjeet River seemed to go on interminably. Enveloped in a green world teeming with life, the pristine waters of the Ranjeet drowned all but the most ebullient

birdsong. The four-hour ascent to Khacheodpalri Lake was an arduous introduction to our micro-pilgrimage. Drenched in sweat, we struggled upwards. Janaka, twenty years my senior, was carrying a heavy backpack and though remarkably fit for his age he was struggling. At one point he seemed to go pale with exhaustion so I briskly took his backpack and gave him the last of our water. We plodded onwards with grim determination. Yet there is nothing quite like shared adversity to deepen an old friendship and I was thrilled that he was with me. It was with great relief that we finally arrived at the trekkers lodge several hours later, having traversed merely 10km as the crow flies.

Khacheodpalri Lake (pronounced *catch-a-perry*) is sacred to Tara, the Buddhist goddess of compassion, and emanates a magical stillness and radiance. A little track leads up from the village past several small temples, including one dominated by a huge *mani-wheel*. The 3m high bronze rotating drum is embossed with sacred symbols and letters evoking blessings. With some effort, its lumbering inertia is gradually set in motion. On each

rotation it produces a resounding clang, which echoes timelessly across the hills. Along the track are stones carved with holy mantras and overgrown with moss. Emerging from the dark canopy of ancient trees you catch a glimpse of the lake. The mirror-like waters, so legend goes, inscribe the goddess' footprint and are encircled by steep protective hills. The jungle drops to the water's edge and the lake is enfolded in an unearthly stillness. The only sound is the fluttering of thousands of prayer flags flapping from tall bending bamboos and strung between the trees. Occasionally, there is a flash of colorful plumage or the exotic call of an unseen bird. The green calm and peacefulness conjured in me feelings of joy, ease and the call of meditation. As we arrived, a young monk in his maroon robes was praying and prostrating by the lake's edge among the stupas and rows of small mani-wheels.

The place where the Three Lamas meet

Our destination on the second day was Yuksom, meaning *the place where the three lamas meet*, a fine example of the efficiency of the Sikkimese language. The three lamas in question are those who came from Tibet in the 17th century and crowned the first Chogyal (Buddhist king), thus converting Sikkim to Buddhism. Hence Yuksom is the spiritual and political foundation of Sikkim, and site of the old capital before it moved to Gangtok.

Thirty-five kilometers by jeep, yet only nine on foot, the path to Yuksom is once again characterized by precipitous descents and ascents, winding jungle tracks, and scattered makeshift habitations. In the absence of any maps (presumably because the area is highly militarized with India and China still disputing sovereignty) we navigated well-worn tracks by compass, common sense and frequent petitions of the locals, most of whom seemed greatly amused at my wild gesticulations and attempts at Sikkimese place names. Tiny villages cling improbably to tumbling hillsides. Narrow terraces of corn, wheat, rice and vegetables are carefully tended by hand. Usually, as chickens scurry away, goats bleat and dogs announce your arrival there seems to be no one in evidence. However, looking more carefully you might notice a face peeping through an aperture (barely worthy of the name *window*) of a rough mud and timber dwelling with a corrugated metal roof. Calling out a friendly *namaste* usually the greeting is returned, especially enthusiastically if little children are about. By Western standards these people are incredibly poor (though occasionally you see a battered satellite dish attached to a roof), but these forest villages don't seem impoverished. Despite their basic subsistence there is a tremendous abundance in this world of children, animals, vibrant flowers, clean air, clear mountain spring water, rich fecund soils and sublime vistas.

Yuksom nestles high on a small plateau surrounded by row upon row of towering forested peaks, a fitting place for a coronation. The *Norbugang*, or coronation throne is perched far above the village. In front of this ancient seat of royal and religious power is a huge and recently-restored stupa said to contain soil and water from all parts of Sikkim. The site is encircled by towering hemlock trees and has an air of dark green majesty. Below the *Norbugang* is the lovely teardrop of *Kathog Lake*, the *soul-lake* of Lama Kathog-Rigdzin Chhenpo who performed the coronation. He is said to have sanctified the lake for oracular practices and each year a special ritual, the *Tru-Sol*, is performed to preserve the sanctity. Janaka and I slowly circumambulated the lake lost in green thoughts and musing on the fading power of a kingdom once suffused with religious ritual. Though barely bigger than a village, compared to the jungle Yuksom seems like a veritable metropolis. Its position at the trailhead for Mount Kanchenjunga means that it abounds in restaurants and guesthouses. Here you will find the essential delights of Sikkimese civilization: a steaming bowl of noodles and an ice-cold beer.

The Magic of Tashiding

Mist and cloud were a hallmark of our travels in Sikkim. Every morning I awoke hoping to catch a glimpse of Kanchenjunga and the mighty Himalayan peaks, and every morning my expectations were turned back by an impenetrable blanket of swirling vapor and haze. We were advised against taking the forest track to Tashiding monastery, since it was slow, difficult to find and, given the rains, likely to be infested with leeches: it was hard to fault the logic. Walking the long, undulating road we fell into a silent rhythmic pace, ideal for becoming absorbed and soaking in the views down the gorges. The road was well-made but not busy, and the one or two vehicles an hour seemed to barely justify its existence. Each year the Indian government pours a huge amount of money into the BRO (Border Roads Organization) in an attempt to stamp Indian sovereignty over the region. Most of the roads cling desperately to the slopes with a tiny verge bounding a sheer drop through the forest. And each year during the monsoon whole chunks simply disappear in landslides. Nonetheless BRO keeps repairing and rebuilding, promoting itself with little slogans dotted along the highways like "BRO can build a road anywhere except the sky", which I found rather charming for a government institution. Along the way we passed the dramatic plunge of Phamrong Falls. The gushing water and scoured rock stirred my psyche with wonder, as if the raw power of the tumbling torrents epitomized a longing to release the wild energy of the mind.

After many hours walking, the road began a long series of switchbacks, and seeking a shortcut we suddenly stumbled upon a stunning view of Tashiding monastery emerging from the haze. Like a fairytale castle, it perches atop a conical peak bounded by deep river gorges, encircled by mountains and connected to the highlands by a slender isthmus. Tashiding is yet another of Sikkim's magical places. Jamyang Khyentse Rimpoche, one of the greatest Tibetan lamas of the 20th century, was cremated here in 1959. The small monastery grounds are astoundingly beautiful. A cluster of elegant old wooden buildings huddle around the main *gompa* (temple) with its yellow roof. Exquisitely executed frescos cover the wall and ceiling, depicting every imaginable Buddhist deity (and some virtually unimaginable ones too). The splendor and exuberance of these frescoes is astonishing. Below the gompa is a grove of *chortens* (stupas) surrounded by tall hemlock trees, elegant bamboos and thousands of prayer flags. The *Thongwa Rangdrol Chorten* is said to be so holy that merely gazing on it will purify one's evil deeds. I decided to put this claim to the test and spent some time gazing hopefully at the great stupa. If purification did indeed occur, then my as yet imperfect states of mind indicate that I somehow managed to accrue some negative karma

rather rapidly afterwards. Enclosing the chorten grove is a long wall whose rocks are carved and painted with mantras and Buddha images. Here you can walk and chant, constantly uplifted by natural beauty and spiritual symbolism.

Though I would happily have stayed in the gompa and grounds meditating and chanting, monks and nuns twice moved me on. This left me a little sad, for I felt a kinship with the Buddhists of Sikkim and wished to express my devotion at their holy shrines. But to them I must have seemed like just another tourist. I wished to be recognized as a practitioner of the Dharma, even if I lacked the external trappings. Then again, Janaka and I certainly looked like tourists even if we didn't behave like them and I realized that the desire for recognition came from some insecurity on my part, and it was best just to let it go.

The Precious Sublime Lotus
Next morning it was a 7.00 a.m. start to catch the jeep back to

Pelling. Supposedly, there are only two times of day when you have a chance of getting a ride out of Tashiding: early morning or late afternoon. However, on this occasion the usual rules didn't apply; perhaps they never apply. An hour later, still awaiting a jeep, a torrential downpour started. As the little group of office workers, manual laborers, sari-clad shoppers, and two bemused westerners huddled under the corrugated frontage of the taxi stand, the heavens opened as never before. Great sheets of water flowed down the steep street of the bazaar. Everything came to a standstill. When, at last, two jeeps arrived about twenty people were waiting and both were already fairly full. In the flurry of activity, gesticulation, shouting and negotiating that ensued, Janaka and I were totally at sea. At one point it seemed that everyone was going to cram on board apart from us. "You'll have to wait many hours", said one young man discouragingly. Janaka and I tried to wheedle ourselves in to one or other of the jeeps but to no avail. Suddenly something amazing happened: a group of sari-clad women got out of one jeep and squeezed improbably into the other, and we were promptly invited to embark. There was just enough space for our baggage and us. Waves of gratitude washed over me. We'll never really know what transpired, but I like to think that some mysterious collective awareness arose of all the putative passengers, including the two clueless strangers, and the seating arrangements kept mutating until a solution was found that suited everyone. I reflected that wonderful things like this seemed to keep happening in India, which is why, against all the odds, the country functions so well.

Back in Pelling another practical obstacle awaited us. Despite having arranged to collect our spare belongings from the Hotel Garuda that morning, it seemed that the owner had gone off with the locker room key for an indeterminate period. "She will be back in the afternoon" is a deeply dispiriting statement when one considers the looseness of Indian attitudes to time. Unable to shave or change out of our rancid gear after three days trekking was exceedingly inconvenient. After breakfast I decided to express the full extent of my displeasure about this unsatisfactory arrangement. The receptionist's face dropped and he started shouting to a little old lady who was at that very moment going upstairs. Suddenly he broke into a big smile and said, "Go now!" I was rather bemused but it seems that the little old lady had a spare key. Why this information hadn't been forthcoming an hour earlier was entirely beyond me. "Well done", said Janaka, as we retrieved our belongings, leaving me to ponder the unfathomable gulf between oriental and occidental modes of communication. Janaka, in his traveler's wisdom, seemed unperplexed just saying, "I'm surprised you haven't had to use that tone more often in India".

High on a ridge above Pelling is the royal monastery of Pemayangtse ('The Precious Sublime Lotus'), seat of abbot Kachu Rimpoche, another of Sangharakshita's teachers. In front of the imposing three-storey gompa is a grassy space where sacred masked dances are performed on special festival days. The

ornate frescoes on the ground floor are faded and crumbling. The second floor is more uplifting: a large shrine dedicated to the semi-mythical founder of Tibetan Buddhism, Padmasambhava. The dozen life-sized statues of Padmasambhava represent in exquisite detail his various manifestations, from peaceful to wrathful, regal to vagrant. As I sat contemplating the piercing eyes of the main statue, a middle-aged Bengali Hindu sat next to me and we fell into easy conversation. He wanted to convince me that the gompa was 3,800 years old. When I declaimed that it was in fact built in the 17th century he asked in astonishment if I were a scholar of some sort. As we sat together looking at Padmasambhava I asked him what he saw. "I see a cruel person", he said swiftly to which I replied "I see a demanding intensity". At that point he seemed a little uncomfortable and we parted cordially.

The third storey of Pemayangtse gompa houses a justly famous three-dimensional mandala depicting Padmasambhava's Pure Land. Each tier of this three meter-high construction is lavishly decorated with tiny figures, rainbows and embellishments. However it was the vividly restored frescoes that really caught my eye. In several places a cloth was hung over the images, hiding from view archetypal figures in sexual union. Bengali women tittered loudly with a mixture of fascination and embarrassment as they lifted each cloth. These images are considered especially sacred in Tibetan Buddhism. The traditional view is that they represent the complete union of compassion and wisdom, represented by the male and female figures. The impact on me, especially of the standing forms enveloped in flames, was somewhat different. The figures were definitely arousing, though not in a pornographic way. Rather I felt a sense of tremendous energy, potency, fascination and aliveness. They seemed to communicate that the inner experience of an awakened mind is full, intense, naked and exciting.

The next day we descended once more to the plains of Bengal

and the insane bustle of India. This land of steep jungles, magical monasteries, great lamas and welcoming people had etched itself onto my heart. I was learning that travelling on foot and in friendship greatly enriches the significance of sacred sites. No true pilgrimage can be severed from the land in which it takes place and the people living there. Every rock, tree, stream and village somehow contributes to the transformative power. Having wandered throughout Tibet on foot, Padmasambhava must have known this and his flashing eyes were communicating to me a glimpse of his vision.

Tibetan Tectonics

The next stage of our journey was supposed to take Janaka and me to Tibet. In particular we had booked with a guide who would lead us on the *kora* (pilgrim's circumambulation) around Mount Kailash. High in the western Himalayas with a uniquely pyramidical form, it is the source of four of South Asia's great rivers (Indus, Sutlej, Brahmaputra and Ganges) and is one of the most revered mountains in the world, sacred to Buddhists, Hindus, Jains and Bon, the pre-Buddhist shamanic cult of Tibet.

Our *kora* was scheduled for first thaw in April 2008, just preceding the Beijing Olympics. Unfortunately a few weeks before we were due to enter Tibet demonstrations began with the aim of bringing the world's attention to the continuing plight of Tibetans living under Chinese rule. The Chinese government cancelled all visas for Tibet and, as I later discovered, severely curtailed any visas throughout China for budget travelers. In the confusion there was no knowing how long the restrictions would last, so Janaka and I were left high and dry. We had gone to Sikkim hoping, fruitlessly as it turned out, that the visa situation would be clearer by the time our Sikkimese pilgrimage finished. Eventually we decided to chance it in Kathmandu, from where our Tibetan pilgrimage was due to depart.

That's how we came to take the grueling fourteen-hour overnight bus from Siliguri to Kathmandu. No budget adventure would be complete without the experience of an absurdly long and uncomfortable bus journey. The physical and mental demands of such a journey stretch you to the limits, and yet the whole experience is contained enough to be manageable. No matter how rough it seems, you know it will end. When we finally set off from the Nepali staging town of Raniganj our bus seemed to stop at every little town to collect yet more people. This combined with the potholes and poor suspension meant that it was going to be a long, jarring and jolting journey. My heart sank slightly at the prospect of the forthcoming overnight ordeal. But help was at hand, in the form of Anatoly, sat adjacent to me and professing a Masters in Spiritual Psychology from the University of Santa Monica. Fortunately, this didn't put me off too much. Originally from St. Petersburg, now married to a young Nepali wife, Anatoly was a genuine spiritual seeker from California. We had an engaging conversation about the Dharma, which inspired me to recollect the power of mindfulness: stay in the present moment and accept the experience of the bus journey without the additional burden of anticipating the long unpleasantness of it. We became friends and were to meet again for a very different adventure.

As the night wore on the bus filled up and we ceased to collect any more passengers. With earplugs and eye-mask in place I went into a strange dream-like space, loosely aware of the vibration and jolting, but also vividly aware of images flooding my mind. It was rather like lucid-dreaming. We stopped every hour or two for a welcome chance to empty the bladder and stretch the legs. Each town along the way looked the same at night: down at heel, deserted but for a tea stand, used by the passengers as an open toilet and with some mangy dogs on the prowl. The skies were clear and starry, a relief after the incessant cloud of Sikkim. I couldn't say that I really slept, but surrendering to this strange lucid-like state was, in a way, refreshing. After becoming cozily accustomed to this unfamiliar boundary between sleep and wakefulness, suddenly around 6.00 a.m. we hit the outskirts of Kathmandu with its chaos of vehicles and people that was more reminiscent of shopping along London's Oxford Street on Saturday afternoon than suburban Asia early on a Sunday morning. Our bus literally dropped off the highway onto a dirt patch and disgorged its disheveled and rudely awakened passengers into the morning dust. Anatoly, Janaka and I shared a taxi as we crawled across the sprawling warren of ill-made streets that constitute modern Kathmandu: a rather typical arrival.

A retreat at Nagi Gompa

Waiting for the Chinese government to make a clear statement about its knee-jerk visa policies is about as thankless as watching bamboo grow. After yet another week without news, and having exhausted the sundry diversions of Kathmandu, we decided to go into the hills above the city to get away from the hustle and bustle and the appalling pollution. In a moment of calculated madness I decided to hike from Kathmandu to Nagi Gompa, a Buddhist nunnery that offers retreat accommodation on the verdant slopes of Shivapuri Peak. Partly I relished the walk up through the forest; partly I wanted to test my stamina in preparation for hiking in Tibet; and partly I wanted to avoid the expensive taxi into the Shivapuri National Park in which the nunnery is situated. However it is a walk of 10km ascending 700m, I didn't know the way or have a map and I was carrying 15kg. To say this plan was ill-conceived would put it mildly. Janaka wasn't coming with me and would follow the next day by taxi if I succeeded in finding suitable accommodation.

Asking for directions in Pullahari village I was approached by a bright-eyed young man called Amare, it soon became clear that

he wanted to be my guide to Nagi Gompa and we agreed a price. Before we took the track to the nunnery, Amare led me to his home in the hills where he deposited his bike. It was a one-room mud hut with an unmade floor where he lived with his young wife and one year-old daughter Jessica, of whom he was immensely proud. During the climb I learnt about his life. He was 24 and worked, when he could get work, as a plasterer. His father had died when he was just 6 months-old and his family was very poor. Without Amare's help I probably would never have found the track to Nagi Gompa. Several hours later, exhausted, weak-kneed and dehydrated, we arrived at the nunnery. The seventy or so nuns were in the midst of their afternoon puja and since there seemed no one else about I just joined them at the back of the gompa. Later one of the nuns found me a room and arranged for Janaka and I to do a week-long retreat.

However we were not the only Westerners in evidence, and certainly not the most unusual. Christiana was a Romanian Buddhist nun affiliated to the Thai tradition. Shaven headed and wearing white robes she was walking across north India. Christiana was indefatigably enthusiastic as well as eccentric. She would happily regale you with stories of her former life as an award-winning director at Cannes, as an Olympic rower and of the spiritual Masters she knew who controlled the stock markets. I was never clear whether these accolades were from her current life or a previous one, perhaps it didn't really matter. She was certainly a kind, generous and friendly person, and it was at her instigation that one afternoon we made a personal offering to all the nuns during one of the big pujas.

Ananda was a diehard Finnish wandering ascetic, aged 28. For several years he had wandered barefoot all over India in just a cotton robe. He proudly told me that he was wanted by the Finnish government for evading his Army Service. He was heading to Shivapuri Peak to do a three-week retreat with an Irish Buddhist monk and a Mexican freelance ascetic (and their porter and cook). They had invited Christiana to join them for the retreat, but in a candid moment she said to me "They are just torturing themselves, I'm not joining them". I climbed with Ananda to his retreat cave, which in reality was little more than a rocky overhang. He was rather touched when I suggested that

we do a Buddhist ritual to dedicate his cave and the retreat. I was impressed by his hardiness and dedication to practice, though his insistence that I email him photos of the cave had a touch of spiritual machismo and the post-modern ascetic.

Janaka and I spent a delightful week, studying, meditating, reflecting, attending unimaginably long and incomprehensible Tibetan pujas, eating delicious nun-cooked meals and gazing out over the glorious vistas of the Kathmandu valley. It was deeply refreshing, but like all Shangri-las this one had a finite life expectancy. The last possible deadline for our Tibetan pilgrimage was rapidly approaching. With grim expectation I rang our guide on the allotted day and received the news that no visas were going to be issued for Tibet and our trip to Mount Kailash was off. Already early May now, several weeks later than originally planned, it was time for action. Unable to continue my land journey eastwards directly from Nepal, I decided that I would again have to compromise my no-fly principle to a limited extent and jump over Tibet by flying to the nearest Chinese city,

Chengdu in Sichuan, and carry on from there. On the designated day I joined the slow queues at the heavily fortified Chinese embassy in Kathmandu only to discover, along with dozens of other startled travelers, that there were new and extremely stringent visa restrictions applying to the whole of China, effectively barring me from entering the country at all.

The news about Tibet was disappointing but expected, but this second rebuttal sent me into shock. Travelling overland from Nepal to Japan without passing through China requires some pretty fancy planning, and my whole itinerary seemed to be crumbling. I wasn't the only one in shock. Looking around the scrupulously clean, white and sterile interior of the visa department I could see several different responses from the rejected applicants. Three English girls on their big gap year trip, with their flights into China already paid for were in denial, just hoping that if they came back another day it would work out. A young Nepali or Indian woman with her father in tow was in tears at her broken plans. A Nepali travel agent, arriving with a swathe of passports to be processed, had a withering look on his face as if to say "Why don't you people just accept the facts and get out of my way?" Other travelers were angry, cursing Chinese bureaucracy. The embassy staff themselves either had a blank *can't do anything* stare or a sympathetic but helpless look of *sorry.* The pathos of others' plight put my own drama into perspective.

The next 48 hours were very intense as I weighed up the options for continuing onwards to Japan. Should I go south and try to get a ship from Kolkata towards South East Asia, working my way around the coast via Singapore, the Philippines and Korea? This was a very long way round and going to involve a lot of ships and a lot of luck. Should I go north from India into Central Asia and try to connect with the Trans-Siberian railway to the Russian Far East? This sounded exciting but was filled with unknowns such as the insurgency of the *Stans* (Pakistan, Afghanistan and Tajikistan) and the notorious Russian visa bureaucracy. Should I abandon my principles and accept the inevitability of a long-haul flight? Added to this I had less than two weeks left on my Indian visa, which I hadn't thought I would need to use again. Suddenly the pressure was on me both externally in terms of organizing a solution and internally as I wrestled with disappointment and looked for a creative response.

It was soon starkly clear that the last of these three options was not tenable. I *knew* that were I to abandon principle and take a long-haul flight out of trouble something of the mythical meaning of the journey would be broken. It wasn't just that I would be admitting defeat at the first big obstacle, though this in itself would be shattering enough. But I also knew that a consequence of the long-haul jump would be to cut me adrift in a sea of uncertainty. Why then go anywhere, why take any particular route? Just get out when the going gets tough, when the experience is no longer enjoyable. My travels would essentially become a very elaborate *holiday*. The significance of the journey was hanging in the balance. At the time this was more a powerful intuition than a coherent reflection. Happily I took notice of that deeper voice amongst the many clamoring for attention during the frantic 48 hours I spent cogitating on the pros and cons of the various possibilities. Finally, aware that time was running out, I decided that I would follow another important principle: *facing an equal choice take the road less travelled, it's bound to be interesting*. So parting with my friend Janaka at Lumbini, birthplace of the Buddha, I headed back to New Delhi in search of transport and visas to Kyrgyzstan, Kazakhstan and Russia. I realized that I would still have to make an expedient flight over the dangerous Taliban badlands of northern Pakistan, Afghanistan and Tajikistan (fresh out of civil war), but this seemed to be in the spirit of the journey.

The coda to this episode was the tragic and appalling earthquake that hit Sichuan province on the 12th May 2008. One of the deadliest earthquakes on record, nearly 70,000 dead, 20,000 missing and 350,000 injured: a colossal loss of life and damage to the infrastructure of the province. Had the Chinese granted me a visa I would mostly likely have flown to Chengdu a day or two before the earthquake hit and been on my way northwest, right towards the epicenter, to visit a Buddhist temple that I wanted to research for a friend. The probability of death, injury or becoming trapped in the shattered province would have been very high. When I heard about the earthquake I was startled to realize that the visa refusal had been a blessing instead of a bane. You can never properly judge events without a little hindsight.

Almighty Almaty

Arriving in Almaty was an almighty dose of culture shock. Although India and Kazakhstan are on the same longitude and have almost the same time zone, my flight was scheduled to arrive at the uncharitable hour of 3.20 a.m.. The in-flight service on Air Astana (Kazakhstan's national airline) was surprisingly good, but even a decent airline vegetarian meal is a bit weird when eaten at 1.00 a.m.. The night flight also meant there was no possibility of seeing the mighty Pamir mountains as we flew over northern Pakistan and Afghanistan. Why don't they schedule the flight for a sensible time? Answer: probably because airport taxes are cheaper for late night departures.

At that time in the morning it was always going to be a challenge arriving in a new country. It turned out to be a bigger challenge than I bargained for. The first hurdle was immigration. I was turned back by the young Kazakh immigration officer who just waved me away and said "Please wait!" in a tone that indicated our conversation was over. Wait for what, where? I eventually found a window called Consular Services where I assumed that I could arrange the transit visa to Kyrgyzstan. There is no direct flight from India to Kyrgyzstan so travelers between the two countries have to fly to Kazakhstan and get a transit to the Kyrgyz capital Bishkek, a couple of hours drive away. My first shock was that the 1-day transit visa cost me $25, whereas my month long Kazakh visa from their embassy in Delhi had only cost me $15. And they wanted payment in dollars, of which I had none. I generally carried little cash, relying on ATMs worldwide and what cash I had was in Euros. Helpfully there was an ATM this side of the immigration control which dispensed dollars and Kazakh Tenge (KZT). I imagine that in the bad old Soviet days had one arrived at Almaty immigration without enough dollars one would have been trapped in a

Kafkaesque nightmare, unable to get through immigration through lack of currency and unable to get currency through lack of immigration. I was spared and the Consular Services even accepted payment in KZT which saved me the irony of having to draw dollars to get into an ex-Soviet republic.

Having negotiated immigration I went to collect my luggage. However, as I tried to leave the baggage collection hall two rough looking guys in uniform started demanding something from me in Russian. For all I knew they could have been mafia men demanding protection money. Eventually it became clear that they wanted the counterfoil to the baggage sticker that was attached to my bag. I have never been asked for this usually insignificant barcode sticker in many years of air travel, and I would have might easily have jettisoned it as rubbish before getting to that point in the airport. Fortunately I was able to produce the relevant sticker, and as it matched the one stuck on my bag the so-called airport officials gave a satisfied grunt and waved me through.

It was now about 4.00 a.m. and the fun was only beginning. The next obstacle was the barrage of men offering me a taxi. Almost to a man they were unshaven, wearing black leather jackets and with the fag end of a cigarette in their mouths. Once again, I immediately thought I'd met the Kazakh mafia, or perhaps a bevy of Borat's relatives. However I had enough presence of mind to refuse their petitions. It was still dark and I would go and sit in a café until it was light and I figured out what to do next.

"Tourist Information" I thought, "They'll help me to work out how to get to Bishkek". A small, plump lady grimaced at me as I asked how to get a bus to Bishkek. She spoke no English and I no Russian, as Tourist Information desks go this one failed at the first hurdle. Just to avoid the assault of the taxi mafia I took the up-escalator to the Departure lounge. Fortunately I noticed that there was another Tourist Information desk on that level. This time the lady spoke a little English. When I explained that I wanted to go to Bishkek she said with complete self-assurance "No flight to Bishkek from here". "I want to go by bus!" "I don't know anything about bus". "Can you help me find out?" With a withering look and a sigh that said "why don't you go away and stop causing me trouble" she scribbled *Sairan 106 or taxi* on a scrap of paper and handed it to me with an air of finality. This cryptic clue turned out to be the name of the long distance bus station and the number of the bus that goes there. I tried to enquire how much a taxi should be but this was clearly beyond the call of duty and I beat a hasty retreat.

Outside was still dark, and from past exploits I knew that waiting at night in the bus station of an unfamiliar city was not a good idea, so I headed to the only available café. I sat down at a table and asked for tea from one of the smartly dressed waiters. He looked me in the eye and then walked off, which I took as confirmation of my order. However after about five or ten minutes another waiter came to me and gesticulated that I needed to make my order at the cash desk a few meters away. It was a far cry from Indian eagerness. The tea came as a cup of fairly hot water and a tea-bag on the side, guaranteed not to brew properly, but I wasn't going to try my luck by sending it back. The next shock was that this tepid brown drink was going to cost 300KZT ($2.00) – a rude awakening to the brave new world of developed economies after paying 5 Indian Rupees (10 cents) for *chai*. "Never mind", I thought. "It's the airport; it's bound to be over-priced".

Waiting for dawn I drank the tepid, brown water and observed the inhabitants of this unfamiliar Central Asian world. Some were Slavs, presumably of a mainly Russian origin: many of the men were portly, vodka drinking and with a sprinkling of black leather jackets. Here and there, elegant mini-skirted *tsarinas* were walking arm-in-arm with their guys. Then there were the thinner faced tartar features of the native Kazakhs with the occasional peroxide-blonde young woman.

As the sun came up there was a big commotion. Two policemen in over-sized caps came running into the café shouting, looking at us all as if we were mad. I had no idea what they were saying. No one seemed to take much notice of them (a response to the police that I noted on several occasions) and in an unhurried manner people started putting their coats on and leaving. The policemen shouted more insistently and I joined the throng. I even heard the word *bomba* bandied about.

The Sting

People started streaming out of the airport and all chaos was let lose. No one seemed to know what was going on. I headed for the first taxi I could find and asked for "Sairan avtow-buss" in my best Russian accent. I asked the price, but the taxi driver grabbed my bag, put it in the boot and with police and confusion everywhere I just got in and off we went. "This is a reasonable country I guess the price will be fair" I thought as I relaxed and enjoyed the view of the city.

Almaty is set against the curve of the northern Tian-Shan Mountains and leaving the airport we had a spectacular dawn-view of them. It was a far cry from the baking plains of New Delhi and I gazed with rapt attention at the snow-capped peaks. The great boulevards were lined with tall, healthy-looking trees

and there wasn't a soul in sight. After six months in South Asia this was a very strange experience. There is never a time of day in an Indian city where you won't see people. In Kolkata, perhaps the most densely peopled of all cities, every niche is someone's home. Even in the affluent suburbs of New Delhi one finds the laborers and rickshaw wallahs around at almost any time of day and night. But Almaty was absolutely empty, though admittedly it was only 5.30 a.m. Next shock was the speed of my taxi. On the well-made Kazakh roads we were driving over 100km/h between traffic lights and at some of those we didn't stop – at least Almaty has that in common with India.

After about twenty minutes zigzagging across town we arrived at the bus station. A posse of guys descended on the taxi as I alighted, obviously sensing a business opportunity. But there was a small problem to address, the fare. When my driver demanded 4,000KZT ($30) my jaw dropped. How could he be charging a London taxi rate here in Kazakhstan? "No way" I said, we were at stalemate. A strange three-way negotiation started between me, the taxi driver (we had no common language) and the other taxi drivers who were wanting to take me to Bishkek. I couldn't figure out what price was related to what and it has to rate as one of the most confusing moments I can remember. Finally a guy called Viktor who spoke English, wore a black leather jacket, was unshaven and holding a cigarette (and perhaps was part of the local mafia), asked me what I wanted. "I want to go to Bishkek, and I'm not paying 4,000KZT for the ride from the airport, that's robbery". He laughed a big hearty laugh, "Yes it's robbery. *We* never use those airport taxis". Somewhat predictably he turned out to be a taxi driver and started trying to arrange a taxi for me to make the 250km journey to Bishkek, which he assured me would only cost 2,000KZT, half of what the other driver was demanding for a 10km journey. The other driver started making threats about the police, I suppose if I had slept a bit more I would have called his bluff, but as it was I decided to try and negotiate. We finally agreed on 3,000KZT, although I knew I was being cheated: there is always a price to pay for culture shock. But I did manage to get to Bishkek for a reasonable price.

Lake Issyk-Kul

Kyrgyzstan is a staggeringly beautiful and wild country; that's why I had taken the trouble to backtrack here instead of heading straight from Kazakhstan to Russia. Mountain wilderness dominates the country, and as soon as one leaves the fertile plains around Bishkek one enters the sublime peaks of the Tian Shan, a Chinese name meaning *Heavenly Mountains*. Khan Tengri, the highest, is over 7000m. A northern branch of the Silk Road threads its way between these peaks, passing by the shores of Lake Issyk-Kul. This was the route travelled by Hsuan-Tsang, the Chinese monk whose journeys are fictionalized in the classic tale *Monkey*, and he nearly met his end here on a high pass where several animals and retainers died in a terrible blizzard. At an altitude of 1,600m, encircled by snow-capped mountains mostly over 4,000m and covering more than 6,000 square kilometers, Issyk-Kul is one of the largest mountain lakes in the world. It has a magical quality of never freezing, even though the surrounding winter temperatures plummet to minus 20°C, because it is slightly saline and heated by underwater hot springs. The name Issyk-Kul is Kyrgyz for *warm lake*. I discovered that this warmth was relative since, after a preliminary paddle, it was clear that to swim even in late May was to risk hypothermia. In the intensely clear sunshine at this altitude Issyk-Kul is a vibrant deep blue, which makes it seem all the more out of this world.

I arrived at the lakeside town of Tamga after five hours crammed into an ageing Mercedes-Benz minibus. As usual the Kyrgyz people on the bus had been unfailingly friendly, and I'd been fortunate to meet a lively young woman called Kunduz who spoke excellent English with a strong American accent. The bus was continuing on to the ex-Soviet military town of Karakol and I was the only passenger alighting at Tamga. The driver pulled up in what looked like the middle of nowhere and indicated that I should get out. There was a bus shelter but no sign of a town. I managed a *"dasvadanya, spassiba"* as I wondered "Where on earth has he dropped me?" To the left immaculate blue waters, to the right hills rising steeply to snowy peaks, forward and back just the road passing through a kind of mountainous desert. A small road veered off towards the hills so in the absence of any other option I took that.

Sasha, owner of the Tamga Guesthouse, was a huge hulk of a Russian – the kind of man you imagine single-handedly uprooting tree stumps to build the motherland. Around Issyk-Kul, which in Soviet times was a thriving tourist resort, there still lived equal numbers of Russians and Kyrgyz. It wasn't hard to see why the Russians had stayed. "Tamga is a very beautiful place", said Sasha. I immediately liked him for his huge but gentle presence, his trusting hospitality (his was the first guest-house in many months where I hadn't had to present my passport on arrival) and his unerring enthusiasm to acquaint me with the delights of this very small town. Tamga owed its existence to a decaying military sanatorium, which had now become a run-down housing estate. Like most modern developments in Central Asia it was laid out on a grid with vast boulevards that seemed completely over specified for such a modest town. But, basking between the lake and the mountains, Tamga was special.

The next day I set out to explore the Tamga gorge. Sasha had hand drawn me a map including directions to a locally celebrated stone carved with ancient Tibetan symbols. The road up the valley was little more than a dirt track and I entered a ravaged landscape. Collapsed sedimentary cliffs, piles of stones and sand had all been washed down by the infrequent rains. The land was utterly parched. Most of the rivers had been diverted into a vast network of irrigation channels making the town and surrounding fields green and productive yet leaving the riverbeds mere dust and stone. After passing several large and well-watered orchards I encountered three local Slavic men in their late twenties. They were very rough, one of them had eyes bloodshot with vodka. Further on a Kyrgyz man bumped past over the rocks and potholes on a horse drawn cart gazing ahead blankly and not even acknowledging my presence. As he passed I saw that in his cart were the carcasses of a freshly killed calf and sheep and I met the misty blue eyes of a calf gazing upward, as if looking for solace.

I wandered alone in these hills for hours, unable to find the ancient stone inscription from Sasha's rudimentary directions. No matter; the landscape was working its way into me. This land was stripped bare by crumbling dryness and as the fawn-sand soils washed away they left an intricate network of branching channels and gullies, rather like a vast lymphatic system. Beyond the peaks stretched the enticing expanse of bolt blue Issyk-Kul. You could walk for days or weeks in these mountains seeing only the occasional mounted shepherd with his flock. I underestimated the fierceness of the sun at this altitude and I was soon

badly burnt and turned an embarrassing beetroot red. As
evening drew on I descended from the hills and stumbled on
Tamga's graveyard with its uncanny juxtaposition of Slavic
monumental masonry, skeletal Nomadic yurts and rough
mounds of earth. Here at last, amid the heaped detritus of this
shattered landscape, it seemed that cultural differences had been
settled and the dead slept together in harmony.

Falling Apart in the Ala Archa

The morning after I had been refused a visa at the Russian embassy in Bishkek I woke up with a gnawing sense of dread in the pit of my stomach. I had catapulted myself from the dusty heat of India into a completely alien world of steppe and mountains, and I was lost. I didn't speak the language, I didn't know anybody, I didn't understand how things worked and by sheer fluke was lodging at a French-speaking adventure holiday centre, whose employees were only too happy to help me yet always for a fee. Feelings of aloneness, isolation and total incomprehension of the world into which I had dropped rippled through me and the questions buzzing incessantly around my head touched my deepest insecurities. "What the hell am I doing here?" "Who am I?" "Where is my life going?" I was consumed by my confusion. I knew that I had brought these difficulties on myself and I couldn't help wondering why I had got myself into this fix. The only sane conclusion was, "I must be mad!"

Practically speaking I *really* didn't know what to do to continue my journey. Should I keep pursuing the Russian visa in Kyrgyzstan, or give up here and try for a Russian visa in Kazakhstan, or forget about my problems and head for the mountains hoping for inspiration and a lucky break? Should I try to meet some English-speaking people who might help, or just admit defeat and get on the next flight somewhere … anywhere? But the practical problems were just the surface and beneath them were disturbing tectonic shifts. The purpose and meaning of my journey seemed to be dissolving, and, as it did so, I was losing a sense of who I was. I literally couldn't understand what I was doing here stuck in Central Asia, paying real money (as opposed to inhabiting the illusion of wealth afforded by South Asian prices) just to survive day by day, locked into a seemingly hopeless bureaucratic struggle for a Russian visa and so far from anyone or anything connected with the putative pilgrimage on which I had embarked. It was not a pleasant situation to be in and I would never I have chosen my current circumstances. The confusion circled round and round until I wondered if I *was*, in fact, going mad. I tried to stay calm and solve the problem, but I was also losing my grip. I wanted to run outside shouting all down the street, "Help, get me out of here!" It took all my willpower to keep hold of a tiny voice that said, "Just get out of this guesthouse".

Alexander, the ever-helpful manager at Ultimate Adventure, had said that he had some contacts in Almaty, who might be able to arrange the visa, and I was expecting him to phone them early that morning and let me know the result. I paced round my little room like a caged animal, as whirling thoughts gripped me. But Alexander's boss had turned up for an important meeting and my little problems were no longer part of his brief. Eventually, exasperated and desperate, I interrupted their meeting to see what was happening and on a whim expressed the desire to visit the Ala Archa National Park, famed for it's beautiful mountain views. Alexander explained he was busy and hadn't rung his visa contacts but agreed to arrange a rather expensive taxi to the Ala Archa. I realized I become overly dependent on my hosts for help and I had to get out of there, but at that moment just keeping myself together was the priority. When the taxi finally arrived, rather late in the day, it was driven by a huge Ukrainian called Vladimir and I was completely unable to decide whether or not to take the taxi. Midday was very late to start a mountain expedition, and Vladimir wanted $40 for the round trip. I apologized to Alexander for my confusion and in the end he just said "It is better that you go today", so I went. My indecision felt unbearably humiliating, but there seemed very little of *me* present with the ability to make decisions.

Vladimir drove furiously through the streets of Bishkek, perhaps a reaction to my uncertainty about enlisting his services.

However as we left the city behind and began to approach the National Park, his driving eased up and I felt some respite. The intense blue sky and the majesty of the Tian Shan peaks lifted me. After I paid the entrance fee to the Park, Vladimir deposited me at the trailhead and said in gruff Russian, "You come back at 5.00 p.m.". I agreed that this was a sensible time and started to climb the high track up to the Aksai glacier in the east of the park. I made this my aim for the day; though in truth it was too late to get there and back by 5.00 p.m.

The Ala Archa gorge is rugged, alpine, carpeted with grass-lands and stunningly beautiful. Enclosed by towering peaks the precipitous gorge splits at the confluence of two fast flowing mountain rivers: the Aksai and Ala Archa. I made my way ever

upwards, following the path to the glacier. At first the blue sky was dappled by clouds that emerged magically from thin air, but soon glimpses of blue sky appeared occasionally through the gloom. The mutable mountain weather and the clouds' encroaching gloom seemed the perfect mirror of my mind. But the breath-taking vistas lifted me out of my self-absorption. I was suddenly flashed back into episodes from my teens and twenties when I had visited awesome natural landscapes seeking for the sublime and felt myself small, insignificant, worthless and overwhelmed by the vastness. That sense of being nothing in comparison to the universe had terrified me. Now it once again felt close as if a specter of eternity was exhaling his cold breath on the hairs of my neck. I felt panic, but just kept walking. What else was there to do? Wave upon wave of self-doubt broke over me, and yet the majesty of the jagged peaks, the roaring torrent below, the carpet of grasses and flowers, and the occasional call of a pine martin seemed to be calling me back. Somehow, things were different this time, perhaps it was the twenty years of Buddhist practice or my greater life experience. There was part of me that didn't despair; it knew I was falling apart and that in a way this was *a necessary evil*. The stories I was telling myself about my journey, my identity and even my life were crumbling and the little mind that tries to hold it all together was losing control. But I caught a glimpse of something deeper, something more, something unnamable. The sense of death was very present. Without any great feeling of concern I thought, "Perhaps I'm going to die up here in the Ala Archa". Or perhaps *part of me* was going to die.

Ascending the trail I was saddened to notice, as I did many times in Central Asia and Siberia, a large amount of human debris: plastic, glass, metal, paper and much more had been tipped here. I so wanted the land to be pristine and beautiful and the carelessness of the litter jarred me. By now I was high above the mountain torrent and heading for a waterfall that descended from the glacier. Above the waterfall, piercing through the mist and light drizzle, were huge, mesmerizing grey teeth of granite, like the jaws of a primordial dragon. I knew I would have to give up my quest for the glacier, time was running out, the rain and clouds were closing in and the last of the other walkers seemed to have had the good sense to head down for shelter. I made my way to the base of a beautiful small waterfall, surrounded by pristine pools that seemed a place of water nymphs and sprites. However these romantic imaginings were again shattered by the human debris, I felt sad that people should be so thoughtless. And all of a sudden a purpose took hold of me; I was here to clean up the waterfall. Slowly and methodically I started to collect the litter, carrier bags, glass, rusting tins, food packaging. Some of it must have been there for years.

Soon it was drizzling heavily. It was time to leave, thoughts of death dissolved and I focused on carefully collecting all the trash I could see and making my way safely down the winding ridge

path. As I descended I seemed to find more and more trash to collect. Soon I had two full carrier bags worth, stuffed tightly, and then it was three carrier bags. Some of the rubbish was very unpleasant: plastic with decaying organic matter, a used nappy and some discarded condoms. I had to overcome my sense of disgust, but my purpose was clear: return the land to its pristine state as far as I was able. And, strangely, as I descended with my bags of rubbish I felt lighter and freer of the melancholy. My Buddhist teacher once said that if you can do nothing else at least you can give: everybody can give! In the psychic disintegration I found a way to give to the land, and my heart was able to open out of the oppression in which it had been locked. It felt like a blessing.

By the time I returned to the car park at the trailhead I was feeling chastened yet more present and alive. With my three bags stuffed full of rubbish I was also rather self-conscious, and I hunted around until I found a bin where I surreptitiously deposited my foul trophies. I got back to the car, almost bang on 5.00 p.m. and Vladimir, napping over his newspaper, seemed a little surprised. Perhaps he hadn't expected me to make it back. We returned to Bishkek and the gloomy moods of my guest-house. Vladimir seemed quite congenial, especially when he got his fee. But I knew that my days in Bishkek were numbered. Two days later, in my quest for a Russian visa I returned to Kazakhstan. I travelled in a shared taxi with a plump middle-aged Kyrgyz woman called Natalia who did her best to marry me to her 42-year-old spinster daughter, Olga, mainly because she discovered that we had both studied mathematics. Having been touched by the sublime, it seemed fitting that I should have a close call with the ridiculous.

Searching for the Soviet Soul

Back in Almaty the effects of psychic dissolution continued to ramify through me. In quiet moments I still felt a chasm of confusion mixed together with a great expanse of freedom. Despite the danger of nihilism and despair, when I listened, or rather intuited, more sensitively there was somewhere in my soul a movement *towards* ... Towards what exactly was hard to say. A movement towards life, towards others, towards freedom and away from the oppressions of meaninglessness, despair, isolation. It was as if I had dropped through the bottom of those oppressions and found myself in a vaster space, more vibrant and alive, though as yet my tenure in this unfamiliar space was unstable. I didn't understand what was happening to me, so I just followed this movement *towards* and threw myself into the next adventure. Perhaps the confusion and uncertainty of travelling in Central Asia and Russia actually helped, since there was always a new problem to be solved whether buying a train ticket or finding somewhere affordable to stay. In this way, the deep processes of dissolution and renewal could continue without my little self becoming too panicked at the prospect and just busying itself with the immediate task at hand.

Every foreigner entering Kazakhstan or Russia needs to register with the police within five days of entry or face a nightmare of red tape and fines when trying to leave. So I went to the infamous *OVIR* office in Almaty, now renamed *Immigration Police*, apparently as much hated by locals as by foreigners. My Kazakh friend Marat had warned me what Cyrillic words to look for to find the right window. "Arrive early", Marat warned me, "and don't be put off by the queues. They move quite fast". Window #3 was just one of a dozen or so windows catering for all manner of registrations and official business.

Most windows open for business at 10.00 a.m. and work for

several hours, a huge improvement from the old days when they opened at 11.00 a.m. and worked for two, and woe betide those too far down the queue! By 9.20 a.m. a sizeable queue was already milling around each window. Having no idea how the system worked I just parked myself as close as I could to window #3 and hoped for the best. The Russian speakers all around me seemed to register my presence and fix my order in the queue. I was grateful that at least someone had noticed that I existed. After years of bureaucratic endurance a sense of queue fairness has developed amongst ordinary people. Those people around me were patient, but bore an air of frustration. I guess it has become a fact of life that you have to spend wasted hours trying to get simple things done. These days, those who can afford it pay others to do the queuing.

As the time got closer to 10.00 a.m. the mood changed palpably, and a kind of jostling for position started. Several people appeared claiming a prior place in the queue to me, and who was I to know whether or not that was fair? I gave way to one young woman and her smile communicated intense relief, though I couldn't understand what she said.

After about an hour I got to the front and presented my papers. Fortunately, the friendly looking Kazakh woman spoke some English; unfortunately she wouldn't accept my passport for registration. "You need to go to the cash window, pay 745KZT, and then come back", she said as she handed my documents. I had a deep sinking feeling that the bureaucrats had me in their power and I wouldn't get off lightly.

The cash window queue had a rather more dog-eat-dog atmosphere. It was significantly longer, since the dozen registration windows were serviced by this one cash window. To make matters worse the sliding metal tray used for pushing documents and money back and forward was jammed, forcing the cashier and her clients to squeeze everything through a small gap. Given the long queue, the atmosphere of frustration, the broken tray and the slowness of her printer, the poor cashier was looking very hassled, and the day barely started. I waited for another hour, the queue seeming even more intractable than at window #3. A woman with a baby used her young charge as a passport to get straight to the front. A man shouting in Russian bypassed the usual protocols, came to the window and managed to receive a piece of paper. He carried on shouting – to whom it was impossible to say – as he marched back to another queue somewhere else.

When I finally got to the front and asked for *registratsya* I got a blank from the cashier. She said something in Russian, but then just ignored me and started dealing with the man behind me. "*Pazalsta, pa-anglisski?*" (please, do you speak English?) got no response. "Can anyone tell me why she won't accept my payment?" I asked in English, but all around just blank, frustrated looks. It is one of those moments when you sink into despair, helplessly lost in a bureaucratic nightmare bouncing from one window to another. A slight sense of panic rose up in my mind, "I could be stuck here for days trying to get through the system".

I went back to window #3 and just went straight to the front, much to the dismay of several bystanders who demanded, "Why?" in Russian. The English speaking official was my only lifeline in the sea of systems. "She won't accept my payment, I don't know why" I explained frantically. With a severe look of consternation she produced a paper with an official stamp detailing the payment I needed to make: it was my ticket to freedom.

Back at the cash window, I went straight to the front, but no one seemed to mind. I guess they could see from my manner that I was desperate, and since the queue had barely progressed they must have witnessed my previous rebuttal. Without even a moments eye-contact the cashier took my chit through the broken cash tray, accepted the money and printed a receipt. As waves of relief washed over me I reflected that for all of us, bureaucrat and citizen, this was a kind of living hell.

I count myself lucky to have escaped the registration hells in just over two hours and with my sanity mostly intact. The experience creates a sense of desperation: "I don't know what I have to do so that they'll let me get out of here". A Canadian man behind me was looking panicked, and I later discovered that it took him several more hours to get through. Of course, in the West there are lots of systems designed to keep us under control. Usually we don't notice that they're being employed; they're hidden behind the spin of this or that threat to our democratic freedoms. But in the ex-Soviet republics the old habits of in-your-face control are still alive, only they are so inefficient that they eat up hours of everyone's lives.

Alone in the Tian Shan

As Marat drove me into the Aksai Gorge National Park south of Almaty we picked up some hitchhikers: a boy called Igor and two very scantily clad teenage girls who seemed to be looking for some attention. We were all going for a day's hiking in one of Almaty's famed beauty spots. As we started walking up from the trailhead we came to the first obstacle of the day. A man in a big four-wheel drive aggressively informed us that the road was private and we could go no further. I was appalled that we should be denied access after having paid to enter a public park. My young friends turned back down the track, but I decided to climb a nearby hill leading to the Aksai Orthodox monastery. The cobalt blue sky, vibrant green grasses and abundant forest flowers were breath taking, mitigating my disappointment.

Above 1,600m the deciduous forest gives way to dark green spruces and firs. The climb to the monastery wends steeply up makeshift wooden steps through the dimly light conifers. The silence was haunting and I felt as if I were entering the abode of Baba Yaga, greatest of the Russian witches. There was not a soul to be seen. The newly-built Aksai monastery is hidden among the trees, the golden onion tower of the main chapel glinting extravagantly in the sunlight. I continued climbing steeply until I emerged suddenly from the forest onto a ridge. Laid out before me was the stunning vista of the snow-capped Tian Shan peaks and the higher Aksai gorge. As I took in the view a figure appeared in the distance, climbing the ridge path laboriously. He was clad in a full-length black habit, wore the traditional circular hat of the orthodox priest and sported a long grey beard. He was clearly struggling with age and the heat, and took a full ten minutes to arrive where I was sitting. Passing, he showed no sign of having noticed me, but as I greeted him he smiled and continued walking silently.

Drawn by its splendor I conceived the idea of climbing one of nearest peaks. It was a rather crazy conception since I had no map, or even much idea how far away it was, but I could see a path leading in the right direction. As is often the case with impulsive hiking, it turned out to be further and higher than I had bargained for. Four hours later, having walked perhaps 12km and risen 800m, I arrived in a basin at the foot of the main summit. In the midday heat I was drenched with sweat and rapidly running out of water. Given the circular contours I hoped this basin might contain a water source. Sure enough as I scrambled over the cyclopean granite boulders I heard the tantalizing sounds of running water beneath my feet. I followed the sounds to the edge of the plateau and suddenly, "Eureka!" I saw a sparklingly clear mountain brook emerging from the rock. Perhaps no joy can really compare with that of a hot, thirsty man drinking his fill from a cool mountain spring. To the south great snow-capped peaks, to the north disappearing into the distance the endless expanse of the Steppe, all around meadows of vivid alpine flowers. As I rested it was almost like being in paradise, but for the increasing numbers of mosquitoes whose attention I was attracting. Eventually they defied my feeble attempts to fend them off, the only alternative to becoming main course in a banquet seemed to be to keep moving.

The final ascent to the peak involved scrambling up a 45° scree slope, grabbing tufts of grass, dislodging loose boulders, stumbling over roots. Yet as much as I labored onwards the summit seemed to get no closer and I felt I would have to turn back. "Just take the next few steps", I intoned repeatedly to myself, staying as present as I could. Often it is the mental rather than physical limitations that cause us to fail. Finally, after an hour I scrambled over a large boulder and unexpectedly found

myself on the summit. Spread out before me was the most sublime of mountain vistas: the Aksai glacier tucked between two grey peaks, a jagged ridge running away into the distance and the beautiful valley carpeted in wild flowers falling away below.

But there was no relief from the ever-thickening clouds of mosquitoes. Despite the intense heat I was now wearing my Gore-Tex jacket for protection and had covered my clothes and face in repellent. But this variety of bloodsucker seemed undeterred, I was the only large animal in sight and they all wanted a piece of me. In the heat of the moment I made a fateful decision. Rather than return by the same path I judged that the descent into the Aksai valley itself was none too steep and I could make it through the grasses. The valley was a feast of meadows and flowers. With a pristine river running down from the snows and gentle glacial contours it seemed like an entrance into a lost alpine world. As I zigzagged down the steep meadows I was dismayed to see the cloud of mosquitoes growing into something like a black swarm. They easily numbered thousands, all hungry for blood. I moved swiftly hoping either that the wind would get up or that the change in altitude would deter their pursuit. I blessed my Gore-Tex raincoat, which like a second skin, provided some respite from the onslaught. As I descended the hillside dropped away and I found myself in a narrow chimney, scrambling over the boulders, and trying to outrun the clouds of bloodsuckers. Somehow the absurdity of the situation prompted my sense of humor, though in reality it was a risky moment. A twisted ankle in such a remote place could be fatal, quite apart from making me into a mosquito banquet. When at last I got to the low meadows I relaxed and started walking fast enough to keep the swarm at bay. The meadows were virgin; tall waist-high grasses and flowers, wide open views of the U-shaped valley, the sound of the river crashing its way out of the heights, a seeming paradise. However, paradise always has its

shadow; I had been warned about the prevalence of encephalitis-bearing ticks in these mountains, and long grass would be their favorite habitat. I'd had the encephalitis vaccination and tucking in my clothing to cover all exposed skin, I tried to put that particular anxiety out of my mind.

I faced one more challenge. There was no path to be seen in the entire valley and as I tracked the river down the contours became increasingly precipitous as the river cut its way through the granite. Soon I was out of the meadows, scrambling through forest and over boulders alarmingly close to a sheer drop over the river. It was 6.00 p.m., only two hours of light remained and I making painfully slow progress through a series of obstacles. For the first time I began to think I was in trouble. "What if I get caught in these mountains at night?" There was one vivid moment as I grasped a root on a tiny ledge above the raging torrent when I wondered if I would slip and meet an untimely end. A sense of panic began to arise, but once again I recalled the Buddhist mind training. Staying focused in the present moment, I brought to mind a mantra, a protective chant, and my mind began to calm.

"What am I going to do next?" I thought. I don't know why, but the answer was crystal clear. "You have to get across the river. This bank is too dangerous". Easier said than done. I could conceivably have waded the river but it was ice cold, waist-deep, and very fast-flowing. My experience of wading shallower rivers was that within seconds your feet go numb and the energy saps out of you. Could I jump across? There were some places where the gap between the boulders was of the order of 1-2m, and the river itself not wider than 10m, but with the boulders soaking wet it would be an athletic feat of great skill. As I slowly edged my way down-stream looking for a suitable crossing point I was astonished to see the skeleton of a footbridge. With no path

leading to it, covered in brambles and most of its slats rotted away, it was clearly no longer in use, but for me it was salvation.

I scrambled across and up a concrete stair now cracked and shattered by roots and emerged, somewhat chastened, into a broad meadow where I could see two large white yurts, some horses and a track. I was home and relatively dry, only one wet boot from slipping into the river. However it was at least 5km to the National Park gate, and after hours of effort and tension I was weary. As the meadow followed the curve of the gorge I suddenly caught a glimpse of Almaty in the distance and picking up a phone signal I sent a text to Marat saying that I was fine and asking him to meet me at the gate. The nomad family greeted me warmly as I passed the yurts, though communication was limited to big smiles. The last obstacle of the day was the same as the first. I had to cross the private land to get out of the valley. Suspecting there would be dogs I kept some big stones in my pocket. I was not mistaken. In a bizarre and deserted ex-Soviet holiday camp there were some large, vicious mastiffs, but happily they were chained up. Decayed wooden buildings were garishly painted with images of children playing. This scene of desolate, abandoned swings and slides could have been straight from a film by Tarkovsky. Lastly, I passed a farmhouse and several gnashing terriers charged out to meet me. The lady of the

 farm did little to call them off as she conveyed to me that this was private land and I shouldn't be there. I made apologetic noises and smiled, she smiled back and off I walked. Marat, bless him, was dozing in the car as I crossed the barrier; I could have hugged all 90kg of him. He said with great irony, "You lazy guy, couldn't you walk the last

12.5km!" And so we returned just as the sun was setting, leaving me to rest my wearied limbs, anoint my large collection of bites and contemplate a brush with death.

The Peddling Provodnitsa

Perhaps no means of transport can quite compare with a slow train across the steppe and taiga. The journey from Almaty to Irkutsk (including a change in Novosibirsk) takes about 65 hours at a leisurely 60km/hour and covers 3,500km. Leaving behind the Tian Shan and Lake Kapshaghay, the immense expanse of the steppe grassland opens up into a featureless monotony, punctuated occasionally by a small industrial town. In the

crushing summer heat, with parched grasses clinging to barren soil, it is hard to imagine how anything but a few hardy grazers make a living here. However there are decaying concrete towns with crumbling factories, sprawling bungalows in various states of disrepair, railway sheds and sidings. Sporadically, as the train passes you see a railway official holding what looks suspiciously like a ping-pong bat. After crossing the mighty Irtysh River at Semey, nearest city to the former Soviet Union's notorious nuclear test site called the *Polygon*, the land becomes flatter but the greenness increases. Huge fields from the collective farm era stretch away as far as the eye can see, lined with tidy rows of poplar and willow.

I had at last obtained an expensive Russian visa from the embassy in Almaty and begun the epic journey towards the Far East. Train life had its own rules and the queen of this itinerant empire was the *provodnitsa*. In carriage #1 on the 302 to Novosibirsk our queen was a short, plump Kazakh woman with an eager manner: eager to make some extra cash from her temporary subjects. Her First Minister was a casually dressed,

chubby man with slightly bloodshot eyes who doled out the sheets and pillow cases for our *plaskart* (known to Russians as hard class) beds. Apart from receiving sheets from him our only real attempt at communication was when he stopped

me on the way to the toilet and said something suspiciously like *baksheesh*. I played the dumb foreigner – "*Ni panimayu*" – and eventually he gave up. Our provodnitsa's approach was more direct. Having taken my passport details her main interest seemed to be my monthly salary in dollars. At the best of times it is hard for me, as a homeless travelling Buddhist, to give a meaningful statement of my financial status, but in this case her motives seemed all too transparent. Once again I was the dumb foreigner saying in English, "It is hard for me to explain". She seemed to pick up that I was being evasive and beckoned me to her small throne room, the compartment from which the Empire of Carriage #1 was run. Here she displayed her collection of Chinese made goods, bags, T-shirts, shoes as well as vodka, beer and cognac. She seemed completely convinced that I needed to buy one of her bags. I explained in English that I had two rucksacks already and that was quite enough, but she clearly didn't understand, and with some frustration repeated, *"Ni panimayu, ni panimayu"*, as if to say "You're just pretending not to understand", which I suppose I was. I wondered if my failure to purchase would have any adverse effect on my status as her temporary subject. A provodnitsa never forgets.

Plaskart, technically third class, is rather like the travelling dormitories of Indian Railways *Sleeper Class*, though a good deal more comfortable since you receive a mattress, pillow, towel and sheets. There is an atmosphere of "We're all in this together", and it's a great way to become part of the family. My first family was nine-year-old Clas, a sweet Kazakh boy, and his parents. Almost as soon as we left Almaty, Clas was keen to try me out at cards. Although we played a dozen games, some of which I won, I never quite discovered the rules, but Clas was happily amused, and the smile with which he would put down his winning cards was worth losing for. I became one of the family since when Clas and his parents ate I was generously included in their meal, sharing salad, bread, apples, but declining the sausage with a "Ya vegetariants", (which got a surprisingly understanding nod). Clas' father, Kanat, had a strong, deeply furrowed face. He sat silently drinking his beer and taking in his son's exploits in an unconcerned way. Clas' mother was plump and short, always with a warm smile and kindly eyes as she played my card hands or offered me things to eat. They all got off the next morning at *Ishigay*, halfway to the Russian border, where Kanat was attending a twenty-year school reunion.

Next I was billeted with Viktor, a warm-hearted 47 year-old Russian, and two young Kazakh girls. Despite having no common language, Viktor and I were soon sharing tea, biscuits, bread and cheese, and having a good laugh at the exploits of our peddling provodnitsa. The girls seemed very shy and spent the midday heat dozing on their bunks, though one of them kept looking at me furtively, and when they got off a few hours later she gave me a beautiful smile and a friendly wave. My final travelling companions were a smooching young Russian couple from Novosibirsk. The man looked brutish and growled at me when he got on. Even taking into account the Russian habit of shouting things in normal conversation I thought he was rather gruff. He asked me to open the luggage locker under my seat and seemed much put out that it was full of my stuff. Amazingly, he later apologized for his rudeness.

Crossing the Kazakh-Russian border by train was a slow process. First, we spent two hours hanging around while the Kazakh police, immigration and soldiers checked everything very thoroughly. Three different officials checked my documents: one for the luggage, one stamped my passport and one scanned my passport into a portable computer. You could be forgiven for concluding that Kazakh immigration was a little over-staffed. Then we spent two hours at the Russian border where they were even more thorough, though mercifully my passport was only checked twice.

When the Russian customs came through to check our bags I unwittingly but judiciously dropped our provodnitsa in it. She had stashed her saleable commodities in the luggage box beneath my berth. Had she expected me to cover for her? For all I knew they could be drugs or firearms and in front of several Russian officials I emotively declaimed that these were *not* my belongings. Later she rebuked me for making her look guilty, but I felt no remorse. Smuggling somebody else's belongings across the Kazakh-Russian border is not recommended. Naturally she got her own back later by cheating me out of some rubles over a "missing" towel. And so train life went on and that night the Siberian mosquitoes first began to drink my exotic, European blood. Having solved the Russian visa problems and negotiated the basics of Siberian train travel I was feeling more relaxed and the sense that I was disintegrating lessened. It wasn't that the deeper problems had been resolved; I knew that they were still just beneath the surface. But the outer momentum of the journey imparted a momentum to the inner processes unfolding in my mind and I felt more able to let that happen without needing to be in control of it.

At Novosibirsk I joined the greatest of all trains, the Trans-Siberian from Moscow to Vladivostok. The carriages were much newer, tidier and unfriendlier than their Kazakh equivalent. After stumbling through a few pleasantries and greetings it became clear to my Russian co-passengers that verbal communication with me would be impossible, most of them just ignored my presence. Our provodnitsa was a young Russian *devushka* who looked like she was still in her teens, wearing a short mini-skirt and fishnet tights. In a moaning voice she complained that I was wearing boots in her carriage, even though they were scrupulously clean. The Russians had brought slippers to wear and she wanted to sell me a tacky pair of Chinese slippers for 200 rubles. I declined her offer and she threw up her arms in exasperation. Later I made a tactical error when she tried to sell me some chocolate. Not feeling hungry I once again declined. From then on it was outright hostilities. When I tried to charge my mobile phone I got a curt "niet", though I discovered that a man from our carriage was charging his phone in her compartment. In the evening as I gazed at the rising moon from an open window I was abruptly moved on from her mopping trail with a sharp "Da, da". I was relieved when her replacement took over, also a teeny provodnitsa with a mini-skirt, fishnet tights and face studs. This time I made a point of buying some biscuits and so was able to partially charge my phone. A classic train tip: never get on the wrong side of your provodnitsa, especially if you're travelling 3rd class and don't speak much Russian.

Our stop in Mariinsk precipitated a sort of platform party. Sandwiched between the *Moscow to Vladivostock* and the *Chita to Moscow* trains, Platform 3 became a sea of Siberian Slavs all out

for a smoke or to see what their cash could buy, which admittedly wasn't much. Mariinsk is an almost inconsequential small Siberian industrial town whose only claim to fame is that it shares its name with the greatest ballet theatre in Russia, the Marinksy in St. Petersburg. Amongst the wares being peddled on platform 3 were, to my great surprise, a variety of large and small lobsters sold raw, here in the middle of Siberia thousands of kilometers from the ocean. Was one supposed to somehow cook them in hot water from the *samovar* at the end of each carriage? I later realized that these must be fresh water lobster from the relatively nearby Lake Baikal (only 1500km from Mariinsk). In any case, the Russian passengers seemed more interested in cigarettes and ice creams, and who could blame them?

After monotonous hours of Siberian Taiga, there were indications that we might be arriving somewhere. Instead of minor stops, little more than a single functional building by a crumbling concrete platform, we passed large factories and sprawling housing estates. Finally we crossed the broad, sparkling and crystal clear waters of the Angara River flowing westwards out of Lake Baikal. We had arrived in Irkutsk, one of Siberia's great cities.

A Day at the Banya

It was a glorious sunny morning at Irkutsk's Raketa ferry port and I was waiting with agitated anticipation. The Russians gathered in clumps and the universal greeting *zdrastvitse* resounded amidst the clasping of hands and generous embraces. We were all looking forward to our journey along Baikal, the world's oldest and deepest lake. We set off forty minutes later than the scheduled time, but I didn't mind. It was just wonderful to be taking a cruise up the Angara River and onwards to Olkhon Island, which is halfway up Baikal, about 300km north of the Angara estuary, and regarded as one of the main centers of shamanic energy in Siberia. I was planning to be there for the summer solstice and to rendezvous with a lovely Swiss woman called Denise who I had met in Irkutsk. The river passage, the lake, shamans and a rendezvous were all guaranteed to put a spring in my step. But the awareness of Baikal's ecological uniqueness and its enormity inspired feelings of great reverence and I had long dreamed of visiting this natural wonder.

The Angara River is broad as it flows the 70km from Baikal to Irkutsk. The huge 1950s hydroelectric dam at Irkutsk has utterly

changed the contours, flooding the valley and sandwiching the river between distant hills on opposite banks. Yet the final passage to the mouth of the river is dramatic, weaving through steep hills that close in on the deepening river. As the ferry navigated the turns we passed rusting hulks driven up onto the gravel banks.

At Port Baikal, our first stop, I was missing a crucial piece of information: I needed to change boat here to get to my destination. With hindsight I have sought long and hard for any clues that might have alerted me to this vital piece of knowledge. The cashier who sold the ticket said nothing, the ticket itself, though giving time and destination, had no indication of a change, at Raketa port I saw no timetable, nor on the ferry itself, my guide book made no mention and the provodnitsa who checked my ticket onto the ferry said nothing. There was a brief announcement in Russian just as the ferry left Raketa, and I listened hard for the magic word *Olkhon*, but since it wasn't named I assumed the announcement didn't relate to my itinerary. In short there was virtually no way for me to discover the information I so vitally needed excepting some good luck, like meeting a Russian who spoke English and knew the ropes. On this occasion my luck was out.

However I enjoyed three hours of blissful ignorance as we headed north up the lake, marveling at the cliffs, forests, the limpidity and sheer expanse of fresh water. When we arrived at our final destination, which clearly wasn't Olkhon Island there was a kerfuffle between the provodnitsa, the gangway boy and myself. They were insistent that I disembark with all the remaining passengers. The place in which we had arrived was barely a one-horse village, little more than a dozen buildings wedged between the beach and the steep forested hills. It was a beautiful little bay, caught between two granite outcrops, but for all I could see not even connected to the rest of Russia by a road. Many of the small settlements on Baikal are only reachable by boat in summer or across the ice in winter. I declined to disembark and be stranded there, showing my ticket clearly marked *Olkhon* which was another 150km up the lake. There followed a rather heated exchange with the provodnitsa as she insisted that we weren't going to Olkhon, and as she kept repeating something in Russian the truth dawned on me "I should have changed boat at Port Baikal". Amazingly, the meaning became clear, even though her words still didn't make any sense.

At this point our jovial Captain intervened, mollifying the provodnitsa so that I wasn't cast away in a backwater on the edge of the Great Lake. I was allowed to remain on board as the crew took a 2-hour break before the scheduled return to Irkutsk. I relaxed a little, though things were still a bit tense between provodnitsa and myself, but our Captain's warm eyes, broad grin, jovial manner and bulbous moustache seemed to say to all of us, "Don't worry, everything will work out okay". I even got a smile from provodnitsa as she said in English, "Lunch!"

Our ferry glided out of the bay, rounded the next headland and beached on an even more secluded and lovely spot. Down went the gangway onto the sand, and off went the uniforms, all

the crew changing into casual dress. Somewhat forlorn, I plodded down the beach with my lunch bag, surveying the world's greatest lake on a gorgeous day, yet staring disappointment in the face and surveying my options. Could I get transport from here to Olkhon? Answer: no, there was no road. Could I get another boat to take me 150km up the lake? Answer: not without paying hundreds of dollars. Should I just make the best of where I'd ended up? Answer: no, since Denise, shamans, solstice celebrations and a hostel reservation were waiting for me at Olkhon. Hence solution: I would have to go back to Irkutsk with the ferry and try again tomorrow. Simple really, except emotions don't work like that. I was filled with a confusing incompatibility of disappointment, frustration, joy and wonder.

After a while lost in my ruminations I became aware of the vast numbers of flying ants that were plaguing the poor cows, who had ruminations of their own, and beginning to get very interested in me and my lunch. As ever, nature's beauty comes at a price, it was time to retreat to the boat. As I climbed the gangway I was surprised to see our Captain (whose name was Mikhail) and able-seaman Maxim stripped bare to the waist, wearing pajama bottoms and carrying towels. With his broad grin the Captain said the magic word "Banya?" and the other members of the crew directed my gaze to a small wooden shack with a smoking chimney. They were offering to introduce me to the Russian equivalent of the sauna, though the word "sauna" hardly begins to describe what was to follow.

My disappointment washed away, like rain soaking into sand. An opportunity for an authentic rural banya on the very banks of Baikal was a good consolation prize. I grabbed my towel and fully dressed ran after Mikhail and Maxim to the smiles of provodnitsa and the other stewardess. The antechamber of the banya had me instantly sweating, itself almost as hot as any sauna I'd ever visited. I hesitated to leave my camera, phone and watch there lest the heat fry their electronics. Naked, I entered the banya proper and the heat was like hammer on anvil. The Captain and Maxim were wearing trunks. "Die Frau!" said Captain Mikhail emphatically with a tone of mild disapproval (we'd discovered that we could partially communicate in German). So I put on my briefs, rather a shame in that liberating setting. The three of us sat together in the heat, as the Captain dowsed himself and the furnace with water, creating a searing cloud of steam. Within minutes we were drenched in sweat. Suddenly Maxim was off, running out the door and down to the beach where he plunged head first into Baikal. I didn't need any encouragement to follow. As my body took the heat shock of diving into the ice cold water, the thought flashed through my mind, "How many Russians die of a heart attack doing this?" At least it would be quick and your body would be nice and clean.

We repeated this cycle several times. The banya was sometimes so hot that I had to crouch as low as possible on the floor with my hands covering my stinging face to make it bearable. The Captain laughed and gestured that I should join him and Maxim on the top bench like a real man. On the fourth occasion I returned to find Maxim lying face down on the top bench. The Captain proceeded to brush him gently with a bundle of hot-soaked birch twigs. And then the thrashing started, all over the back, thighs and calves; Maxim loved it. Next it was the Captain's turn. As the thrashing proceeded his back became ever more intense shades of red and he seemed to both congratulate and castigate Maxim for the vigor of his lashes.

After the next plunge Maxim asked me in Russian if I would like the birch treatment. How could I refuse? As I sat catching my breath from the last plunge he said in English with a smile, "Lets go!" The bench was almost too hot for my skin, so Maxim kindly dowsed it. He shook the excess water out of the twigs and started to brush my back and thighs gently, but with steadily stronger strokes. And then with a sudden shock the lashes began, he continued to the point where I thought my skin would be flayed.

As the pain went over the bearable threshold I groaned and rolled over. Maxim immediately drenched my back with cool water and the whole process began again. Twice was enough for me. Clearly Maxim was doing me a great kindness (at least in his eyes) by administering this torture, so I thanked him profusely in Russian as I fled from the banya and plunged, again contemplating sudden heart failure, into icy Baikal. Is this insane ritual one of the reasons that the Russians have remained unconquered by the armies of Genghis Khan, Napoleon and Hitler? It must breed fortitude into these tall Slavs with their hint of Tatar genes. I suspect that Maxim was a master in administering the birch, so I feel greatly privileged to have suffered at his hand.

Thus my journey to Olkhon became a day out at the Baikal banya. It was a rather expensive way to experience this quintessential Russian rite of passage, via a 12-hour roundtrip on a boat, but nonetheless indisputably a taste of the real thing. And as I wondered at the ferocity of the Russian sauna and if the red blotches on my skin would be gone by the morning, I also contemplated the complete lack of information that a luckless

tourist faces in such a situation. Perhaps this is another source of Russian strength: the need for self-reliance and good preparation. You had better know what you're doing before you embark on it because, sure as hell, the bureaucracy and public services won't help you.

Ulan Ude Idylls

The rain fell in torrents as train 240 from Novosibirsk approached Ulan Ude, capital of Siberia's Buryat Republic, a Buddhist enclave southeast of Lake Baikal. Once again, I, was bound for the Unknown, and felt the familiar mix of excitement and anxiety that assailed me with every new Russian city. My poor Russian and unfamiliarity with the culture meant there was always the possibility some completely basic need would elude me. Would I find somewhere affordable to stay, would I meet anyone with whom I could communicate, would I stumble on some decent vegetarian food, would I figure out the public transport system? These seemingly trivial tasks loomed like Sisyphean obstacles to be overcome again and again. Yet I was learning a deep and reassuring lesson: that somehow things always work out, albeit in the most unexpected of ways.

For instance there was the wonderful banya on Lake Baikal, and eventually the pleasant days spent with Denise on Olkhon Island, though we were looking for different things. Here in Ulan Ude it took me three days to do some laundry. My first attempt was to ask at my hotel. I prepared my vocabulary meticulously, writing down the words for *laundry, cool wash* and *no tumble dry*. But I was staying at the Hotel Barguzin, cheapest of the cheap, and after my virtuoso performance in halting Russian for the floor *babushka* I was given the key to a room with an ironing board. Returning with my laundry in hand I tried to explain to her that I needed to do washing not ironing but I got the familiar, blank *can't help you* stare. She was much more interested in what was on TV. My next idea was to seek out a launderette but they seemed to be an extinct species in Ulan Ude and from the outset this idea was even more doomed than asking at the hotel. By now most of my clothes had been slept in, covered in Siberian mud and sweated through for at least two weeks and virtually able to stand of their own accord. So when a couple of days later I moved into the city's Zungond Darshay *datsan* (temple) for Buddhist women, I thought I was in with a chance to do some hand-washing. I went to a supermarket to look for hand-washing liquid or powder. Siberians obviously delight in economies of scale for most of the packets I could find were 2kg or 5kg bags, not very appealing to a round the world traveler. The smallest I could find was a 500ml bottle of what looked like liquid soap. I attempted to ask one of the supermarket assistants if it was for washing clothes, by using a combination of mime (pretending to wash my T-shirt whilst wearing it), a few Russian words and the appropriate English words. She obviously enjoyed the perfor-mance and smiling gave me a confident "da" as she nodded. So to my great relief I picked up the bottle and headed for the checkout. The only problem was that when I finally managed to borrow a bucket at the datsan (which in itself took some miming and mangled Russian) and soak my clothes there was no lather and no suds, in fact this magic fluid seemed to just disappear into the water leaving no trace but a faint synthetic perfume. At last Zorigma, my Buddhist hostess who spoke a little English, turned up and I explained the problem to which she exclaimed "you buy anti-static!" and burst out laughing. Fortunately she actually needed some anti-static and had some hand-washing powder, so we did a swap. Sometimes, after all the trials you really need a lucky break.

Amid this utterly unfamiliar sequence of experiences, time seemed to inexorably lengthen. I felt like a child for whom each day was immensely long, and a week seemed like eternity. My incomprehension of the simplest things turned me inside out. I both loved and dreaded this aspect of being in Russia. It felt so alive and fresh, but there was no place to hide from the uncer-tainties and confusions. In moments like this, knowing how little I knew, something profound came alive in me.

I had made contact with Zorigma through the Buddhist

network. She arrived forty minutes late at our first meeting and rather flustered. I had all but given up hope of her appearing. In fact, Zorigma was often flustered. She was a warm and generous single mother, with two lovely young daughters, a big smile and an air of busyness. Zorigma also ran the Zungond Darshay datsan for women and in her generosity had invited me to stay in their spare room. This datsan wasn't a nunnery by any stretch of the imagination; in fact it seemed that what really made it the women's datsan of Ulan Ude was that all the people who worked there were women. Zorigma was the manageress, Olga ran the shop and Svedlana – a perplexing mix of elegant, long flowing hair, stilettos and a maroon monastic gown – did the fortune telling. Almost all the women that I saw in Siberia dressed attractively, sometimes even provocatively in skimpy, curve-accentuating garments.

Facilities in the datsan were basic. On one side of the temple was a small room with a desk and an appallingly hard wooden bench that became my bed. On the other side were a kitchen and a toilet. Unfortunately, there was no shower, so on my first day Zorigma deposited me at the nearest municipal banya. Here I joined the men of Ulan Ude in their ritual steamings and thrashings, which was a bit strange as the outside temperature was about 28°C. The banya was about a twenty minute journey by public transport from the datsan and this rather dampened my aspirations for regular personal hygiene. In the end I resorted to locking myself into the tiny toilet and doing my best to have a bucket bath without drenching the floor. But the datsan was a very friendly place to stay. Olga and Albertin (the security man) greeted me warmly and, although we had little common language, we managed to have many 'conversations' about practical matters and the weather. Every morning there was a puja from 9.30-11.00 a.m., and I would sometimes join Zorigma as she led the ritual. The chant was in Tibetan or Mongolian with much ringing of bells and beating of drums, and it felt very much like the Tibetan temples I had visited in Nepal. When I offered to lead a Western puja for them, there was much interest and excitement until we were interrupted part way through by a group of voluntary workers who'd come to paint the ceiling.

Buryat Peregrinations

Svetlana of Narayan Tours was a short round woman, an absolute bundle of vitality, with a deep love of Buryatia and a desire to show its highlights to others. What more could one want from a tour guide? If I'd met her twenty years ago I don't think I could have kept up with her. As it was the first day we spent together nearly wiped me out. When, at the end of it, she

proposed that we start an hour earlier the following morning, and follow an even more ambitious itinerary I couldn't help but accept. Probably fifteen years her junior, and certainly fitter, it seemed like a challenge not to be missed. What kind of traveler was I if I couldn't keep up with Svetlana? Answer: definitely not the sort of traveler I wanted to be.

Slava was an excellent driver. In fact he was so good that he drove every kilometer of Buryat road as if he were in a Trans-Siberian motor rally. On the unmade sand and gravel roads, with frequent dips and potholes, he averaged about 80km/hour, but on the single-carriageway metalled roads, also with frequent dips and potholes, he averaged about 110km/hour: a speed at which I only drive on a well-made motorway. The experience of being driven by Slava was like having one's organs and ligaments prized apart inside a small vibrating box. But the amazing thing about my two-day tour of the Buryat Buddhist sites with Svetlana and Slava was that I was actually paying them in excess of $175/day to be driven to exhaustion and shaken to pieces. I wouldn't have missed it for anything.

On our first day we headed for the famous datsans of eastern Buryatia. Under a glorious blue sky I felt a leap of joy as we left the contained sprawl of Ulan Ude and hit the wide-open steppe of the Uda valley. Our first venue was a ridge top cafe, where we stopped for a timely breakfast. There were looks of dismay as it emerged that I didn't eat meat, chicken or fish (somehow chicken was classed as a flesh in its own category). "How can you stay warm in the Siberian winter without eating meat?" Svetlana wanted to know. I declined to answer with the obvious "Use central heating and eat lots of carbohydrates". Svetlana interrogated the waitress, as only a native speaker of her gusto could do, and proceeded to order everything on the menu that didn't contain meat or fish. On learning that I was vegetarian many Buryats seemed to assume that I needed to eat vast volumes of food compared to meat eaters. So I breakfasted on borscht (beetroot soup which had some suspiciously meaty flecks in it), cabbage piroshki (dumplings), coleslaw salad and sweet pancakes. Not the most obvious selection of flavors and textures, but wholesome enough. Heartily full, we drove onwards and Slava wound down his window and threw out 10 kopeks as an offering to the local spirits. He repeated this ritual every time we crossed a pass between two valleys.

The Astagat datsan is famed for its once-great library. Like almost all the datsans of Buryatia it was destroyed during the purges of the 1930s, but the library was preserved and sent for safekeeping to the museum in Ulan Ude. The self-proclaimed Head Lama was a well-built man who sported a sort of cowboy hat. He was married with a family, and fixed me with a firm gaze as Svetlana translated for us. Since all Buryat Buddhists are part of the Gelug tradition in which lamas are celibate I asked how he came to be married. He explained, rather nonchalantly, that whilst it was true that ordinary lamas had to be celibate, the more advanced ones could marry. One had to admire his brashness.

After advising me to become a monk, and suggesting that we travel together to Tibet, he took us to a small waxwork museum dedicated to Lama Agvan Dorzhiev, most famous of all Buryat lamas. Dorzhiev became well-favored by Tsar Nicholas II and was responsible for building western Russia's first Buddhist temple in St. Petersburg. Amazingly, it survives to this day. He lived at the Astagat Datsan for many years until his death in 1938 at the hands of Stalin's secret police.

Svetlana prided herself on never forgetting how to find a place previously visited, no matter how long ago. Our journey to the remote datsans of Buryatia was to test her to the limits, but she always got us there in the end. The Aninski Datsan was the most wonderfully remote. Slava drove us off the metalled road onto the open steppe where we followed furrowed tracks and, when these petered out, just drove off-piste across the grass. Aninski was built by a well-known Irkutsk architect in the 19th century and had the honor of being the first brick datsan ever

built. It was styled on a church design and in its prime must have been very impressive. Now however it was a ruin, blown up by soldiers during the 1930s.

As we approached we saw two cars full of monks driving across the grass in the opposite direction. One of the cars stopped and out got the portly and beaming young Lama Leksok, head of the datsan. He happily joined our car and took us on a tour, explaining the history and detailing the plans they had for rebuilding it. Across the plain were some wooden buildings, the current monastery, to which he invited me for a retreat when I

had the time. Lama Leksok had plans to build 108 stupas all around the vast valley, each one paid for by a different local family, and already about a dozen straddled the horizon. These stupas framed against the dark grey sky gave the steppe a rather unworldly aspect, as if the local spirits were gathering for a séance.

Buryatia's most holy Buddha statue is the *Sangden-Jo* or Sandalwood Buddha. The faithful believe it to be 2,500 years old, having been carved when the Buddha was still alive. However it appears to be of Tibetan or Mongolian origin and perhaps a few hundred years old. In any case, the age is unimportant since it is a beautiful wood-carved standing Buddha with a serene face and uplifted gaze. In the new purpose-built shrine room at the  Evinski datsan I made an incense offering and chanted some sacred verses. This caused a bit of a stir and several people including two young monks gathered to listen. The new shrine hall was still being finished for the forthcoming grand opening and we were amazingly fortunate to actually see the *Sangden-Jo* which had only been installed on the previous day.

A Buddhist Hero

On our second day we visited more datsans and the remote, unassumingly beautiful Sartaktey valley, which is only 30 km from the Mongolian border. Rolling forested hills clasp a narrow valley with a lovely river and flowering meadows. From time to time a rocky outcrop bursts through the forest to shatter the flowing contours and add a sense of the dramatic to the picturesque landscape. As we progressed further and further up the valley the unmade road became a dirt track, the dirt track become two mudded furrows, and finally we drove across open fields. We were pursued by swarms of vicious looking horseflies up to 3cm long and with fearsome probosces that would easily extract a small chunk of flesh. I was immensely thankful for the protection afforded by our car. The herds of cows and horses we passed from time to time were sorely plagued.

Slava literally drove us as far as he could up a hillside, and we

discovered a roughly made stupa surrounded by flags amidst the pines. Three Buddhas were represented in bas-relief: blue, red and yellow. Nearby was a tiny cabin with some Buddhist images and a wooden staircase that climbed steeply up the hillside. Ascending 246 steps to a tiny clearing on the forested slope we found a small hole in the ground, about 70cm square, topped with a grassy covering and decorated all around by flags. Climbing inside I found myself in a space about two meters square and one meter high, lined with untreated timbers and furnished with just a small brick stove. There was just enough room to sit up in one corner.

The site commemorates the life of Hambo Lama Darmaev. The Hambo Lamas are the head lamas of Buryat Buddhism, holding a position similar to the Dalai Lama for Tibetans. During the Stalinist purges of the 1930s all the Buryat lamas were either killed or imprisoned. Lama Darmaev was sent to the gulags, but at some point he was either separated from his transport or managed to escape. The guards left him for dead, but he was found, barely alive, by local Buryat people and they built this tiny hole in the ground to shelter him from the secret police. Here he lived for three years, facing the bitter Siberian winters and the vicious summer bloodsuckers in his little cave. It is hard to imagine how, but he survived and in 1947 he became the Hambo Lama, founding one of the most important new datsans in Buryatia, the monastic study centre at Ivolga. Here he trained a whole new generation of monks. Were it not for him Buryat Buddhism would almost certainly have died out under Communism.

Nailed to a nearby tree, a bleached and blistered photo in a plain wooden frame showed a man gazing out. Only one eye remained recognizable, yet within that gaze was a hint of directness and kindness. He wore a plain jacket and shirt buttoned at the neck, the left side of his face dissolving ethereally into the whiteness of the paper, as if he were materializing from

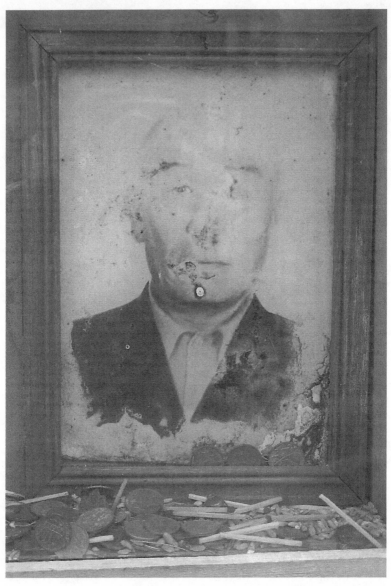

another dimension. This little shrine had been decorated with coins, grains of barley and, curiously, even matchsticks.

Cramped but comfortable, I lit a candle and serendipitously found some dry incense with which to make an offering. I chanted some Buddhist verses to celebrate Lama Darmaev's amazing feat of survival and the life that he had lived for Buddhism. Contemplating his struggles and successes moved me deeply, how the life of one man may sometimes encompass the fate of a whole culture. What must he have endured in those grueling years of hiding; what vision sustained him during his ordeal and what gave him the energy to rebuild a shattered lineage? Lama Darmeav is truly a modern Buddhist hero.

The Journey to the Far East

Siberia is staggeringly, ungraspably large. Crossing east to west by train it takes over a week to reach the Pacific coast and Vladivostok, the Lord of the Russian East. From north to south it is even larger, stretching from the mountain borders with Mongolia and China to the Arctic Ocean. The only way to even begin to comprehend this vast landscape is to journey through it tree by tree, river by river, valley by valley, mile by mile, day by day. There are many moods to the Trans-Siberian railway. The taiga, relentlessly encircling the northern hemisphere, is an unfathomable wilderness, the breathing lungs of our planet. This primeval forest remains virtually unchanged from the dawn of time. The taiga cradles the railway in a tunnel of conifers: tall, short, standing or fallen. But after hours of forest monotony, the procession of pine, birch and larch feels almost claustrophobic. With a palpable sense of relief you suddenly emerge into the sublime emptiness of the steppe: vast green meadows speckled with flowers, gently rolling hills, huge open skies, and a glimpse of the horizon. Another mood is the river valley, of which there are many in this vast territory, the train dodging hills and ravines as it weaves its track alongside a swift torrent. Built in an era of vastly more sedate travel and crossing such varied terrain, very little of the railway is in fact straight. Lastly there are the hamlets, towns and cities: lonely outposts in the immense wilderness. The first sign of an approaching conurbation is a thinning of the trees, tidy little vegetable patches eked out from the forest and the discovery of a mobile phone signal (though for the greater part of Siberia you can forget about anything other than satellite communications). Next come the dwellings: at first just a single blackened log dacha surrounded by a weathered grey wooden fence and all manner of rusting scrap. Then the houses gather in little clusters until finally you reach something resembling a town. The concrete cities are so far apart that they feel like rare visitors to a vast nature reserve.

Long distance train life revolves around the station stops, sleeping and the ubiquitous *lapsha* (instant noodles). When it comes to sleeping and *lapsha* everyone follows their own routine, which in any case is being constantly usurped by the regular transition of time zones, usually an hour a day. Some sleep by day and eat by night, others try to keep abreast of the changing time. At the station stops the provodnitsa opens the door, wipes the handles with a hygienic flourish and we all queue to be down the four steep steps and onto the rough concrete slab that serves as a platform. The first out is the first to get to the station *magazin* or shop and thus the first to buy whatever is going. The other urgent reason to exit from the train is the call of the cigarette, a habit that is alive and well in Russia, though thankfully all the train carriages are non-smoking. Usually there are some elderly *babushkas* walking with slow effort along the platform selling their home produce, which is invariably more interesting than the shop produce, but a little more risky. The *babushkas* sell anything from hard-boiled eggs to meat filled dumplings. You feel that you ought to buy their wares regardless of whether you want them. Supporting *babushkas* is something of a national pastime, especially since the collapse of the Soviet Union has left so many of them with little security in their old age.

The pre-eminence of the noodle is unrivalled on a Russian train. From dawn to dusk a steady stream of people, clasping their pots and bowls, make their way to the samovar. Here the noodles are doused in boiling water (usually at 90°C) and with a hallowed reverence, slowly transported back to the appropriate berth. The shared reverence for the noodle is amazing. People move carefully out of the way and children are shushed to the side as if a holy icon were about to pass. Or is it just that carrying boiling water on a jolting train is liable to create scalding accidents? Either way, the noodle is a central feature of train life and the closest thing to a collective ritual. Naturally, there are noodles and there are Noodles. Some come in large polystyrene trays replete with flavorings, assorted and indistinguishable freeze-dried bits, vinaigrette sauce and even a small plastic fork. These are the kings of *lapsha*. Others are plain in little plastic covers, the gourmet required to provide his own bowl and fork. Where the ingenuity really shows is in the additions that each person makes to his or her noodle feast. Mayonnaise is very common, and also chunks of tinned meat (which, to my vegetarian eyes, usually bore a close resemblance to dog food). The most common flavor is chicken, entirely synthetically flavored and almost indistinguishable from my favorite: mushroom. Thus you can cheerfully pass the long miles of forest and steppe sustained by instant e-numbers.

Making Friends

Embarking on Train 054 from Kiev to Vladivostok, I was billeted with two sturdy Russian men, Vlada and Sasha. They gave the barest acknowledgement of my *zdrastvyute* but I recognized this as a typical beginning for Russian acquaintanceship. A Russian friend once gave me some very helpful advice: "At first Russians seem really cold and unfriendly, but once they know you, you'll be accepted as one of their own". In *plaskart* accommodation there is nowhere to stash your pretensions; you see each other in all modes and moods. In fact, most Russians seem to take a *plaskart* journey as a way to let their hair down in public. In summer the men are often bare to the waist, exposing their vast dumplinged bellies unabashed. The women dress in pajamas or skimpy shorts, as if they were pottering about the house prior to a visit to the beach. Yet though there are certainly some attractive *malchiks* and *devushkas,* all this bare flesh isn't the least bit erotic. It represents a kind of shared family life in a safe public space. So the station stop exodus can be quite a remarkable spectacle. Suddenly hundreds of semi-naked beings erupt onto the platform and mix in complete unselfconsciousness with correctly presented railway staff and formally attired new travelers who haven't yet *gone native*. No one seems to be in the slightest bit aware of the incongruity of these two modes mingling, it is a just a natural part of Russian railway life.

With Vlada and Sasha I bided my time, it's best not to try and make friends too fast. Soon Vlada, a solid hulk of a man at 56, got interested and started to ply me with questions in Russian. We managed with some effort to get through the essentials. He and Sasha were going to Vladivostok to buy Japanese cars which they would transport to Novosibirsk for resale. Judging by their familiarity with all aspects of the journey it was one they had made many times. Vlada seemed to take a paternal interest, furnishing me with tea and biscuits, wanting to know why I wasn't married, and offering to procure me a Russian wife. Though in reality only thirteen years my senior I had acquired a temporary new father. As the dominant alpha male in our berth of five men and a woman, it was up to Vlada to take the lead, and Sasha, in his mid-30s, was more reserved. When on occasion I joined in with a four-way game of cards, without any real understanding of the rules, Vlada kept a close eye, giving me winning advice at key moments and trying to stop the others from sneaking a glimpse of my hand. Fortunately there was no vodka drinking so I didn't have to decline insistent offers. Vlada was the main drinker, downing about two or three bottles of beer as the evening wore on.

Sailing to Sakhalin

Arriving at Port Vanina to take the ferry to Sakhalin Island when you have a reservation is an appalling experience. Arriving without a reservation is downright hellish. Since neither my guide book nor the travel agent with whom I enquired gave me any reasonable hope of being able to make a reservation I was destined for roughly twenty hours of hell, the time it took to acquire a ticket and be herded on board.

My Caucasian travelling companion Oleg (who was really from the Caucasus) and I spent sixteen hours of this time queuing  for a ticket, and up to the very last minute I had no idea whether we would actually embark. The details of the brutal ticketing system are tedious in the extreme. From our train's arrival at 8.00 a.m. until midnight, just one hour before the scheduled ferry departure, we queued in a dingy ticket hall with intermittent breaks when the cashier disappeared. Even the worst that Indian and Nepalese public transport can throw at you pales in comparison to the SANES (Sakhalin ferry line) ticketing process. Virtually no information is forthcoming, there is just one cash desk, a grindingly slow process for each person, a stony faced cashier, no idea of your chances of procuring a ticket, or even when or how to try.

This wasn't just because I was an eccentric English tourist way off the beaten track and lost in the Russian bureaucracy. The savvy Russians who knew the system and could pronounce with confidence the magic word *brony* (reservation) also had an awful time of it. By 2.00 p.m. the cashier was issuing tickets to the privileged *brony* holders, but the scene was not a pretty one. A semicircular scrum had formed around the cash window, with shouting and physical presence being used to the utmost effect to get pole position. It was every man for himself, or perhaps I should say every woman, since the formidable middle-aged *zhenas* seemed to be dominant. The pack had a visceral feel, and as one person got their prized little white slip there was a sudden surge to take her place, leading to one hefty *zhena* almost punching her way out with her ticket in hand. Predictably, those who were most unpleasant seemed to fare better, the more generous spirits, of which Oleg and I were but two, finding themselves always at the back.

Watching the people, one could see frustration, anger, despair and finally relief or triumph when they received the magic paper. Some had a selfish look: "I'm getting my ticket so get out of my way"; others had a sympathetic look: "This is really awful isn't it". As the hours passed I was constantly aware that my Russian visa would expire soon and that there was little margin for error with my onward voyage to Japan. I found myself passing through an ebb and flow of hope and hopelessness. Someone would say that unreserved tickets would go on sale at 4.00 p.m.: hope. By 6.00 p.m. we were no nearer getting a ticket: hopelessness. The darkest hour was just after 6.00 p.m., when hopelessness reached a peak and Oleg decided to give our passports to a complete stranger who would keep our place in the queue. I was understandably very nervous about this, protesting and continuing to queue to make sure that he didn't disappear with our precious documents. Oleg tried to convince me with, "This is Russia, it's okay". In the end I bowed to his greater experience, and there seemed little hope of any other strategy other than just giving up and trying to get a train to Vladivostok instead, forty hours away. There followed a buttock clenching couple of hours when the stranger did in fact disappear with our passports and I contemplated the Russian police, British consular services and trying to explain why I'd given up my passport to a total stranger. Oleg was utterly unconcerned and somewhat amused at my regular "When do we get our passports back?" He was of course right. Faced with a legacy of appalling queues the Russian people have developed the concept of the queue *person on duty*. One person, usually a total stranger, will look out for the places of a number of others who are then free to go and do other things with their time: a very humane and communally-spirited response to the appalling bureaucracy.

Another response I noticed was looking for someone to blame for our collective suffering. I couldn't really blame the aggressive men and women for their selfishness since under these conditions such behavior was bound to come out. I couldn't really blame the cashier since, though slow and stony, she was just working within a brutal system. For a short while I tried to pin the blame on to Oleg. "Why doesn't he push harder and get to pole position?" Of course, if he had been that kind of guy we wouldn't have become friends, and I wasn't prepared to act like that myself. My blame was absurd. I confess that my least charitable thoughts were for the management of SANES ferry line. In my imagination I had them all sent to a gulag where they perpetually queued for the basic necessities of life without ever knowing if they would receive them. But they were probably just running a company that had had no investment for a decade. Finally, I blamed myself. "*Why* did you come here?" But self-blame isn't my forte, so in the end there was no one to blame; just the awareness that we had all ended up here because we wanted something, a journey to Sakhalin.

Towards midnight the hope and hopelessness oscillated increasingly rapidly. Our man on duty got to the front of the queue, but he gave the passports back to Oleg; Oleg got to the front of the queue, but a late person with a reservation arrived and took priority; Oleg gave the cashier our money, but she queried my British passport. The oscillations were so rapid that I almost lived the emotions in frozen moments of time. "This is ridiculous, it's just a goddamn boat ticket!" Finally Oleg emerged with our tickets, I felt some relief but I was also sad at the collective frustration we'd all been through and aware that many people still didn't have a ticket.

The story didn't end there. Two hours after the scheduled 1.00 a.m. departure there was still no information about when our ferry would be ready. Some bright spark realized that the transit bus was outside, so like a flock of sheep we all marched out to spend a freezing thirty minutes in a car park; the bus was locked up with no driver. Eventually, people drifted back into the warmth of the waiting room until around 5.00 a.m. we got the announcement that the bus was ready to go. It was clearly too small to take everyone and there was the same animal frenzy to get in that I'd seen at the cash window. "Crazy Russia", was Oleg's comment. By this time, tired and cold I just joined the mêlée and pushed my way on. In fact the frenzy was totally pointless since at the other end we waited 20 minutes on a freezing foggy quay for the second bus load to arrive before the crew let us on board. Here was another small act of carelessness, why couldn't the crew be prepared to welcome us straight away? This time I imagined having the whole SANES management shot. At last the hells began to recede. Some relief came as we found our bunks in the smelly bowels of the ship, were given linen and collapsed into sleep after twenty hours doing battle with the ferry company systems.

The epilogue is that the 22-hour crossing was rather pleasant: calm waters, a sedate rate of knots, alternate fog and brilliant sunlit seas, passable canteen food and a friendly young provodnitsa. We were woken up at 3.00 a.m. with every expectation of disembarking at 4.00 a.m., but the fog around Kholmsk was

viscously thick. In the gloom our ferry stopped its engines and drifted offshore waiting for an opportunity. Occasionally there was a distant blast of a foghorn from Kholmsk harbor, a kilometer or two away. As I stood on the freezing deck, the damp air chilling to the bones, the sea was deathly still. Somewhere out there was an intermittent snorting and my mind raced with possibilities from dolphins or whales to mythological giants ready to pull us down to Davy Jones' locker. Finally, I caught a glimpse of a beautiful sleek seal. In the end, the fog delayed us another ten hours, drifting to and fro. A journey I thought would take about twenty hours had in fact taken us fifty-six hours. As Oleg said, "Eta zhivu!" ("That's life!").

Heading to the Land of the Rising Sun

Sakhalin Island, nearly a thousand kilometers long, fought over by Russia and Japan, now dripping in oil money, is outstanding for its rugged wildness. A powerful ridge of hills runs like a long spine from the northern tip in the Sea of Okhotsk to the southern tip, just 100km from Japan. Here the range breaks into two spurs so that the capital, Yuzhno-Sakhalinsk is caught in a pincer between them on a large plain. This makes for a dramatic cityscape where as you gaze along the long straight boulevards east and west the view terminates in steeply forested slopes. Crossing the hills by bus you weave through the valleys following the path carved by the fast flowing rivers. And Sakhalin in summer is indescribably green and fecund. Everywhere in these rain-drenched hills plants grow profusely, trying to get as much as they can out of the warm season before the winter snows arrive.

At Korsakov immigration I had prepared myself for a fight. Tales abound of foreigners being fined when leaving Russia for not having enough registration stamps in their passport. These are remnants of the old system with its suspicions of what you have been doing in Mother Russia. These days it seems to be more about making money than security. You are obliged to get a stamp from every place you stay for more than three days, but, of course, in practice it is impossible to get a stamp from everywhere, and for my four weeks in Russia I had only managed two. "Where have you been for the rest of your visit?" is the obvious ruse of an immigration officer wanting to make a bit of extra money out of a departing tourist. As the only English speaker in this far flung part of the Russian Far East I was an obvious catch. In anticipation I had kept every train and boat ticket, hotel receipts and even a left luggage slip. I had evidence to account for my whereabouts for each day of my stay. But there was the nagging doubt that a scrupulous official would find some obscure reason to relieve me of my cash. So I was only carrying a small amount of rubles about my person, my stash of emergency Euros hidden in the deepest recesses of my luggage.

In the event the immigration was a mere three-minute formality, the officer even met my *zdrastvyute* greeting with a slightly warm acknowledgement. His buddy eyed me closely from the barrier as we went through the paperwork; I looked at him directly once so as to communicate "I've got nothing to hide" and then avoided his gaze. I was even a little disappointed that there was no call to produce my impressive collection of train and boat tickets, some of them obtained at no small cost.

The difference between the quality of service in Russia and Japan is graphically demonstrated by the difference between the SANES ferry to Sakhalin and the Heartland ferry to Wakkanai. Buying my ticket for Wakkanai took little more than five minutes in a comfortable downtown office in Yuzhno-Sakhalinsk, and the agent even phoned round to book me a cheap taxi to Korsakov port the next morning. After Russian immigration we boarded a smart new coach in an orderly fashion. An elderly Japanese lady thanked me profusely and embarrassingly for letting her sit next to me, and at the quay most of the Japanese crew were standing by to welcome us personally on board, bowing gracefully as we passed. After weeks of battling through Russia this was a bit of a shock. Inside the ferry was spotless, modern and full of light. Economy class consisted of shoes-off seat-less bays where you could sit or lie down. We left within ten minutes of schedule. The five-hour crossing cost six times more than the scheduled twenty-two hour crossing from Port Vanina.

The sea was glassy still as the little Japanese ferry *Eins Soya* (I found myself wondering if it was made of a single piece of tofu) made a dash for it through the fog. The boundary between sea and sky was lost, giving a horizonless sense of the infinite out there. There were just two shades blurring imperceptibly into each other: white-grey meets green-black, like a huge natural Rothko abstract. There was something deeply mysterious about the stillness and the invisibility. Occasionally I glimpsed a close-knit flock of petrels floating by in the thinner patches of fog. One or two would chase the ferry as if to relieve the monotony. Or an air blow would break the calm waters as I saw the disappearing head of large seal. Amazingly, this freezing watery wilderness was teeming with life, as evinced by the large clumps of seaweed that sporadically drifted past.

I arrived in a grey, rainy Wakkanai: a reckless adventurer with no language, no guidebook and no real destination in Japan's most northerly town. Fortunately, this being Japan there was a tourist information desk with a young woman who really wanted to help me. However it wasn't all plain-sailing. There was a conference in the town and almost every room was booked out; the banks all closed at 3.00 p.m. giving me just twenty minutes to find an ATM; in the youth hostel the manager physically ejected me from the front desk for not taking off my shoes; and my request for a vegetarian meal at a fish restaurant had them laughing me out the door. Had I imagined that the journey would be easier just because I was now in a developed country?

Japanese Dewdrops

First Impressions

Although I arrived in Sapporo, Hokkaido's bustling capital of two million souls, around midday I was still too late to bag a cheap hotel. As ever, the girls at the tourist information were faultlessly polite and trying hard. After several "Fully booked" rejections my assistant, Chihiro, said, "You know Cap-sool hotel?" My heart sank; yes, I knew about Capsule hotels. "Very cheap", she added as if to offset my look of dismay. "Well I suppose it will be okay for one night and I ought to find out what they are really like" I tried to convince myself. After so many weeks of Russian dormitories on trains and boats sampling the Japanese equivalent wasn't high on my agenda.

There is something unnerving about the experience of staying in a Capsule hotel. It is hard to say whether this is because your possessions are spread between lockers on different floors, or because you are allotted a personal space not exceeding two cubic meters, or because of the shockingly explicit and neatly laminated pornographic images in the lift advertising the paying adult TV channel (the sort of thing I would only expect to see in a Soho backstreet). Whatever the reason, it's unnerving. This is an emphatically male environment, since most Capsules, which seem to be a feature of every major Japanese city, don't accept women guests. With clinical Japanese precision, everything is arranged down to the smallest detail. My key for the shoe locker was deposited in a pigeonhole labeled 506, which was also the number of my basement locker and my bed space on floor five. Machines were embedded into the fabric of the building offering alcoholic and non-alcoholic drinks, internet access, instant, highly-plasticized food, cigarettes, clothes washing facilities and vouchers for the porno TV channels. It was possible to satisfy all one's human needs, and desires, without ever interacting with another human being.

My capsule was a prefabricated unit: really just a bed with built in TV, radio, light, alarm clock and air-conditioning. On the fifth floor, in the space that might accommodate one or two medium sized hotel rooms were enough capsules for 40 men,

one-up and one-down on both sides of a central corridor. The densities weren't quite at South Asian levels, but it wasn't far off the crowding of a Kolkata street. Yet it was neat and clean and every man has his own tiny private space. The best part was the communal bath. On the seventh floor was a smoke-filled TV lounge adjacent to the bathroom. The vestibule housed yet more lockers,

though in this case you could pick any locker you liked: a shocking lapse of orderliness. The bathroom consisted of six sit down showers and a large 4m by 3m bath sunken into the floor. Here I joined the band of Capsule guests, stripped off, lathered up, showered and soaked in this generous bath which I had mostly all to myself. It was very refreshing. There was no verbal communication, every man attending scrupulously to his own hygiene, and yet I felt a strange bond between us, as if entering this utterly male preserve I was receiving some kind of Japanese initiation.

Back in the communal TV room it was football, beer, cigarettes and adult *manga* comics. And some of then were decidedly *adult*. Explicit sexual imagery seemed to be much more acceptable in Japan than in the West, yet I later discovered that the relation between the sexes was wrapped in formalities so presumably sex was too. Here was one of the many apparent contradictions facing a foreigner visiting Japan. Unsurprisingly, with all the sexual imagery around, and having recently arrived from far more strait-laced Eastern Russia, the place stirred erotic feelings in me. I guessed I wasn't the only one, but to my relief, the Capsule hotel seemed to be a totally devoid of cruising men. By contrast, going to a communal male bath in England would be tantamount to looking for a gay pickup.

Surprisingly, I slept remarkably well, at least once the earplugs were in, and I even managed an early morning meditation, though my hair brushed the top of my capsule as I sat cross-legged. I can't say that I liked the Capsule world, and the next day I checked into a budget hotel, but it wasn't as bad as I had feared and, yes, it is cheap by Japanese standards.

Heading for Honshu

It was raining ninjas and turtles as the Toyako to Muroran bus dropped me in the middle of a neat industrial estate with copious car parking and big green spaces. Even though I ran for it, trailing my wheelie backpack through the puddles, in the 40 seconds it took me to get to some shelter I was completely drenched. No wonder Hokkaido is so green and lush.

I had gone to Toyako to see the beautiful volcanic lake and bathe in the natural hot springs, and was now crossing south from Hokkaido to Honshu, Japan's largest island. What I expected to be the ferry terminal, the bus' supposed terminus, turned out to be an open air sports stadium, though the only customers were a bedraggled flock of sodden seagulls. The two receptionists seemed bemused at the appearance of this lone *gaijin* (foreigner) dripping in their foyer and complete with luggage. There followed a linguistically challenging few minutes while they communicated that this was not a ferry terminal and I asked if I could sit out the rainstorm in their lobby. We eventually understood each other and the manageress kindly offered me a tasteless but hot cup of instant coffee and, later on, an umbrella. Her generosity touched me deeply. Since I was in

Japan I had expected joined-up thinking in which the bus would drop me at a spanking new ferry terminal, rather than in a parking lot next to a sports stadium. Another illusion was shattered. Actually there was a spanking new ferry terminal, but it was 300m away on the other side of the lorry park, and there was no way of knowing this other than asking strangers or just wandering around in the rain hoping to stumble upon it.

No matter how many times I convince myself that taking a local bus for an intercity journey is a good way to see local people and the real life of a country, I always end up regretting the grindingly slow procession of suburbs, shopping malls and housing estates that seem to comprise real life. The bus took about 135 minutes to cover just 50km: for Japan that was agonizingly slow. In this case there was no other option other than a very expensive taxi. As I was the first to board and the last to exit, I concluded that not many people make this trip. And that is hardly surprising since Toyako is a very chic spa resort, close to Sapporo city and served by two airports, whilst Muroran port is the economy ferry option to Honshu from Hokkaido. In fact Toyako is so chic that it hosted the G8 summit just before I arrived. Another opportunity to rub shoulders with the great and the good missed.

Meeting the Poet

Travelling in Japan's Deep North I met a kindred spirit, a poet called Basho. Though he died three hundred years ago, he offered me his friendship through careful observation, deep emotion and delight in the small things along the Way. This was a man who, seeing a five hundred year-old ruin would weep for the long-dead warriors who had died there; a man whose dream drove him to sell his house and propel his old body, which he called a "weather exposed skeleton", on to the open road. He left with no idea if he would ever return, exhibiting remarkable fortitude. Ultimately, no travelers know whether they will return.

I wrote Basho a haiku to cement our friendship:

Ah, so wonderful
To meet a friend along the Way
The boats and trains
Grow weary of my solitude.

Basho travelled throughout Japan, but his most famous and longest journey was captured in a masterpiece of Japanese literature *The Narrow Road to the Deep North*. Since I was travelling from the Far North, in fact the Farthest North, I decided to follow a small Basho pilgrimage and visit some of the places that he described.

I wonder what haiku Basho would compose, now that his beloved Matsushima is overrun with hotels, amusements and retail opportunities. A Japanese sense of decorum prevails, none the less, the seaside tat is of the more tasteful variety and Matsushima is scrupulously neat and clean. Regarded as one of Japan's great natural wonders, Matsushima Bay is home to about 250 pine covered islands, and with gentle lapping waves and miniature beaches, it is unbelievably picturesque. Avoiding the

crowds I spent much of the time sitting on Oshima Island, one of three connected to the mainland by a bridge, and gazing out across the bay towards the Pacific. This was a place frequented by monks and carved into these ancient rocks, entwined in pine roots, were dozens of little alcoves each with its own Buddha image. Basho wrote a famous haiku here, which is inscribed on a rock at the centre of the island:

Breaking the silence
Of an ancient pond
A frog jumped into the water
A deep resonance

Dewa Sanzen

After a stay in Sendai, capital of the northern Tohoku province, Basho recommended that I climb the holy mountains of the *Dewa Sanzen*, and how can you to disregard the advice of a 17th century Japanese beatnik and literary genius? So I took the cross-country bus via the remarkable feat of engineering that is the Yamagata Expressway, with tunnels and viaducts all the way, and an abrupt change of weather as we passed through a 3km tunnel under the mountains from the finely drizzling east to the humid, sun-drenched west.

The Dewa Sanzen, the collective name of the three holy mountains of Haguro-san, Gassan and Yudono-san, has been a place of pilgrimage for over 1,000 years. In particular it is the main destination for *yamabushi* pilgrims, followers of a rather eccentric fusion of Buddhist and animistic Shinto beliefs. The Ideha Bunka Kinekan, a sonorous name for a museum, has a delightful video installation that projects two yamabushi actors onto a real miniature waterfall. They start by emerging from a rock in formal costume blowing shells and horns before bashing sticks, and then they reappear in loincloths squatting and grunting. For a modest fee of $300 you can attend a weekend course and learn to be a yamabushi.

When I met Mr. Masamito he was hunched over something in the bushes; in fact, he could even have been relieving an urgent call of nature. Seeing me peering at him, he jumped up, as if discerning my uncharitable suspicions, and spoke some rapid Japanese. Somehow from his gesticulations I gathered that he was looking at flowers, which turned out to be his great passion. As I strolled on he matched my pace and we naturally fell into walking together. In fact, Mr. Masamito was exceedingly fit, striding up the 2,500 steps of Mt Haguro two at a time. When he told me that he was 73 I bowed deeply in respect and made sounds of amazement. I often met seniors of his stamina. The Japanese age remarkably well.

Mr. Masamito spoke not one word of English, so my dozen words of Japanese were the only verbal communication we were able to share. Yet we enjoyed one another's company for two hours, either walking in silence or me listening to his enthusiastic Japanese explanations of history and nature, whilst making appreciative "Hmms" and "Ahhs". Discovering that I was a friend of Basho he took me on a detour to visit the ruins of an ancient temple where a famous Basho haiku had been composed. Basho had been overcome with emotion at the ruins:

I drenched my sleeves
In a flood of reticent tears

Mr. Masamito was utterly delighted when I produced the English translation from my backpack. The temple's decay was even more complete than when Basho had visited and all I could see were a few piles of stones. I too felt a sudden surge of emotion at the ephemeral nature of life, my link with a long dead poet and companionship with a contemporary flower lover.

The forest ascent of Mt Haguro was quintessentially Japanese. There were vast, looming conifers, deep green mosses and ferns, carefully placed rocks with elegant kanji inscriptions, streams with delicate wooden bridges, a towering five-storey pagoda, aged wooden shrines and an uneven ancient stone staircase. Add to this all manner of wild flowers, a chorus of birdsong, the cacophony of cicadas and the hint of a fox and you were transported to a timeless, magical Japan where the natural world teemed with benign and malign spirits. Some of the malign ones

took the form of vicious biting flies, or tiny kamikazes that flew into my eyes.

Halfway up the 400m climb was an old tea room. I was going to pass it by but Mr. Masamito indicated with his open palm that we should sit for a tea. From the verandah you could gaze out over the Tsuruoka valley, and just beyond the haze, discern the waters of the Sea of Japan. We were served a free cup of iced green tea – wonderfully refreshing – a traditional service to the pilgrims of the mountain (at first, I was offered many expensive choices of tea à la carte). It was stiflingly humid, and both Mr. Masamito and I were sweating profusely. We reached the summit and made a quick tour of the temples, bowing and clapping in the traditional manner that Mr. Masamito showed me, but really it was less about the destination than the ascent itself. After ten minutes or so we agreed to go back down, and shared a silent communion as we descended through the forest. Eventually we parted with a heartfelt two-handed shake and mutual delight. We never met one another again.

At Oquibo I had landed in a working pilgrim's rest house or *shukubo* complete with shrine room, white clad yamabushi and hordes of children on a summer school trip. The owners were unfailingly polite and welcoming, but they were rather perplexed at the arrival of a lone English Buddhist. I was given my own bedroom and separate dining room while the other guests slept in large groups and ate together. I would have been happy to join the communal meal, but that clearly wasn't the done thing. Catering was a major event and there was a large canteen kitchen to prove it. On my first night I waited for an hour in my private dining room while the groups were served.

The yamabushi are famed for their ascetic practices: walking barefoot through cold mountain streams, sitting naked under icy waterfalls and eating vegetarian food before undertaking the pilgrimage to the Three Holy Mountains. The culinary hardship reflects the intense Japanese love of meat and fish. At Oquibo rest house I was furnished with an ascetic banquet of vegetarian delights. Served in individual bowls were a dozen different flavors and textures, colors and aromas, all exquisitely presented: from fat udon noodles to rice, from pickled radish to miso soup. Some of these remarkable dishes took me far from my familiar food zone. I was merely puzzled by the small shriveled-brown leaves in clear jelly and wondered why anyone would want to eat something so bland and nutritionally worthless? Then there were the clear wormlike noodles in lemon sauce with hot, grated ginger. But most startling of all was the crème caramel desert with a sweet-looking yellow topping that turned out to be blisteringly hot mustard. My exclamations of surprise must have passed through several paper walls, since the following evening the crème caramel came topped merely with a glacé cherry. I was both relieved and disappointed, and a little suspicious that I had been the object of a culinary practical joke. Add to all this lashings of tofu, salad and freshly steamed vegetables and it was one of the best meals I have ever eaten … and the kind of asceticism I could really learn to endure.

Mme Joshu was a delightful and diminutive woman of latter years. She shuffled in a traditional way with her toes pointing together, and had an infectious laugh and smile that lit up her whole face. As proprietress of Oquibo, which can host up to a hundred pilgrims a night, she was certainly a capable person, yet you wouldn't guess it from her air of charming absent-mindedness. Her husband was the Head Priest at the rest house, performing morning drummings and evening worship, but he seemed distant and aloof. The real heart and soul of Oquibo was Mme Joshu. She delighted in showing me around the *shukubo* from the shrine to the ancient ropes and lacquer-ware and we even exchanged tips on how to bow correctly to a Buddha. On seeing the way I made a bow she exclaimed with amazement a rapid "So, so, so, so". In fact a stream of "so's" was her favorite exclamation for anything from, "Yes, you've got it!" to "How interesting!"

When we parted she gave me two gifts: a printed dragon cloth and a little guardian bell that I attached to my rucksack to ward off evil spirits as I walked. I didn't know the form for parting so I shook her hand, but she offered me her cheek, which I kissed lightly and then she embraced me with her tiny frame. As I walked down the road to the bus stop she stood waving from the *shubuko* gate

until I was out of sight. How wonderful to meet someone of seventy so full of zest for life!

Ascending the Holy Mountain

The Japanese public transport network is phenomenal. It is phenomenally effective and phenomenally expensive. Wherever you want to go there will be a train or bus going there sometime soon. From the sleepy village of Haguro, a local bus arrived to the minute of its scheduled time and collected me, the only person on the street. On board were a few fit looking middle-aged Japanese decked out in the latest hiking fashions. The driver had already discerned my destination. "Gassan?" he questioned and I nodded appreciatively. At Haguro summit we collected one passenger, Stephane, a French solo traveler and intellectual (at least he certainly smoked like a French intellectual). He looked startled when I greeted him with, "Bonjour" but even in Japanese his French accent was unmistakable.

The bus laboriously wound its way up 22km of hairpin bends through the forest and deposited us at the trailhead for Mt Gassan, a dead end road. I was shocked when the driver wanted nearly 1700 yen ($20), which was hardly a local fare, but I was still immensely appreciative that any sort of bus would make this trip, without which my intended hike would have been impossibly arduous or prohibitively expensive. It was Stephane who suggested that our meeting was more than pure chance, and I felt it too in my heart. In the swirling mists and intermittent rains a solo hike to Gassan and Yudono-san would be somewhat perilous, so we were both in need of a companion. Yet more than that, we met as kindred spirits exploring an unknown destiny. I had seen Stephane the previous day as he made sketches at the children's cemetery on Mt Haguro. He said that the contrast between the tragedy of a child's death and the brightness of the colorful bibs, clothes and shoes affixed to each form, had arrested his attention.

As we plied our way to the summit of Gassan, highest of the Dewa Sanzen peaks at 1984m, visibility was down to a few meters. This created an eerie atmosphere, shapes suddenly emerging from the cloud: a small wooden *torii* or symbolic gate, a statue of Jizo (Bodhisattva Ksitigarbha) clad in a red bib, a pilgrim plodding silently wearing a round straw hat and propped up by a strong wooden staff. As we passed through flower strewn alpine meadows, the bundles of lilies were lovely even in their shroud of mist. Often we would hear the jingling of the pilgrim's bell several minutes before seeing a mature party clad in white cotton tunics. Only the most dedicated were making the journey under these conditions. The path was easy to follow, laid as it was with large rocks that made a kind of pavement, but the mist and rain had made it treacherously slippery. At one spot an elderly yamabushi took a nasty tumble, but he just got up silently and continued on as before. The hardship of the pilgrim's journey is intimately bound up with its sacred purpose. If you could make the climb in stilettos and listening to an iPod then the journey would lose its meaning. At times we had to cross well-trodden snow fields, the snow black with grit and dripping with

melt water. Lower down the temperature was a humid 22°C, yet amazingly many of the snow fields persisted. I couldn't think of a convincing scientific explanation so I plumped for the magical one: these mountains were inhabited by various cold-hearted spirits who froze the waters.

At Gassan's summit there was a *shugendo* shrine which could not be entered without first going through a purificatory rite. So Stephane and I paid 500 yen ($6) to an enrobed man in a tiny damp ticket booth, who then proceeded to chant and shake a large paper pompon at us. The whole ritual took less than a minute leaving my conscience no lighter than before. I couldn't help feeling that the ritual had become an empty commercial rite. As we were about to head off into the fog, attempting the more navigationally challenging route to Yudono-san a Japanese woman stopped and asked in perfect English if she could help us. From her mountain gear she was obviously a seasoned walker and proceeded to produce a map, something we hadn't been able to procure at the tourist office. To my surprise and immense gratitude she gave it to us saying that she could easily get another one: yet another anonymous kindness.

When we finally dropped out of the clouds Stephane and I discovered we were walking in a lovely green valley with precipitous forest clad slopes, and equally precipitous rusting metal ladders for the descent. We came upon a dwarf pine clinging to a large rock that seemed to encapsulate the essential Japanese wilderness. The next day we rendezvoused and took the train south. Stephane had dreamt a big dream after our hike and was feeling a deep call to change some of the fundamentals in his life. We talked of meaning, love, philosophy, religion and forged one of those deep yet transient connections that are the soul food of solo travelling. When we parted I felt a sudden intense pang of loneliness; the delicacy of the feeling was curiously Japanese as if taken from a novel by Soseki, the most celebrated of Meiji writers.

Searching for Saints

Seeking Shinran Shonin

Pilgrimage is essentially a state of mind, a way of perceiving the journey, imbuing it with wonder and opening yourself to an inner resonance. The external particulars of a journey may be identical for two travelers, but the pilgrim looks for a way to express delight at life's mysteries and devotion to people and places worthy of reverence. As I meandered through northern Honshu, led by Basho's epic journey to the Deep North, I realized that, while one pilgrimage was coming to an end another was opening up. Basho's guidance had led me to the northwest coast of Honshu and from the depths of remembrance came the recollection that this very coast was where the great Buddhist teacher, Shinran Shonin (Shinran the Saint) had been exiled in the 13th century. This turned out to be the most spiritually creative time of his life and during his exile he completely recast his understanding of Buddhism. He rejected his twenty-year monastic training and founded the Jodo Shinshu, now Japan's most prolific Buddhist school. He is one of the four Japanese teachers most revered within my own Buddhist community, and it dawned on me that here was a clear invitation to visit his temple. I had found the key to the next stage of my pilgrimage around Japan: to seek out these four saints and pay them my respects.

One of the ironies of traveling in Japan, given the Japanese' insatiable appetite for technology, is that the telecommunications were the most difficult of my entire trip. My PDA phone, deep-fried by the irregularities of Russian train voltages, was obsolete by Japanese standards. Nowhere could I purchase a spare battery and, worse still, it was incompatible with the 3G network. Add to this a paucity of internet cafés and internationally-enabled payphones, and I was struggling to write, research or stay in touch. Traveling down the coast by bus and train I spent two days hunting for an internet café where I could research Shinran's exact whereabouts. In Niigata station, prefectural capital and local transport hub, I finally found a free internet point, and with jaw-dropping amazement discovered that this was exactly where Shinran had been exiled. A touch of destiny seemed to have deposited me there.

At Niigata tourist information there was great consternation when, amidst the stream of people wanting trains, buses and hotels, I asked for information about Shinran Shonin in the locality. Miko, the young assistant, spoke some English and kept apologizing profusely that she knew next to nothing about Shinran. She seemed very ashamed by her lack of knowledge. Doing a rapid research job of kanji webpages, she informed me that Shinran had lived out most of his exile near Naoetsu 80km to the south. There were, however, seven miracles associated with Shinran's time in Niigata town. Miko giggled nervously as she retold the story of Shinran casting a grilled fish into the sea, which then swam away, as if to say, "But only a child would believe it". I tried to reassure her that this was exactly the sort of story that I wanted to hear about, but perhaps I only managed to convince her that I was a very eccentric gaijin. The sites commemorating the seven miracles around Niigata were all accessible by bus, but the information was typed in kanji, my guidebook had not a single reference and the local department bookstore had no English language books on Shinran. I imagined myself wandering around Niigata, trying to get off at an unknown bus stop and find a monument to a miraculous grilled fish all in an unintelligible language, and gave up the idea as a little too crazy even for me. So I settled for a stay in Naoetsu, once a tiny fishing village and now a commercial port, where I was assured they had lots of information about Shinran.

It was a grey, hot and humid morning in Takada, near Naoetsu, as I walked slowly but with great anticipation to Jokoji

temple. When I arrived the precincts were deserted, but the statue of Shinran in his pilgrim's hat and holding a rosary was unmistakable. The main avenue leading to the *hondo* (shrine hall) was lined with gently twisting gingko trees, and in some huge pots grew large flowering lotuses. I bowed to Shinran and entered the hondo. The interior was a classic Japanese combination of dark wood, tatami, black lacquer and gold. On the shrine was a lovely standing Amida Buddha. The solitude and beauty put me in a devotional mood, so I lit some incense and chanted a mantra to Amida, the Buddha of Infinite Light, who is the presiding figure for the Jodo Shinshu. Eventually a woman appeared and proceeded to mop the verandah of the hondo; we bowed respectfully to one another as I left.

Shinran founded Jokoji having been exiled for the heretical views which he enshrined in the *Kyogyoshinsho*, the seminal text of the Pure Land schools and a ground-breaking work of Buddhist thought. At Jokoji he completed this work, and that of remaking himself after his seemingly fruitless years as a monk. He was inspired and happy here and, having studied the *Kyogyoshinsho* some years previously, I, too, was inspired to be at the place where the master had worked. I was touched by the particulars of Shinran's life: his courage in recreating himself after a spiritual crisis, his emphasis on surrender to the Buddha Amida and his abandonment of attempts to use *self-power* as a means of spiritual growth seemed to resonate with my own unfolding journey. I too was learning to intuit direction from forces outside my control and let my life be shaped by what Shinran called *other-power*.

I went in search of the office to see if I could gain access to some of Shinran's personal affects including his skull (a rather macabre touch), which was reputedly kept at Jokoji. I met the wife of the Head Priest and managed to convey in broken Japanese and English that I was a Buddhist and student of Shinran's writings. She seemed delighted to help and unlocked the small room containing scrolls, cabinets and paintings associated with Shinran. The skull, it seems, had been lent to another museum. Inspired by the visit I wrote two haiku.

Jokoji temple
Happy happy the place
Where the Buddhist Saint
Completed his great work

The lotuses of Takada
Bending in a summer breeze
Blush gently
Shy of their own beauty

Dogen's Legacy

Eiheiji monastery was founded by Dogen Zenji, one of the greatest of the Zen masters. Carved out of a steep hillside, it is surrounded by towering ancients of cedar and pine. Water cascades under old stone-arched bridges. The traditional wooden meditation halls merge seamlessly with the trees, ferns and mosses. It appears to be a natural and spiritual paradise.

Yet I didn't take to Eiheiji. Unusually for Japan the welcome for gaijin seemed rather inhospitable. The rather expensive ticket came without further information and I was simply directed towards a large modern office block with a confusing number of entrances. At the first doorway an old lady who was sweeping shouted at me and pointed to a different doorway. Here I entered what looked like a Buddhist airport departure lounge. In several directions were long counters with monks and laywomen sitting behind computers and telephones. Many civilians were filling in forms or making payments. In front of me was a big sign, the only part of which I could decipher was "1500 yen", and old ladies selling yet more tickets. I wondered if I'd bought a ticket to the wrong thing. In vain, I asked for the way to the old temple, but no one could help and there was not an English sign in sight. After asking at all the desks I was eventually directed to a monk who gave me an English pamphlet about Eiheiji. But he immediately told me that I could *not* go to see the introductory video in a nearby room since it was only for Japanese. He gave no reason for this inexplicable prohibition. He motioned that I should ascend an unlikely looking staircase, the sort that might serve as a fire exit for a university faculty building. He became very insistent until I just ignored him and sat down to read the pamphlet. Inserted before the contents page was a leaflet called *Rules for Visitors* neatly typed and giving eight rules; things like, "Don't leave the wooden walkway because your socks will become dirty and bring dirt into the temple". If the paying visitors get eight rules for a short visit, you begin to wonder how many rules the monks have to follow.

The unpromising staircase led to several unpromising neon-lit corridors. Eventually, however, I emerged into a beautiful, sunlit cloister with weathered timbers and abundant plants. Here was old Eiheiji, with its traditional wood carved *hondos*, elegant covered walkways, graceful curving roofs, and carefully crafted stones. From time to time, amidst the throng of tourists a monk would come and go, usually genuflecting as he passed the main hondo: a mark of respect to Dogen. Some of the monks smiled warmly as they went on their way, others were less friendly, like one who shooed me out of a hall included in the tour with a dismissive wave of the hand. The *daikuin*, or kitchen, was one of the main places I wanted to visit, it being the inspiration for

Dogen's most approachable writings on Zen practice at work: *The Advice to the Tenzo* (monastery head cook). Unfortunately you were only allowed to see the vestibule, not the *daikuin* itself.

I couldn't resist breaking at least one rule. With naughty-boy delight I padded in my stockinged feet down some stone steps to get a better view of the impressive main gate, it being impossible

to see it properly from the wooden walkways. I did, of course, brush, all the dirt off my socks before returning to the temple walkways. But no alarms went off, the Zen police didn't descend on me. Perhaps the rules weren't to be taken so literally after all. What would Dogen have made of it all?

Meeting Kobo Daishi

The baffling sequence of trains that connect Kyoto to Koyasan (no less than four trains and two different railway companies) only take you 80km. But the change in environment couldn't be more pronounced: from urban intensity to mountain retreat.

However, Koyasan isn't the mountain retreat that it was when the temple was founded by Kukai (known honorifically as Kobo Daishi) in the 8th century. The isolation of this remote mountain forest plateau has been eroded through the course of centuries by the arrival of nearly seventy temples, lots of souvenir shops and a spectacular funicular railway. The train ride through the winding mountain gorges and the final funicular ascent are remarkable in their own right. Despite its evident transformation into a tourist destination, Koyasan remains magical.

As I boarded the connecting bus at the Koyasan funicular terminal I was accosted (no lesser expression does it justice) by a lively and garrulous middle-aged English woman called Sheila. Where was I going, where had I come from, what was I doing in Koyasan? Sheila vigorously informed me, and anyone else we happened to meet, that though she was English she was currently living in China and had done so for the last few years. It turned out that we were staying at the same temple, Haryoin, so we made our way there together.

Arriving at Haryoin we rang the bell and waited for what seemed like an age before the sliding door was unlocked and a physically disfigured man appeared before us. He was bent over in a hunched shape, and dragged his right leg along as he walked. Sheila quickly ascertained that he had suffered from some kind of brain trauma that had left his body rigid and misshapen. He greeted me politely but was sterner with Sheila. Though she had booked she had forgotten to reconfirm on a certain date and he made it very clear that she was at fault. I waited to see if she would get a room or not, but in the end it turned out fine. I reflected that his attitude wasn't altogether welcoming, something that was to be dramatically confirmed for me later on.

In a gentlemanly sort of way I decided to wait for Sheila, even though she chattered incessantly and, as soon as the formalities of arriving at Haryoin were over, we set off to see the sites. She plied me with many questions, some of them quite deep, about my life. I hesitated, but eventually decided to attempt a meaningful answer to her questioning. However, just as I was articulating one of the deeper motivations that had led me to travel the world, Sheila disappeared. Turning, I found she had darted into a shop and was fascinated by a lady weaving at a loom. I waited for a few minutes and then bade her farewell. She nodded momentarily and then seemed to forget I was there. I was rather relieved to be on my own again. As I made my way through the village, passing the many trinket and souvenir shops, my purpose was clear, I was here to meet Kobo Daishi. The most important shrine in Koyasan is the Okunoin, the inner sanctuary, which is situated at the far side of Koyasan's huge and ancient forest cemetery. Here, it is said, Kobo Daishi is still in meditation, awaiting the next Buddha whose message he alone will be able to interpret for humankind.

To approach the road through the cemetery one passes many of the temples, and one in particular, Shojoshin-in, caught my attention. Whether it was the wood-carved gate, the beautifully manicured pines, the little stream running by or something altogether non-rational, my feet propelled me into the temple grounds. Here, a Japanese man who was mindfully sweeping the wooden verandah greeted me. I removed my shoes and wandered down the corridor. On one side was a wonderful garden, on the other elegant rooms each with a different shrine. Eventually, I came, at the very end of the corridor, to a dimly-lit classical Japanese room with painted sliding screens, tatami floors, and in the centre a formidable image of Kobo Daishi, holding a *vajra*, the symbolic thunderbolt, to his heart. Surprised to be meeting him face-to-face like this, I felt a surge of gratitude and joy and spontaneously chanted some devotional verses. When I had finished these ministrations, Kobo Daishi was smiling at me broadly. I left that small, dim room feeling quietly elated.

Walking through the forest cemetery and visiting the Okunoin was one of the most atmospheric and moving moments of my entire time in Japan. Amongst the immense pillars of towering cedar (cryptomeria japonica) are a million or more tombs of the great and the good of Japanese history. In the deep green light the mosses and ferns cling to the stones and you pass into a timeless world, at once delightful and reflective. The majestic beauty and monuments to the dead call up reflections on your own life and death. The effect is one of deep aesthetic awareness and intro-spection. The paved way to Kukai's mausoleum meanders slowly,

each turn revealing another striking monument or mighty giant of the forest. Eventually, you arrive at a small complex of traditional wooden buildings where the faithful purchase their offering plaques and prepare to make their devotions.

Amidst the afternoon throng of visitors I joined in and anointed the arrayed Bodhisattvas at the entrance by splashing them with mountain spring water. Further along the track was the *Miroku-ishi*, a stone locked in a cage whose weight is determined by your impure deeds. Aspirants attempt to lift it from a lower to a higher shelf. I put my arm through the tiny gap and tried to lift. It was indeed a strain, but by taking off my watch I was able to squeeze my second arm through the gap and then the lift felt as light as a feather. No one said that you had to lift purely with one hand.

Finally, I ascended the steps to the Okunoin hondo. Inside the clouds of incense were thick and thousands of paper lanterns lit a large shrine space, at the centre of which a Shingon priest intoned a puja. I removed my shoes and joined the small crowd of worshippers in attendance. As the bells rang and the drumbeats resounded, a sort of peaceful one-pointedness descended on us. At a certain moment in the ceremony we individually took turns to offer some incense and bow to the shrine. It felt like the most natural thing in the world. After the worship had finished I walked around the hondo and spent time gazing at the mausoleum where it is believed that Kobo Daishi still sits meditating. Many people came and went, making offerings in a spirit of joy and sincerity. The atmosphere was uplifting and inspiring. The Okunoin was the most tangibly holy place I visited in all Japan.

Back at Haryoin I washed and joined the other guests for dinner, but I was feeling rather uncomfortable. The feeling came from the little details of the place. Though the amount we were paying made this a fairly expensive night's stay for me, Haryoin seemed quite ungenerous: the dinner was meager, there was no guest towel, the rooms were stuffy with no mosquito screens so that opening the windows was not advisable, and when I asked for some cold drinking water I was refused. Since I had run out of change for the drinks machine this left me very thirsty in the heat. I began to feel that the place was rather oppressive and decided to go out for a walk.

In the night-time dark the streets of Koyasan village were deserted. I had no idea where I was going, but just that I needed to get out of Haryoin. My feet intuitively guided me in the direction of the Okunoin and forest cemetery. I felt a frisson of fear and excitement as I entered the forest. The path was lit with elegant stone lanterns, but deserted and at night the forest was an altogether different place. The silence was complete and arresting. From the shadows forms seemed to take shape and then dissolve again as I walked past. Occasionally, a sudden sound would startle me, but the atmosphere was strongly benign. I began to enjoy being in another world and an exhilarating intensity and one-pointedness filled my mind. I wanted to continue all the way to Kobo Daishi's mausoleum, but, as it would take a couple of hours to get there and back and I didn't wish to inconvenience the temple, I turned back halfway. As I emerged from the forest a party of young boys were entering led by their teacher. They looked at me somewhat startled and amazed, as if I were a wood spirit, before erupting into calls of, "Hello", "Good-bye", and "How are you?" I smiled at them, exchanged greetings and walked on.

When I arrived back at Haryoin it was about 9.15 p.m. Though I had told them I was going out and would return soon, the gate was well and truly locked. I knocked vigorously for some minutes, and eventually heard some noises from inside. Our disabled host finally arrived and unbolted the gate. As I took off my shoes he was clearly very agitated. "You must obey rule!" he said several times before finally asking me forcefully, "You understand?!" to which I had to say, "No". Finally it dawned on me that they must have a locking up time and I had come back too late. As I turned to go to my room he again said forcefully, "You must say, *'Very sorry'*". The fact that 9.15 p.m. didn't seem outrageously inconsiderate, that I had been unaware of their locking up time and his aggressive manner meant that I didn't feel particularly sorry, but he was clearly upset, so I offered a mild sorry and walked back to my room. There I reread the rule sheet I had been given on arrival and there was indeed a sentence which included the number nine but since it was written in kanji, there was no way to guess that it said they locked up at 9.00 p.m. I wondered to what extent the rigidity of our host's adherence to rules and the rigidity of his physical form were connected. My feelings for Haryoin as an unfriendly and somewhat oppressive place were confirmed. Next morning, foregoing the temple ritual, I went to visit the Okunoin one last time. At this early hour the forest and Okunoin had yet another atmosphere: cool, refreshing and silent. Some early pilgrims were out, but the main throng of tourists had yet to arrive. This holy place had a different mood morning, noon and night.

Over the centuries many pilgrims have come to Koyasan to ask for Kobo Daishi's blessing before undertaking the hardships of the 1200km pilgrimage to the 88 temples on the island of Shikoku. I too was planning to do part of that pilgrimage and it seemed quite natural be at Koyasan seeking to meet with Kobo Daishi. The tradition of the Shikoku 88 temples says that you never undertake the pilgrimage alone since Kobo Daishi is always at your side, often symbolically represented by the traditional walking staff. As I basked in the atmosphere of Koyasan's Okunoin and forest cemetery I began to feel that, indeed, I wasn't fully alone. Occasionally, this would bring tears of gratitude to my eyes. All of us are travelers on life's difficult journey and, perhaps more than anything else, a human being needs to feel the companionship of a kindred spirit.

Thinking about my experiences at the temples of Koyasan and

Eiheiji I was struck that in this faultlessly polite and welcoming country the only two places where I felt unwelcome were two of the holiest Buddhist sites. What a strange irony! I was left reflecting on the detrimental effects of high reputation and hordes of tourists on religious institutions.

Looking for the Wild Ivy

Latter-day Shoinji, nestling near the slopes of Mount Fuji, isn't the haven of peace and tranquility you might expect from the temple of a formidable Zen master. Rinzai master Hakuin was abbot here for fifty years. This was a man who demanded a rigorous meditation discipline and who famously locked himself in a shrine at Eiganji temple and meditated continuously for seven days before having a significant realization. Hakuin had returned to Hara, the village where he was born, to escape the incessant politics of the Kyoto temples in the early 18th century. He established Shoinji as an important and reforming centre for Rinzai Zen. But the urban sprawl of modern Japan hasn't favored Shoinji, now sandwiched between the JR railway line and a major highway.

In the front of Shoinji was a very old and beautiful tree named the Suribachi pine: a wonderful example of the Japanese appreciation of plants as part of their cultural heritage. The temple complex was partially a building site, with new foundations in the process of being laid and large piles of building materials filling the gravel entrance. I wandered around trying to find Hakuin's tomb, which the city plan indicated was in the temple grounds. Amidst the hundreds of stones I was unable to decipher enough of the kanji to be sure that I'd found the right one. I asked a man, who might have been a gardener, but he just waved me on in a vague way leaving me none the wiser. Finding no one who could enlighten me about Shoinji and Hakuin I took to the hondo and decided to offer some incense, chant some traditional Buddhist verses and meditate. The hondo was small and had a friendly atmosphere. On the main shrine were a classic line drawing of Hakuin and a photo of an elderly monk laughing.

As I meditated I felt very contented and peaceful. Contemplating Hakuin's unique contribution to Buddhism moved me deeply. From his biography it is clear that he was a sincere seeker of the truth. Though he is said to have become 'enlightened' while still a young monk, he judged that his experience was only partial as he was unable maintain the insights he'd had in the bustle of the day-to-day. He strove intensely to integrate his understanding with everyday living. In his autobiography *Wild Ivy* he says, "I feel like a physician who possesses a wonderful knowledge of medicine but has no effective means of curing an actual sickness". Hakuin's uncompromising commitment to meditation practice, his willingness to abandon religious institutions, and his self-honesty gave me inspiration for the path on which I was embarked.

Refreshed and uplifted I once again went in search of someone and met a tiny old nun with a kindly face and dressed in a blue-grey pajama suit. She led me to a little hall with a neatly lined set of meditation cushions. At the far end was a raised

cupola and ascending the stairs I saw a beautiful shrine with a strikingly lifelike wood carving of the Zen Master. "Hakuin-san" she said with a great smile in her eyes. I gasped and bowed deeply. She left me alone with the Master as I lit some incense and chanted sacred verses. I couldn't resist taking a photo of Hakuin gazing at me, though he gave me a stern look as I did so.

Contrary to my usual habit of leaving only a token donation at the temples I visited – many of which were already immensely rich – the simplicity of Shoinji, the unfinished building works and the humility of the old nun moved me to leave rather more. As I offered her a 1000 yen note she gasped and asked me if I would like some tea. Unable to speak together we sat in silence as I drank some delicious ice-cold green tea. As I parted she gave me a present of a simple plastic fan on which was printed an iconic image of Hakuin. As if to capture the specialness of my visit to Shoinji, when I set off for Hara railway station I caught a glimpse of Mt. Fuji through the August haze. I gazed in wonder at the majesty and grace of its silhouette, no longer clad in winter snows. Within thirty minutes Mt Fuji had disappeared again, enveloped by cloud. I felt touched by a blessing from the mountain.

A case of Zen Digestion

After many weeks slowly making my way south on the highroads and byroads of Japan I finally felt ready for an encounter with the cultural heart and ancient capital: Kyoto. The city boasts so many exquisite masterpieces of architecture, landscaping, art and historical artifacts that every visitor is in danger of being overwhelmed and succumbing to cultural indigestion. I decided I would explore the city in small, bite-sized chunks.

Steve and I met by chance, solitary strangers on a bus, and in the easy way of the solo traveler we fell into a pleasant camaraderie, sharing the delights of Kyoto's Zen temples for a day. Steve was a young Cambridge graduate in English, now a teacher doing a part-time MA and with a zest for travel. He was wearing bright-yellow Indian trousers, clutching his Lonely Planet Japan tightly to his breast, and simultaneously trying to keep control of his various bags as well as a soiled paper cup. I thought this combination of artifacts a little strange for a seasoned traveler, but of course you don't say that to a complete stranger. It turned out that he had been trying for some time to find a dustbin in which to dispose of the cup. For somewhere so incredibly tidy one of Japan's strangest omissions is the great lack of public dustbins. His cup was actually symbolic of responsible waste disposal.

After enjoying a morning in the bamboo gardens and temples at Daitoku-ji we arrived at Ryoan-ji housing perhaps the most famous and admired of all Zen rock gardens. I generally take the adulation lavished on the Zen aesthetic with a pinch of salt. The Ryoan-ji blurb confidently informed us that the Zen garden evoked "a complete sense of the natural world without any trees, grasses or flowers" and that the fifteen rocks in the garden had been "expertly placed". Yet entering the rectangular walled garden I did feel a tangible sense of beauty rising in my mind. Despite the crowds of admirers, something about these rocks, mosses and gravel was indeed uplifting. Steve and I sat there for a while, just gazing at these carefully placed granites and slates. I am certain that, with typical Japanese care, every last detail was significant. Some of the rocks were smooth, others were jagged; some were tall, others were flat. But, sadly, a prosaic description leaves you no wiser. However, the effect was intensely pleasing. After a while, we both tried to get the perfect photo, along with dozens of other tourists, and I have to admit feeling slightly embarrassed by my shameless attempt to digitally capture the intangible quality of Zen beauty. But as Steve put it rather succinctly, "One's got to do it really". Having wandered around the temple for a while, there really wasn't much else of note beside this tiny patch of rock and gravel; how amazing that thousands of visitors a day pay to come and see it.

My exit from Ryoan-ji was spectacularly incongruous, though very few people noticed. This being the third Zen temple of the day, I had managed to achieve a near perfect state of spaced-out *satori*. In this altered state of awareness I managed to put on another man's shoes, which admittedly had a strong resemblance to my own, and even walk a few paces before realizing that I was wrong-footed. The only people who seemed to notice my rapid re-hoofing were the two ticket ladies, who gave me very strange looks as I swapped footwear. What a wonderful irony, a seasoned meditator exiting the most refined of Zen temples and walking off in the wrong pair of shoes. Surely a dangerous case of Zen-digestion!

Realizing that we were both seriously *Zenned-out*, Steve and I decided to forgo any more temples and head for the famous bamboo grove in Arashiyama, at the base of Kyoto's western

hills. What is it that is so enticing and fascinating about bamboo? Amongst Asia's wonderful flora, bamboo seems to hold a privileged place. We passed from the toy town tourist promenade of Arashiyama village into the deep green grove of giant bamboos. Though small (a ten-minute walk was enough to emerge at the far side), these groves evoked a kind of timeless oriental realm. Steve and I, trying to find a suitable description of the essence of bamboo played an associative word game: deep green, dense, delicate, linear, powerful, soft, dark, magical; the abode of foxes and deadly assassins.

The last pilgrimage of the day, and the most physically exacting, was finding a particular *onsen* (public baths) that had a cool pool as well as the usual hot tubs. Steve had been before, but the journey by public transport from the bamboos of Arashiyama was rather complex. In Kyoto's heavy humid heat we ended up with a walk of several kilometers down the main roads before finding this shangri-la bathhouse: a suitable reward for a hard day's sight-seeing. The onsen was certainly worth the effort with nearly a dozen different ways of soaking, heating and cooling the weary body. Cheap and compact it was clearly a favorite with the locals, for many Japanese men were scrubbing or soaking when we entered. I showered and dived into the nearest bath: so very relaxing! But Steve was looking distinctly uneasy and confused. "It's definitely the same building, but this isn't the place I came before". Was Steve also suffering from a severe case of Zen-digestion, was he having some strange flashback or déjà vu? After some minutes puzzlement we figured out that the men's and women's baths had been swapped over since his last visit, as evinced by the completely pink toilet facilities, which had struck me as rather out of keeping in a men's public bathing facility.

The last shock of the day was yet to come. Steve waded into a particular pool and suddenly jumped out again. "I've just had a strong electric shock!" he said. I tried it too and yes, an unpleasant tingling started all over my immersed skin. "This isn't good, maybe there is a loose wire somewhere". But no one else seemed in the least concerned, and one Japanese gentleman had been happily sitting in the same pool before Steve got in. Using impeccable group logic Steve concluded that since no one was worried about it, it was probably meant to be like that. I wasn't so sure, but in any case both of us eschewed that particular dip.

Finally, we returned to Kyoto station, where Steve had a train to catch, and, as it was already late, we wandered about rather desperately trying to find a vegetarian meal. In a dimly lit bar we had a passable supper and talked about our lives. At one point Steve brought up the subject of sex, but then said rather embarrassed, "Oh, but I shouldn't talk about sex with someone I hardly know". I said I didn't mind since sex was a very interesting subject. Looking round at the beautiful couples in the bar I added rather innocently, "After all, probably everyone in this bar is here because of sex". Steve looked rather startled and we changed the subject. On the way back to the station Steve being gay, invited me for a late night liaison, which I, being straight, politely declined. He was clearly disappointed but we parted warmly, having shared a day of unexpectedly Zen moments.

In the footsteps of Kobo Daishi

Beginnings in Bando

The unforgiving midday sun was baking the little town of Bando as I arrived. At last, after all the preparations, I was about to begin the long dreamed-of pilgrimage to the Eighty-Eight Temples of Shikoku Island, one of the oldest and longest pilgrim routes in the world. All I knew about the practicalities was that one starts at Ryozenji (Temple 1), where I hoped to find what I needed to continue. In the oppressive August heat Bando prompted a momentary cultural hallucination by reminding me of a deserted hacienda where a sombreroed bandit might come riding lazily down the street as a haunting spaghetti western melody echoed in the air. Without a map I groped my way to the temple where a few pilgrims, known as *henro*, were making their offerings. I entered the *hondo*, the main shrine hall, and lit some incense for the Buddha, unsure what to do next. In the shop next door a busy little Japanese nun stood behind the counter. When I approached and explained in mangled Japanese what I intended, clearly looking rather new to the Shikoku pilgrimage, she gave me her full attention. Immediately I was given a gift of a sleeveless white cotton henro shirt: "Present from Ryozenji" she said smiling. Soon I had an English language map book, a volume for collecting the temple stamps, a small container of incense, a classic straw henro hat, and the offer of a *Kobo Daishi* walking stick. Though at a rough calculation these items should cost about 10,000 yen, she only charged me 3,000, for which I was very grateful. The henro path can be unpredictably expensive. Shirt and hat are the distinctive garb of the pilgrim. Wearing them you are immediately recognized both by other henro, with whom you feel a bond of kinship, and by ordinary people who may want to help or perhaps just to greet you. The hat is also good protection against the sun and the rain. "Bigger is better" said my nun

friend. I immediately felt like I'd joined the henro family, having been recognized by one of the pilgrim mothers. This was the first of many such kindnesses on the *Shikoku hachi ju-hachi* (The Shikoku 88). The people of Shikoku have been practicing *osettai*, or receiving and supporting henro for over 1,200 years, and sometimes their generosity is breath-taking. Often, when you are most in need, as I was at Ryozenji, the giving just occurs naturally. Such is the magic of pilgrimage. By the time I set off for Gokurakuji (Temple 2), walking along the busy Highway 12, I was feeling elated. The dream had begun, I was really on the Way, and every step felt like meaningful progress. In the intense heat I was soon utterly drenched in sweat, as I would be for much of the next seven days. Yet my elation wasn't dampened; it just grew stronger: I knew on a deep level that this was exactly what I should be doing with this moment of my life.

Why have the people of Japan been donning the shirt, hat and stick and undertaking the hardships of walking the 1,200km Shikoku pilgrimage for so many centuries? Wherever possible the pilgrimage route takes in the glorious beauty of Shikoku Island: its mountains and forests, cliffs and rivers, the sky and the sea. But this is not just a pleasant ramble. It is hard-graft walking, often along busy highways and sometimes without even the protection of a sidewalk. The official reason is that through undertaking the pilgrimage one enlists the aid and support of one of the greatest of all Buddhist saints, Kukai or Kobo Daishi as he is honorifically known in Japan. Kukai was born on Shikoku in the 8th century, was enlightened at Shikoku's southern Cape Muroto, and was the founder of Shingon Buddhism, Japan's equivalent of the Tantric Buddhism of Tibet. Kukai's writings and the Shingon temples contain a high degree of symbolism and esoteric teaching. *Hotoke* (Buddha images), *mandalas*, ritual implements, bells and drums are ubiquitous. Kukai is attributed with founding most of the eighty-eight temples on the pilgrimage and many of them have magical stories about his visit: here he conquered a dragon, here he carved a Buddha, here he created a stream that always runs pure.

Yet in a sense there is no general answer to the question, "Why?" The answer must be sought in the heart of every would-be or actual henro. For those to whom such an undertaking seems like a fruitless waste of time, no answer will ever suffice; for those who long to undertake it, no reasoning is really necessary. My

own desire to undertake the Shikoku 88, or at least part of it, stretched back over eight years, to the time I first heard about it from a friend. A young Japanese man told me that he had seen a TV program about the Shikoku *hachi ju-hachi* and on the spot decided that he wanted to do it.

At each temple there is a traditional formula to follow.

Arriving you find the water basin, often elaborately decorated with a dragon-headed water fountain, wash your hands and drink. Next you ring the temple bell to announce or celebrate your arrival. Then you go to the hondo, make offerings and chant to the presiding Buddha figure. Each temple has a different presiding Buddha and I fell into a ritual of chanting the mantra or invocation of that particular figure, though traditionally Japanese henro chant the same sequence of scriptures for each Buddha. The penultimate ministration is to visit the Daishi Hall, a temple building dedicated to Kobo Daishi and to make further offerings and recitations. Here peering through a small window I often saw an elegant woodcarving of Kukai in his classic seated position holding a vajra, the symbolic diamond-thunderbolt, to his heart and a rosary of 108 beads. Lastly, you repair to the temple stamp office to collect the official emblem of each shrine, proof of your visit. This delightful little ritual is easily completed in thirty minutes.

I loved watching as the red stamps and elegant black strokes of traditional calligraphy were inscribed in my little volume by the temple stamp officers. Some fast, some slow, some rough, some smooth: it was like receiving a personal gift. You also receive a delicate block print of the temple's presiding Buddha. However, the 300 yen stamp charge at each temple means that the cost of visiting all 88 temples is more than $300 in stamp fees alone: hardly a minor consideration. At Gokurakuji, I was still a henro greenhorn and I naively didn't realize that you had to pay for the temple stamp. I imagined it was a gift from the temple to the henro for the hardships being undertaken. Thus two rather sweet elderly Japanese ladies protested loudly as I headed out of the stamp office debt unpaid, a rather embarrassing start to my temple visits. With 150,000 people a year making the pilgrimage, the henro stamp money and temple offerings are big business.

For a walking henro, though the 88 temples set the form of the pilgrimage and are the crucial goals and resting places, they are not the heart of the pilgrimage. The long, often solitary hours, of asphalt or forest track, belting sun or pouring rain, steady progress or grinding effort constitute its essence. It is here that the gold and dross of the mind are separated and joy and despair meet face to face. It is here that inner and outer obstacles are confronted and the heart chooses between the selfish and the selfless. These days it is the car or bus henro who are in the majority, and perhaps for them the goal rather than the journey is most important.

Reflections on the Route

Though the origins of the Shikoku 88 pilgrimage go back to Kukai's life in the 8th century, the first guidebooks were only written in the 17th century. Thus there are many geographical quirks and historical accidents that have shaped the route. For instance, the walking route usually makes more sense than one driven by road. There also seems to be a spiritual rationale to the walking circuit, an inner logic to the sequence that is both testing and encouraging. For example the first nine temples are all situated on a meandering east-west curve that proceeds along the coastal plain north of Tokushima. In two days walking it is easy to visit all nine without much strain. It is immensely encouraging to know that you have 1,200km to walk and eighty-eight temples to visit, and yet to find that in the first 35km you have already achieved ten percent of the total. The Shikoku 88 gives the new henro a confidence boost right at the start where it is most needed. Kirihataji (10) is both demanding and heart-ening. It constitutes the first strenuous climb, rising over 100m above the plain, and a small taste of what is to come later. You begin to feel the real weight of your backpack and the impact of your boots, by now the first blisters or sores are emerging. Leaving Kirihataji you know your body a little better: where are the weak points that will need attention in the days ahead. This is the first real test of the stamina needed to complete the journey.

Another essential factor that defines the pilgrimage is the impact of the mythic or secret dimension. In particular experiences and realizations along the way you sometimes intuit a deeper pattern and glimpse the interplay between the outer and the inner terrain. A seemingly intractable outer obstacle is suddenly perceived as a psychological or spiritual dead-end. So when a new pathway eventually opens up, as if Kobo Daishi were at your side pointing to a hitherto unforeseen doorway, the liberation extends in both directions. Outer progress mirrors inner freedom. These insights may come in the form of new understandings, images or simply seeing things clearly. More often than not they are triggered by seemingly trivial incidents: a tiny gift from a stranger turns into a blessing from the Universe; momentary laughter at your own frustration turns into a gateway to unlimited freedom; a small act of generosity can turn into boundless love for all that lives; forbearing a difficult stretch of road becomes unshakable determination.

The Henro Haircut

In the humid August heat the climb to Kirihataji had me drenched in sweat. A sharp, steady feeling of pain from the skin of my thighs dramatically brought home to me Kirihataji's lesson on stamina and endurance. It took a while to find somewhere suitable to drop my trousers. I was shocked to see that after only two days the sweating and rubbing had combined to leave my skin utterly red, raw and oozing fluid. It looked like a wound ripe for infection. I managed to create a makeshift antiseptic bandage from the materials in my first aid kit, but it was clear that I was going to have to expend some time and energy to prevent the sores from getting worse. The pilgrimage was beginning to bite. Soon the pain gave way to feelings of numbness. I had a long but easy walk to complete in the remainder of the afternoon, wanting to arrive at Fujidera (11) before it closed so that the following day

I could make the tough climb to Shosanji (12) in the cool of the morning and with a fresh pair of legs.

Wandering through the village lanes that cross the plain to the southern mountains I suddenly saw the spiraling red, white and blue of a reassuringly familiar barber's shop. I was feeling rather top-heavy in the summer heat, so on a whim I opened the door and entered the cool, air-conditioned shop, thinking I would be out again in twenty minutes. Inside three middle-aged Japanese were chatting easily but at the appearance of a heavily sweating gaijin dressed as a henro the conversation stopped abruptly. They stared at me with blank amazement. Suddenly one of the men got up, made some parting remarks and left. The other two, I guessed husband and wife, attended carefully as I attempted to mime receiving a haircut, and repeated, "Haircut" in English several times, as if repetition would make it more comprehensible. Given the context it wasn't too hard to work out what I wanted. At my "Ikura des ka?" the woman pointed to a long indecipherable pricelist on the wall. I just chose the cheapest option hoping this would be a simple haircut, rather than a wash and dry. She nodded and I was installed in a sumptuously soft barber's chair. What followed in the next hour must rate as one of the hairdressing highlights of my life.

The man proceeded to give me a slow and methodical cut, going over my head several times with different types of scissors. Each time that I thought he had finished he changed, to another, more delicate, implement, last of all giving me a blood chilling shave with a cut throat razor, prompting gruesome Sweeny Todd fantasies. Since every hair on my head had now been ministered to I rose from the chair to leave, but his wife urgently indicated that I should sit down again. She then proceeded to recline the chair until I was more or less horizontal. "What now?" I wondered, deciding that it was best just to relax and completely give myself up to their treatment. And what a treatment it was! In the next thirty minutes she practiced her art upon my scalp, starting with a head massage, then a refreshing face mask made of sterile cloth with nose, mouth and eye apertures, followed by cool pads on the eyes. The finale was a scalp shower using a pressurized container of fluid that gave an ice-cold sensation all over as she rubbed it in. At last I was allowed to arise, certain by now that I had been the recipient of *osettai*, since I am sure that their cheapest haircut wouldn't usually include such services. I thanked them both profusely, bowing and intoning, "Arigato gozaimas" as I paid and re-donned my henro gear. My scalp was still tingling freshly as I walked off cheerfully down the asphalt road, wondering what they had thought of this gaijin apparition.

As usual, I had no idea where I would stay that evening, making it all the more urgent to arrive at Fujidera in good time and find some accommodation. Since I was still getting used to the pilgrimage and what distances were viable each day I had consciously decided just to chance it each evening and see what appeared: something good always turned up. After completing the requisite rituals I was sitting by the temple gate wondering what to do when a bright young Japanese henro arrived. His name was Hiramichi. I asked him if he was staying somewhere nearby, and in near perfect English he told me that he had booked into a *ryokan* just down the road, so we agreed that I would come with him to see if they had a free room. At the ryokan I was given a pleasant Japanese-style room and joined two men, Yasu and Mr. M, for dinner; Hiramichi was self-catering to save money. Yasu had lived in Canada and his English was faultless, so we talked long into the evening about travelling, the pilgrimage, Kobo Daishi, Buddhism in Japan and our lives in general. It was a wonderful meeting and I felt as if Kobo Daishi were by my side bringing me good luck.

At the rear of Fujidera temple is a small footpath that immediately starts with a steep staircase cut out of the hillside and held in place with gnarled roots and rotting faggots. The 13km walk to

Shosanji works its way up through the forest, occasionally affording stunning views of the plain and rising 700m or more. I

set out early and walked alone, filled with delight at this ancient track through the forest. It is certain that pilgrims have been following this very route for over a thousand years. The Shikoku forest mixes mighty cedars with slender pines, shimmering poplars with serrated maples. Wherever there is a break in the canopy, flowers and bushes grow profusely on the forest floor. Everywhere one hears the whirring and clicking of *semi*, the Japanese name for a large species of cicada, at times drowning out all other sounds. The track to Shosanji takes about five hours at a steady pace, climbing and falling, alternating between deep green tunnels and sunlit broad tracks. At one point it follows a narrow ridge, no more than a meter wide, through a tunnel of trees falling away steeply left and right. It is incredibly magical, conjuring in my mind images of shamans, samurai and dragons. Shosanji is also one of the great tests of the Shikoku 88. After a steep climb for about three hours, one has to spend the next hour descending rapidly in order to cross a mountain river, before the final, grueling ascent. It is a test of stamina, strength and

patience. However the exertions of Shosanji are amply rewarded. Perched on a high cliff and approached by a snaking pavement adorned with lovely Buddha images, Shosanji is indeed a mythical setting for a temple. The *sanmon*, or temple gate, stands at the head of a steep stone staircase, grand and imposing, and in the temple compound, which clings to the mountain on several levels, grow some of the largest cedars in Japan, towering high into the canopy above.

On arrival I rang the great temple bell, swinging the large horizontally suspended log clapper. The resonance echoed across the valley. There was a kind of party atmosphere as, one-by-one, the walking henro arrived, each feeling the great achievement of attaining Shosanji. After resting for an hour or more, Hiramichi and I set out for another ryokan a few kilometers on, seeking accommodation. August is the off-season as it is considered too hot by most people, but one big advantage is that accommodation is almost always available, unlike the peak season when thousands of people pass the temples each day.

Just when you thought...

The next day, my fourth, was to be a day of shattered assumptions and powerful spiritual lessons. Firstly, instead of the clear skies and blistering heat it was welcomingly overcast as Hiramichi and I set out. Soon the cloud cover had become impenetrable mountain fog which turned into drizzle and finally became torrential rain. Despite our wet-weather gear, the rain was so heavy that at times we were obliged to take shelter. After days of being baked by the sun, the rainstorm was exhilarating, though it slowed us down considerably. From time to time we were granted a tantalizing glimpse of the mountains and valleys through the mist: jagged, forested and mysterious. I had assumed that Hiramichi and I, having developed a warm friendship, would walk together that day. So when he needed to stop to adjust his pack (which was considerably heavier than mine) I always waited for him. Several times he suggested that I go on without him, but I didn't take this seriously, assuming that it was just Japanese politeness. Thus I was very surprised that when I needed to stop Hiramichi didn't wait for me, but just kept on going. "Oh, we're not walking together after all!" I recalled one henro saying to me "everyone goes at his own pace". Nevertheless, for me it was rather strange that Hiramichi and I kept passing each other on the road, no longer as walking companions but more like strangers.

The long road down from the mountains to Dainichiji soon dropped out of the forest and became a hike on Highway 31. Hour after hour I trudged the asphalt, the road becoming busier the nearer I got to Tokushima. Dainichiji was tucked into a bend on the highway and you had to risk life and limb dodging the cars as you entered the temple gate directly from the carriageway. Finally arriving at this small and unpretentious temple after so many hours walking was something of an anti-climax. After a brief pause for a snack and to redress my wounds, I took to the road again. The next four temples were all within a few kilometers, so I thought, "After the last two days serious hiking this will be a doddle, I can knock these on the head really quickly". But there was a surprise in store. As I began to meander through the suburbs of northern Tokushima travelling from temples 13 to 17, navigation started to become difficult. Suddenly there was a profusion of small lanes and the way markers almost completely disappeared. I struggled with the directions, confused and lost. Several times I was forced to retrace my steps to ensure that I hadn't missed a key junction. On one occasion the pathway to Jorakuji (14) involved walking down an unmarked road that looked like the private driveway into a schoolyard. It was uncanny just how confusing the route became and the journey took considerably longer than I had anticipated. I couldn't help feeling that it was almost designed to be like that, as if Kobo Daishi were saying to me, "You've become too focused in the goal, this isn't the point". The Shikoku 88 was once again teaching me a lesson about making assumptions and getting complacent; I chuckled at myself. Eventually, the way-finding became easier and I was at last blessed by finding a drugstore where I could stock up on bandages and surgical tape.

The temple stamp officer at Idoji (17) gave me a map of how to find a nearby *zenkon-yado*. The tradition of *osettai* finds its zenith in the *zenkon-yado*. Here a local family offer to lodge henro for one night without expecting payment. It is seen as a way of making merit. Usually, as well as somewhere to shelter, you will find clothes washing and basic cooking facilities. And they really don't expect any payment: it is an extraordinary act of generosity. As I was waiting for Hiramichi to arrive, to see what he was intending to do for the evening, a large party of bus henro arrived at Idoji. I watched them making their offerings at the hondo and Daishi Hall and was impressed with the energy and sincerity they poured into the ritual. I pondered how extraordinarily different an experience of the Shikoku 88 they must have from the walking henro. Instead of the long solitary hours on the asphalt they sit in a large air-conditioned bus chatting and socializing together. It seemed rather like a spiritual package tour. I was in no doubt that I would rather be a walking henro. While I was musing in this way, a woman from the party approached me and asked, in good English, where I was from, how long I had been in Japan, and what I thought of Shikoku. She was delighted to discover that I was an English henro and follower of Kobo Daishi. As we parted she gave me a small envelope which I guessed contained a card or image of the Buddha. Imagine my subsequent amazement when upon opening this envelope and found it contained 1,000 yen, yet another unexpected *osettai*. Here also I met Kozai, a young man with whom I had shared a lodging four days previously, and he offered to show me the way to the *zenkon-yado*. One of the joys of walking the Shikoku 88 is that you tend to meet the same henro again and again since, fast or slow, we are all constrained by the limits of what can be comfortably walked day after day.

At last Hiramichi arrived seeming rather frustrated and in a hurry, I guessed that he'd got lost and it had taken him an hour or two to find his way. I asked him where he was going to stay and he had in mind a place nearly 7km away. That was too far for me, having, once again, walked nearly 30km that day, and I suggested that he come to the nearby *zenkon-yado*. "I don't want to go back", he said in a grit-your-teeth sort of way. Finally, he turned to me and said, rather forcefully, "I have to go and pray now!" That was the last we saw of each other. I slightly regret that I didn't persist with persuading him to come with me. His state of mind seemed to be a rather painful one for him. The Shikoku 88 was teaching him a lesson and he was learning it the hard way, just as I would have done when I was 23.

There was a wonderful atmosphere of camaraderie in our greasy garage garret above the busy Highway 192 into Tokushima. Up some rough wooden stairs was a single room, the walls plastered with henro name tags and Buddha images. Our host family lived in a downstairs room adjoining the forecourt. By Japanese standards they were extraordinarily poor, yet they gave unstintingly of what they had. The five of us lodging there that night took turns to use the washing machine amidst the piles of clothes. We shared our food, and discussed the trials and joys of the Shikoku 88. In a further act of generosity our host offered to take us to see the traditional Awa Odori dances. Every August Tokushima becomes the venue of a formidable street dancing festival attracting hundreds of thousands of visitors. Awa Odori is danced in a troop, requiring extraordinary co-ordination. Men and women dance separately, though sometimes the troops oppose or highlight one another. The dances are slow, rhythmic and include elegant yet powerful movements of the hands and arms. A band of drums, flutes and Japanese-style guitars creates a strong, resonant and haunting backdrop. As the troop advances, weaving back and forward, suddenly on a particular beat the leader calls out "Aya-Owha!" and the troop drops into a powerful tableau. Then, slowly, the beat picks up again and the troop moves on, weaving and advancing. I found the dance utterly captivating and hypnotic, a cross between Flamenco power and Balkan communality.

The Test at the Barrier Temple

It was a beautiful morning as I left my friends at the *zenkon-yado*. Though only 6:40 a.m., Highway 192 was already buzzing with cars and lorries, but I happily made my way along it. I knew that ahead of me was four hours of serious highway walking, yet I was feeling quietly elated at the prospect. The challenge was to find something inspiring even here in the fumes and the heat. With early morning optimism I found it in the blueness of the sky and the open vistas as Highway 192 crossed the broad Akuigawa River. However I am not a complete masochist, so when the opportunity for a shortcut through the forest arose I took it. The relationship to road walking is very different for the pilgrim and the rambler. The rambler wants to get out into nature, away from the smelly, noisy and artificial world of asphalt and internal combustion engines. For him to spend a large part of his excursion walking a major highway would defeat the whole purpose. For the pilgrim the walk is inherently meaningful whatever the conditions because it is dedicated to a higher purpose and to deeper self-realization. To pick only the cherries from experience, such as lovely forest footpaths, would be to miss the opportunity of coming face-to-face with your dislike of certain aspects of the world. You might inhabit more beautiful states of mind for a while, but be more prone to becoming depressed when the conditions deteriorate. In short the cherry-picking pilgrim is likely to make less progress than one who takes things as they come.

The densely forested Mt Bizan dominates Tokushima's skyline. Though only 290m high it rises steeply from the coastal plain and penetrates deeply into the heart of the city. Almost all of the city's thoroughfares skirt around this rocky intrusion. However, the arduous Jizo-goe path takes you directly over the saddle, and this was my chosen shortcut. Eventually, amid the suburban streets I found a highly missable opening into the forest indicated by a tiny red arrow. Climbing steeply, I was suddenly in a new world: a finger of a long lost realm reaching down into the city, reminder of times past. The intense blue of the sky was suddenly dimmed to a dark, cool green. The whirring and clicking of the *semi* drowned out the droning engines and there was a mysterious echoing of bamboo. After a while I came across a carefully tended spring, obviously a hallowed spot. Already sweating heavily, I drank deeply and refilled my bottle. Further up the path I was amazed to find an intricate network of bamboo aqueducts, waterwheels and hammers that would slowly fill and then suddenly tip, resounding heavily with a distinctive concussion. This wonderful work of nature art had seemingly no other purpose than to delight the beholder, or propitiate the local spirits. Soon the forest grew denser and darker, the path strewn with cobwebs, covered with ferns and shrubs; the Jizo-goe was clearly not a popular route with henro. However the most striking aspect was the powerful odor of the forest: the smell was that of a strong warm spicy red wine. I kept sniffing deeply to check that this wasn't some kind of olfactory hallucination; but no, it was definitely red wine. Why the forest should have smelt this way was beyond me. Perhaps the local spirits had been indulging in some forbidden merriment.

Although the Jizo-goe path put off the inevitable for as long as possible, eventually I joined Highway 55, the main north-south highway from Tokushima all the way to Cape Muroto. Though the four lanes were lined with sidewalks anyone with any sense was traveling Highway 55 in an air-conditioned car. I met two other henro who were sheltering from the midday heat in a little hut constructed by the city council along a particularly fearsome stretch of the road. A bizarre feature of this hectic motorway was the momentary calm that descended when all the synchronized traffic signals changed to allow the minor routes to join. For maybe thirty seconds an eerie silence prevailed, you could even here the call of the odd bird, or the grating of a badly lost *semi*. Once a beautiful blue and black butterfly fluttered by, unaware of the deadly onslaught that was about to be unleashed when the lights turned to green. Somewhere along the way a haiku fell out of my heart:

August in Shikoku
Too hot for o'henro
Only the *semi*
Buzz around the island

Another vital ingredient of the henro path is *Pocari Sweat*. The marketing department who named this soft drink are either abject idiots or paramount geniuses. I guess it must be the latter since the drink is found in roadside vending machines all over Japan. It boasts the replacement of electrolytes lost through sweating and claims to have exactly the right balance of sugars and salts for your body to absorb quickly. Though I mainly associated electrolytes with chemistry lessons, this didn't diminish my enthusiasm for the salty-sweet ice cold drink. Throughout my travels Pocari Sweat became my soft drink of choice. Upon discovering a vending machine, like finding a hidden oasis, I would dive for shade and gulp down the cool, life-preserving fluid.

After many arduous hours on the asphalt, just a small step away from instant death under the wheels of a lorry, I ascended a hill to the lovely temple of Onzanji (18). The contrast between the worlds of Highway 55 and Onzanji couldn't be more pronounced. Elegant wooden buildings surrounded by bamboos, all appointed in the most aesthetic and uplifting way; typically Japanese. As I left the temple a small opening led into a forest of tall bamboos. This ancient narrow track was strewn with elegant, delicate needle-shaped leaves and dappled with diffuse blue-green light as the rays of the sun tumbled over the foliage. Protected by a large hill, the incessant rumbling of Highway 55

had finally abated and I was transported into a quintessentially Far Eastern realm of spirits and foxes. A sense of timelessness and happiness melted into me, such a blessing after the hours of alienating tarmac. The calm of Onzanji seemed like another dramatic teaching of the Shikoku 88: after forbearing the harsh ugliness of things, the unexpected discovery of peace is all the more sweet and refreshing. The joy of this ancient bamboo grove will long stay in my heart.

Eventually the track emerges from the bamboos and snakes along back roads into the small town of Tatsue. Tatsueji (19) is one of only four *sekisho* temples amongst the Shikoku 88 – a checkpoint or barrier temple. You cannot pass the barrier unless your motivation is pure. The story goes that a woman who had killed her husband in order to take up with a new lover came to Tatsueji, but when she tried to pray her hair got entangled in the rope of a temple bell. She broke down, confessed her evil deed and spent the rest of her days as a nun. Though the barrier was clearly symbolic, nevertheless approaching Tatsueji I began to feel apprehensive. How could I know if I had passed this barrier? As my time on Shikoku was running out, I had decided to make Tatsueji the last temple that I walked to unaided. From here I planned to catch a train south some 70 km to leave enough time to walk to the cave where Kukai was Enlightened. I felt that perhaps I was short-circuiting the inner spiritual logic of the pilgrimage and leaving the barrier unassayed.

Tatsueji is a large and wealthy temple in the centre of town. Perhaps its barrier status provokes extra generosity from visiting pilgrims. As I entered, washing my hands at the dragon fountain, I was stirred by the solemnity of this testing moment, and the transition I was making after five days on foot. Ringing the temple bell, I listened reverently as the sound peeled out, in a mood of expectation. As usual I approached the *hondo*, dedicated to *Jizo*, and started to chant the appropriate mantra. Suddenly as I was chanting, I remembered that I had uncharacteristically left my rucksack unattended by the temple gate. This being a busy temple, and the gate opening straight onto the main road it seemed quite possible that the rucksack would disappear. I felt a pang of anxiety, but in the very same moment it dawned on me that *this* was the barrier test. If the rucksack was stolen I would have to go to the police, get certificates for the insurance, and buy new equipment; in short my pilgrimage couldn't continue. My heart started to beat increasingly rapidly. I had to force myself not to rush, but to complete the devotions in the proper manner. With adrenalin high in my blood I walked back to the gate and turned the corner: the rucksack was still there, propped up against a bench where I had left it. The likelihood of it being stolen from a temple in Japan was of course slight, but that didn't diminish the inner feeling of passing the test. It is strange how symbols work on the mind if you are open to them.

The Road to Muroto-misaki

Arriving at the small JR Station of Tatsue I felt sad to be breaking the walking discipline of the Shikoku 88, rather like leaving an important retreat before the end and I took off my henro garb, feeling that it would somehow be false to still appear as a henro on a train. It was decidedly odd to suddenly be back in the world of commuters, shoppers and school children twitching their mobile phones. One elderly man was in a very confused state. He kept getting up and changing his seat, putting the sunblind down and then up again and looking about with rapid darting eyes. At the all-change stop he got on to a train going in the direction from which we had just come. I felt as if I had just arrived from a different universe.

At Kannoura station I started to search for *minshuku* (guesthouse) *Inoue*, marked in my guidebook and asked two elderly ladies if they knew the way. There ensued a baffling and wonderful interchange. In one moment I felt that I understood completely what they said, yet in the next I was utterly confused.

In rapid Japanese they seemed to suggest that *Inoue* was not a good place to stay and I should try somewhere else further down the coast. They wanted to know, did I already have a phone reservation, to which I confidently replied "Iie" ("No"). How I comprehended this, far beyond my meager dozen words of Japanese, I don't know. But then my intention to stay in Kannoura would reassert itself and I would doubt if I had understood them at all. What was wrong with *Inoue*, and how on earth would I find somewhere else to stay if I didn't even know the name? Finally, it struck me that one of the words they kept repeating was a dwelling on my map: *Ikumi*. An inner tussle took place between sticking with my original plan and following the direction of two kindly strangers. Happily the latter prevailed, though it was getting late and I really didn't know where I was going. As I headed off down the beautiful Pacific coast for another few kilometers, the complete rightness of this choice impacted upon me. Here was a way to reconnect as a walking henro. Re-robing, there was now nothing but my feet to carry me the last 40km to the hallowed ground of *Muroto-misaki* (Cape Muroto).

Ikumi minshuku is a secret Shangri-la. The proprietor Ten (who introduced himself as, "One more than nine") was a warm-hearted flower-power surfer running a super-value guest house and café on what must be one of the loveliest beaches in Japan. Ten and I immediately took to each other, and he adopted the honorific Riju-san whenever he called me. Though I arrived too late for supper, on discovering that I was vegetarian he arranged to rustle up something special since he said I wouldn't find anything else on the beach. As it dawned on me what a jewel of a place *Ikumi* was, I realized that those two old ladies of Kannoura must have been bodhisattvas or guardian angels. They had not only helped me to reconnect with my pilgrim's purpose, but, in addition, given me a teaching on being unattached to pre-conceived plans and ensured that I arrive at a lovely resting place. So I stripped off and hobbled, as best my poor, blistered feet would manage, down to the mighty Pacific breakers and plunged headlong into the surf.

Next morning the Muroto peninsula was an intense azure. Sky and sea met in a thin vanishing line, merging into a complete universe of blueness. I hit the road early as it was going to be a scorcher on the asphalt. At the small town of None (pronounced *no-ney*), I found plenty to sustain me for breakfast. Sat on the breakwater munching vegetarian sushi and gazing out across the beach and harbor, I noticed a large family of eagles, perhaps two dozen in total, perched on the electric cables. They eyed me carefully and soon took to the skies, soaring upwards on the morning thermals. With a backdrop of tumbling forests and the clear sparkling waters of the None river, they were a mesmerizing sight. I have long felt an affinity with eagles, the lords of the air, and on that sun-drenched morning I felt I was part of their family. The feeling was amply confirmed when I found a long, graceful eagle feather lying on the road in front of me: a sort of welcome home gift from the skies. Muroto-misaki was already starting to work its magic upon my soul. It is hard to capture the

solitary experience of these two intensely hot days walking the last reach of Highway 55 to the cape. At times the heat was so crushing that there was no choice but to seek shelter. At times, sitting astride a rock watching the breakers roll in, I contemplated the vastness of our universe and thought of Kukai gazing out at the sky and sea all those centuries ago. At times I would walk with a grim determination, utterly drenched in sweat, all blisters and sores, shoulders aching, but in a perverse way delighting in my endurance and the knowledge that I would never give up until I reached the goal.

Cape Muroto

It isn't hard to understand why Kukai came to Muroto-misaki. Surrounded by the far horizons of the Pacific in three cardinal directions, it is an awesome setting. Gazing into the distance the sky is intensely bright, and the deepening Pacific waters shade from aquamarine to dark blue. Hovering above the vanishing point are towering cumulonimbi, the Kings of the Clouds, poised ready to unleash a thundering storm. Drenched by a tropical

sun, the Muroto forest is a shiny green. The raucous sound of the *semi* echoes across the jagged hills. Rock, sea and sky come together to give you the feeling of teetering on the edge of the known and staring reverentially towards the Unknown.

The name Kukai means *sky and sea* and Mikurado cave, where he lived over 1,200 years ago, is where he had a pivotal mystical experience that was to leave a permanent impression on him. In his writings he says, "The morning star, which shines in the sky, entered my mouth". Apart from the concrete plinth and granite altar the cave had probably changed little in the intervening centuries. Dark, damp, dripping and attended by an assortment of fantastically colored crabs, from intense blood red to bruised purple and yellow, it had an otherworldly atmosphere. As I stood there for some time intoning sacred verses, the crabs lost their inhibitions and started to creep out of every crevice. They were very beautiful as they performed a sort of scuttling dance of bright colors around the altar. Forward, stop, left and right, stop, back again; it could have been the Ballet Rambert. They were the true keepers of this sacred place, surveying the offerings of the faithful and tidying away the donations. As soon as a party of tourists arrived they all disappeared, only to re-emerge cautiously when the party had gone. Apart from myself no one seemed to tarry long in Mikurado; I suppose that a dark, damp, crab-infested cave isn't the most enticing of tourist attractions. But it was indeed a special place, for here the master practiced deep mystic meditations and founded an unshakeable intention to work for the well-being of the world. It was also a cool haven from the intense heat of radiating asphalt.

The final labor of ascending the cliffs to Hotsumisaki (24) felt like a crucial and cathartic struggle, at once grueling and rewarding. Here at the southern tip of Shikoku the forest truly becomes jungle, with its tough leaved evergreens, spicy smells and thunderous chorus of insects. Hotsumisaki is perched on the summit of a huge finger-like cliff, gazing into the distance, a lone outpost of the Buddha's teaching at the far extremity of the world. Arriving here was for me close to an ecstatic experience as all the effort and exertion of the previous week coalesced in a single moment. Of course, many of the other visitors had driven by car or bus and were no doubt on their way to somewhere else. For them Hotsumisaki was just another temple, and the irony of this contrast was not lost on me. Had I expected there to be bells and banners just for my little achievement? After the usual devotions I sat gazing for a long time into the vastness of the ocean. The transience and profundity of this moment seemed both beautiful and tragic. I realized that feelings of deep significance always pass and are themselves something to which I could become attached. Eventually, I slowly made my way down the cliff.

Muroto City clings like a limpet to the narrow seaboard strip, the smallness of the habitable area a reminder that nature is pre-eminent in this far-flung wilderness. I stayed in the tiny *ryokan* Fukuyo-maru, which I later found takes its name from a famous boat caught in one of the A-bomb blasts. My hosts were a lovely elderly couple who, despite being rather perplexed by my dietary requirements, cooked a splendid attempt at a vegetarian supper. Unfortunately the rather chewy carrot tempura turned out to be made of squid. This being the end of my Shikoku pilgrimage, I wanted to celebrate and share the triumph with someone, but there was no one with whom I could communicate what these seven days had meant. There were no beaches at the far point of the cape, just rock meeting ocean, so my evening plunge into the surf was taken in a rock pool. There I communed with the crustaceans and they alone were my witness. That night I watched a spectacular sunset over the western ocean, perhaps the most fitting end to any pilgrimage, and composed a haiku:

Mistaken as a tree
The *semi* cicada

Jumped onto my lip
The taste wasn't good

Hiroshima

It was a hot August day in Hiroshima. The sky was a faultless blue, peppered with clouds. The city, cradled by its many rivers, looked lovely in the bright sunlight. Everyone was going about their lives, but something utterly unforgettable was about to happen. On an August day just like this one 63 years ago the fury of nuclear war was unleashed here. I came to Hiroshima as a kind of duty: to see the unseeable, listen to the unspeakable, comprehend the incomprehensible. How, why, what was it like to have been part of the hellish tragedy of Hiroshima?

In the 1950s with great foresight the city fathers, as they struggled to rebuild their broken and shattered world, decided to build a memorial park and museum in the very centre of the old city where the fullest force of the bomb had vaporized buildings and people. The renowned Japanese architect, Kenzo Tange, won the competition to design the park and memorial buildings. The result is a juxtaposition of beauty and horror, aesthetics and sadness. The Prefectural Exhibition Hall, now known as the A-Bomb Dome, was originally a much loved city

landmark built by a Czech architect in 1915. It has been preserved just as it was on the day of the bomb: a skeleton of a building prominently offset by a lovely park, the Motoyasu River and modern towers of glass and concrete. The incongruity is intentional and complete.

Two museums tell the story in different ways. The Victims' Memorial Hall tells the subjective account of thousands of *hibakushi* (A-bomb survivors) as well as an aesthetic yet harrowing post-blast panorama made from 140,000 little tiles, one for each of the estimated number of people who died from the immediate effects of the bomb. Everywhere there is running water in remembrance of the thousands who died crying out for water. For some inexplicable reason many of them were denied water for fear that it would kill them; most died anyway in intense agony. In the multimedia suite you can view thousands of hours of interviews with survivors. The architecture and technology elegantly support the experience of trying to understand this personal side of the Bomb. The Peace Memorial Museum gives the objective account. What is impressive is that the displays start by clearly retelling the Japanese war policy of the early 20th century, which set the stage for the Bomb's use on Japan. The American role is told with almost total historical objectivity, and no interpretation or judgment is given. You are left with a strong feeling of horror of war rather than hostility to a particular nation.

None the less, as you view original photos of horribly burnt and disfigured bodies, barely clinging to life, or contemplate the gruesome waxworks of people whose skin hangs from their bones, or see pictures of the appalling radiation diseases, it is hard not to feel anger for the politicians, bureaucrats, scientists and generals who coolly made this happen. The memoranda and letters show the precision and calculation that went into the execution of the A-bomb drop on Hiroshima. Their heartless rationality is terrifying: Why did these men unleash such horror on a city largely made up of non-combatants? Yes, there was the need to end the war with Japan as quickly as possible to avert further loss of life and before the Russians had a chance to extend their influence; yes there was the need to justify the immense cost of the Manhattan Project with a significant strategic victory. But what the hell were they thinking when they decided to snuff out the lives of so many innocents in this way. Why couldn't they have chosen a purely military target, why couldn't they have demonstrated the Bomb's power somewhere uninhabited and used this as a threat to end the war? No extenuating circumstances can justify for me what these men did on 6th August 1945.

The careful monitoring of the after-effects of the Bomb by the Americans in occupation shows that they were desperately keen to know the result on human beings. The harrowing testimony of one *hibakusha* says, "They monitor us, but they don't treat us". The survivors of Hiroshima were seen as scientific specimens rather than suffering human beings. Hiroshima was the first sacrifice to the nuclear age, a controlled experiment to see what power mankind had unleashed.

As I left the halls filled with images and objects of hellish destruction and suffering, Hiroshima was still looking beautiful: children were running and playing, people walking and talking: a reminder of the renewal that follows even from atomic hell. In the blue sky was a huge cumulus cloud, towering above the baked August landscape, as if echoing that fateful cloud that rose sixty-three years ago. Silently the tears rolled down my cheeks. Yes, Hiroshima is utterly unforgettable; may it ever be so!

Pacific Passage

Sayonara Japan

It was a sultry morning in Yokohama as I made my way along the broad avenues to the Immigration Office. Here, barely 150 years ago, the European colonial powers set up their first trading bases and the transformation of Meiji Japan into a modern techno-logical power began. I was feeling sad to be leaving Japan after nearly two months. It had been an astonishing journey ranging from the wild north to the humid south, from the Pacific in the east to the Sea of Japan in the west. I wandered about looking for somewhere to spend the last of my small change, finally settling on the *7 to 11* convenience store and a bottle of Pocari Sweat, a suitable memento of my Japanese travels. With some regret I abandoned my strawberry umbrella in the communal umbrella stand (bought while stranded in a Kyoto deluge) before embarking. Seamen are very superstitious people, and umbrellas area anathema onboard, especially strawberry umbrellas.

The Yokohama Immigration Office was housed in an utterly improbable building, tucked into a small corner of an inconse-quential block that was sandwiched between a triangle of roads. I walked right past it a number of times. At the desk there was consternation at my immigration card. None of the officers could pronounce or recognize the kanji for *Eins Soya*, the vessel on which I had arrived from Russia. In the end one of them just shrugged her shoulders and stamped my documents. Clearly, arriving in or leaving Japan by ship was not a common occurrence. The embarkation procedure was swift and simple. Soon my co-passenger, Jens Graeulich, and I were in the port and alongside the massive Hanjin Madrid. As the huge cranes shuttled containers to and fro, the familiar smell of cheap-grade fuel oil filled my nostrils: how I love travelling by container ship! Once again, being a vegetarian on a commercial freighter felt like being a fish out of water. My first meal on the Hanjin Madrid was a plate of white rice and a green, exceedingly bitter vegetable of Filipino origin that looked like a cross between a pineapple and a pepper. It was edible enough, but hardly a balanced meal. When the steward offered me the same again for supper, I declined and he invited me to meet the cook to discuss my dietary needs. I tried to explain that a balanced vegetarian meal would involve some sort of vegetable protein like beans, lentils or soya products but clearly the cook didn't really get it. After listening politely for a while he expressed his exasperation by saying, "It is the first time we've had a guest who doesn't eat anything!" Behind me Jens was chuckling, this telling remark showing what assumptions I was up against. In the end we agreed that the next day I would cook my own lentil dish to show him what I had in mind.

Captain Jaworski took great pleasure in explaining our 7,000km route to British Columbia. The trajectory would take us into the Bering Sea, skim the northern coast of the Aleutian Islands, thus giving us some shelter against the North Pacific swells, and we would re-enter the Pacific by passing through the Unimak passage. The whole transit would take eight days. Once again, the mealtime seating arrangements were fixed, so Jens and I got to know each other well. Jens, in his thirties, was a tournament cyclist who worked in computers. He had an even crazier love of the road less-travelled than me, having cycled across the whole of Siberia with his netbook and foldout solar panel. Having found difficulties taking his bike by air he had decided to travel by sea and was embarked for Vancouver with his trusty steed. His tales of monstrous blood-sucking insects, disintegrating roads knee deep in mud and camping rough in the wilderness weren't for the faint-hearted. We got on famously.

The karaoke party

Captain Jaworski, like Captain Ziems of the Hanjin Chicago, was a jovial man with a relaxed attitude in his command of the ship. One of his priorities was ensuring that the passengers and crew enjoyed themselves and you got the feeling that no exceptions to this rule would be tolerated. Nowhere was this more evident than during the mid-voyage karaoke party. In a mild drizzle, trestle tables, a barbecue and precariously dangling electrics were hastily erected on an observation deck. The sausages and

beer were followed by a sequence of wailing performances in which the Captain nobly led by example and Jens and I were not to escape unscathed. Bowing to the Captain's insistence, I stepped up to the microphone. "Do you have anything by Sting or The Police?" met with blank stares from our Filipino DJ. "The

Rolling Stones, Led Zeppelin, Jimi Hendrix…?" fared little better. An air of impatience hovered as I looked through his collection of karaoke CDs and felt keenly my age and lack of knowledge of contemporary popular music. As I hunted for something I recognized, the Captain reassured me, "We want you to feel comfortable", though I was feeling anything but. In the end the only song I knew well enough to attempt was John Lennon's *Woman* which went off okay apart from the sustained pitch of "I looooove you, now and forever".

Monday 1st September 2008 was a very unusual day, it happened exactly twice. However much you reflect on the logic of crossing the International Date Line eastwards, it is still something of a shock when it actually happens. In the midst of the ocean where the daily routines are identical it seemed that we had finally succumbed to *Groundhog Day* and were destined ad nauseam to relive the same events over and over. I kept wondering if there wasn't some elaborate scam one could pull by living the same day twice. Surely a stock-market coup would be possible with the foreknowledge from the previous 1st September. A little reflection told me that were such a scam possible, some marketer would have exploited it long ago. And, of course, traveling westwards you lose a day. Was that day forever lost? Were you now destined to live one day less than your natural term? Should you have to pay utility bills for a day never lived? These and other imponderables clattered around my brain as I cogitated on the strangeness of time.

The Unimak Passage
The Aleutian Islands are a chain of volcanic carbuncles running from the wildly remote Alaskan peninsula to the even wilder land of Kamchatka. Though the Aleutians are on the same latitude as Scotland and Scandinavia they are indescribably bleaker and more isolated. The barrier they form between the North Pacific and the Bering Sea has a significant effect on the

regional tides and currents and here nutrients are stirred up from the depths, supporting a rich ecosystem. The islands have exotic names, reminiscent of ancient Inuit traditions: Unalaska, Atun, Akutan, Unimak, Ugamik, Tigalda. On the largest of these,

Unalaska Island, is the port of Dutch Harbour, home to one of the most lucrative American fishing fleets. It even has a container terminal at which some of the freighters deposit cargo.

On the afternoon of the second Monday 1st September we caught our first sight of these wild cliffs and gazed in wonder at the profusion of creatures that come here to feed and shelter. Seeing a whale for the first time and glimpsing the telltale spray of the blowhole and the huge tail rolling down into the water is utterly arresting. The size and grace of such a being inspired me with feelings of awe. By the time we got close to Atun and Unimak islands whole pods were swimming close to the ship. Clearly, the ban on commercial whaling has emboldened the whales of the North Pacific. Occasionally, amid the twisting of fins and thrashing of tails, one of the whales would emerge full-body from the waters and then splash down mightily. You couldn't help feeling that they were doing it for fun, and even showing off a little. The skies were filled with huge flocks of sea birds. Some flocks were so large, numbering thousands of individuals, that they showed up on the ship's radar. In these cool waters they must be hardy fishers, though there clearly are rich pickings to be had. From time to time large beds of seaweed floated by, offering a perch for many of the birds. Large numbers of seals also bobbed their heads above the water inquisitively and then disappeared beneath the waves. Given what could be seen above the surf, what was below had to be even richer: these waters were teeming with life.

Force Nine in the Gulf of Alaska

With a deftly-calculated maneuver, the second mate turned our ship (all 70,000 tons of her) through a few degrees and she passed through the very centre of the Unimak Passage (a mere ten nautical miles wide) like a skillfully-threaded needle. Back in the Gulf of Alaska a storm had been brewing and we were heading into the eye. For two days force nine gales buffeted the ship creating fearsome waves up to five meters high whose peaks were blasted into clouds of white spume. A lesser vessel would have been in severe trouble. But the Hanjin Madrid merely began to oscillate from side to side in a regular harmonic motion through an angle of thirty degrees. I wondered whether we would start to lose containers off the deck, but the Captain assured me that there was no danger until the oscillations reached a tilt of forty degrees. The Chief had carefully adjusted the seawater ballast to control the timing of the oscillation, causally declaring that otherwise many of us would start to void our stomachs. I was once again impressed by the skill and knowledge required of a seaman. While I was spared any seasickness, the rocking of the ship took some getting used to and made for interesting effects when playing table tennis with Jens in the ship's gym.

After 48 hours being pummeled by the Pacific squalls it was a relief when we began to approach the relative shelter of the Dixon Passage, the waterway between Prince of Wales and Graham Islands that marks the entrance to British Columbia's wilderness coast. Our first port of call was Prince Rupert, named for the eponymous Prince of the Rhine, and developed in 2005, for obscure political reasons, as an alternative container facility to Vancouver harbour. A less likely site for a container port one could hardly imagine. Set amid the beautiful and remote islands and fjords of Canada's west coast, thousands of kilometers from industrial and urban centers, Prince Rupert port is a lonely commercial anomaly caught between the primeval forest and the wide blue yonder.

The first lesson in Canadian geography is this: Canada is unimaginably big. I had decided to disembark at Prince Rupert and make my own way to Vancouver rather than continue on the Hanjin Madrid. A cursory glance at the map had led me to believe, through a gross miscalculation of scale, that the onward journey would only take half a day by public transport. It transpired that the route was 1,000km by ferry and 1,500km by highway. I wasn't going to arrive there any time soon. The next problem was that the Canadian Immigration officers didn't seem at all interested in my arrival in their country. The lack of red tape was indeed refreshing after my sojourn in Russia and Central Asia, however I felt uncomfortable arriving on a new continent without any evidence of how I had done so. Given the puritanical zeal of US Immigration officials, who I would be meeting later, I thought it best to get some kind of stamp in my passport. Eventually not one but three officers arrived on board to authenticate my disembarkation. Was it my imagination or had their uniforms been hastily donned? The superior officer was a woman in her 40s, slightly overweight and casually coiffured, with the manner of someone rather relaxed putting on a professional persona. To her probing of my particulars I answered politely adding the word "Ma'am" frequently. The young man was yet more overweight and more informal, enlightening me that Prince Rupert was in "God's Own Country" but now the population was growing it felt a mite crowded (some 12,000 souls grace the town), and he was considering moving further north to get away from the bustle. Eventually, the informalities (sic) dispensed with, he turned to his boss in a charmingly naïve manner and asked, "Which way round do I hold the stamp?" The black smudge that ensued from this endorsement was all but illegible, though the words *Customs* and *Douanes* could just be made out.

To say that Prince Rupert is a one-horse town would be unfair, it is likely that two or three horses could reside there comfortably. Jens accompanied me on his bicycle as I walked two kilometers through the forest from the port into town. I began once again to feel the dizzy impact of culture shock. All the more remarkable since I was now in a culture closer to my own, in language and history, than any I had been in for the last nine months. I arrived at the bus station just fifteen minutes before the departure of the daily Vancouver Greyhound service so I promptly bought a ticket and got on, Jens kindly furnishing me with a few Canadian dollars. I was to have twenty-four hours with Greyhound in which to contemplate this brave New World and the amazing creatures in it.

Some thirteen hours later I reflected that the passengers awaiting the midnight bus at the terminal in Prince George (a nondescript town lost somewhere in British Columbia) were not beautiful. There was the obese man with a lopsided face, battered metal walking stick and plumy English accent who, with faultless politeness, was bothering everyone. There was the woman in her late fifties, overweight wearing a zebra pattern boob tube and very heavy makeup who was trying hard to be younger and more attractive than her years warranted. There was the young woman with long curly hair and ugly sores all over her mouth. I guess that beautiful people don't take the midnight bus from Prince George. They have large pickups or sports cars or fly with their expensively-attired partners. Since I was taking the midnight bus from Prince George it dawned on me that I also was not a beautiful person with my worn travelling clothes, disheveled hair and pimply forehead: a sobering realization with which to arrive in North America.

New World Blues

In my time in North America I often felt that I was closest to the spirit on the continent when I was travelling by public transport. The Intercity coach from Vancouver to Seattle confusingly deposited us on a back street some distance from the city centre and my first Seattle local bus set the tone. A black man with a very camp voice berated me for struggling past him with my backpack on the crowded bus. "Why are you so anxious? There's plenty of seats down there!" he said as he wandered off.

On my next journey I witnessed a shouting match between an inebriated white and a black further down the bus. Though the white was the more aggressive, the black was egging him on. Next to me a Chinese old lady started to join in. The Chinese bus driver brought us to an abrupt halt, walked down the bus and spoke in a firm but polite way: "Sir, you are too loud. Either you quiet down or you get off this bus here!" The white fell silent and then apologized profusely to the whole bus. It was moving but slightly embarrassing to witness his abject shame. As the Chinese old lady chipped in her tuppence-ha'penny the driver turned to her also "Ma'am, you too are too loud!" She giggled nervously and was silent for a few minutes attending to her knitting. While she knitted she seemed completely unaware that she was regularly stabbing me in the ribs. I was wondering whether to protest when she started to tell me about a car accident she'd had, and how the health insurance hadn't paid out, and then proceeded to give a potted story of her life. I turned to look at the elegant elderly black woman beside me and she smiled saying, "You're really getting it today". I smiled back saying, "Well, I've just arrived in Seattle". I came to love the 358 Express to Aurora Village for the characters that you invariably met and learned that the best place to sit was up front since that was where the strangest and loudest passengers seemed to congregate. This was

North American life raw and unadulterated.

On a tightly crammed rush-hour bus a political debate was in progress between standing and seated strangers. "They gonna smoke his ass", said a young black dude. "The CIA have already got a plan to have him killed" chipped in another. The main protagonists, a burly black and a robust white, were vigorously debating Barrack Obama's chances of becoming the next President and soon the conversation had passed to the wars in Iraq and Afghanistan, where it turned out the robust white man, who was originally from Essex, had served as a soldier in the British Army. "I gave ten years of my life to that country" he said bitterly, "and have nothing to show for it, I suffer from PTS (Post Traumatic Syndrome), and they gave me nothing". His face was indeed exceedingly gripped as if the muscles had become permanently frozen in a blank expression. Hidden behind his glasses were blue eyes and exceedingly small pupils. He explained that he was intending to move to Canada and find work as a security man, and started to extol the virtues of Canada over living in the USA or UK. "I can't go to Canada, I am a convicted felon" said the burly black, the second time that he had loudly announced to the whole bus that he had a criminal record, with a certain swagger in his voice. "I did my time, but I can't go to Canada" he reiterated. The young black dude threw in some more cynical remarks about the government, and was and met with general approbation. I joined in the debate with some random remarks about the gap between rich and poor and the unfairness of the healthcare system. Despite the inflammatory comments, our discussion was rather amicable, as if we were building a bond that breached the barricades separating lonely souls on an impersonal transport system. When I got off at the same stop as the ex-British army man he grabbed my hand firmly, looked me straight in the eye and said "God Bless you, God bless you!" I felt quite emotional as I wished him well with his move to Canada. We were strangers connecting in a lonely universe.

After several more colorful journeys I reflected that in Russia and Japan I had only seen one or two strange people in several months. Why were there so many strange and interesting characters on the public transport systems of North America? Or perhaps I should ask where were the strange and interesting characters in Russia and Japan?

A Buddha on 45th Street

I met Hank in Starbucks on 45th Street, or perhaps I should say I observed him, since he was slumped semi-conscious, wearing worn-out army slacks, in one of the generous armchairs, with his long, grey beard sprawling across a crumpled copy of the *Seattle Post Intelligencer* sports pages. I immediately had him tagged as an urban hobo making the most of his Americano Grande to get a comfy seat for the afternoon. Still, with his wizened face and rough tattoos he looked like an interesting character. I took the armchair next to him.

Hank awoke abruptly and started muttering about how awful the writing for the *Seattle PI* had become, and how much better the Spokane local papers were. Since he was talking out loud and I was the only person in the vicinity I asked him in what precise way the Spokane papers were superior: they gave you detailed facts rather than opinion, understood the context of each team's history and made an intelligent analysis of the strengths and weaknesses. This remarkably lucid and reasoned critique of what constitutes good sports journalism surprised me and my interest was further awakened. We proceeded to discourse on his conspiratorial theories of politics, which Hank succinctly summarized as "these guys are really just repeating the Crusades of a thousand years ago". Hank then regaled me with his views on Richard the Lionheart ("a sadist and a Jew hater"), medieval censorship and Church power, the Gnostic Crusades against the Cathars, Constantine's conversion to Christianity and the Council of Nicaea at which Catholic dogma started to proscribe what could be said or even thought. It turned out that Hank was one of the city's most educated vagrants. Most of Hank's views were tinged with conspiratorial and anti-establishment insinuations, whether about the Church patriarchs or contemporary politicians.

When I said that I was heading down the coast he said, "You'll like San Francisco" and then his voice dropped to a hush. "It's the only place on the West Coast that you can still get good marijuana". I laughed deeply. Finally on discovering that I was a Buddhist, Hank declaimed that there was just one thing that he really wanted to know about "Boo-di-zum". Was there any way

to get off the endless cycle of the wheel of life? When I informed him that any human being could achieve this by becoming a Buddha, he rapidly interjected "I am a Buddha!" with an intensely serious glint in his eye. This revelation seemed to shock us both, for he went abruptly silent while I, wondering just how far off the edge he had gone, continued as if nothing had happened. Finally, I asked permission to take his picture. He repeated the great American cliché, "You have a nice day", adding, "And don't go into Belltown after dark it is a dangerous place". With that he put on his wrap-around shades, announced to the world that he was off to collect a microwave oven, and departed.

Amtrak Adventures

"Oh you're not together, do you want to sit next to him?" said the conductor to Jeanette as he attempted to seat us in seats 37 and 38 on the upper storey of the double-decker seating car. "Er, sure", she said hesitantly, as though she wasn't at all sure. Was I perhaps a homicidal maniac or sexual pervert? It was one of those social situations where none of us knew what to say. As I climbed the stairs I noticed that the lower level was almost exclusively taken

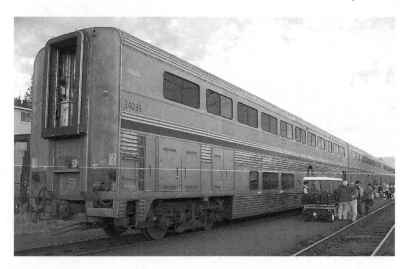

up with tired-looking games machines. All were switched off and none of the passengers seemed in the least bit interested in their grimy entertainment. These useless lumps of metal and glass were just endlessly shunted up and down the West Coast to no one's benefit.

The seats on the two storey Amtrak carriages are astonishingly generous and spacious, with more width and legroom than any train I can remember, as if you were a first class passenger. This is especially amazing when you consider that a journey of nearly a thousand miles cost me only $95. I reflected that this generosity of space was probably of both a consequence of the intense competition that Amtrak faces with the airlines, the family car and the bus network, and the average size of Americans' butts and legs.

Amtrak 11, the *Coast Starlight*, was packed out on this average, rainy Monday as we made our way south, an encouraging sign that rail travel in the USA is no longer an endangered species. We were a typical cross-section of American society with one significant omission: all the middle-aged professionals were missing. The conductor of our train was scrupulous in keeping us informed of every aspect of the journey, from the reason for a short delay at a traffic signal, to the extensive security measures we were asked to observe. The most insistent announcements concerned the non-smoking status of the entire train (with the threat of being put off if found in breach of this rule), and requests for passengers to wear their shoes when walking about the train. This was repeated so frequently that I began to imagine a long and sordid history of barefoot Amtrak passengers running amok with their odorous pinkies.

Jeanette was a pretty eighteen year-old student of Interior Design travelling to her college in Albany, Oregon from her family home in Seattle. We chatted a little, or rather I asked her about herself and listened to her stories about visiting her cowgirl sister on a ranch in Montana and her mom's travels in

Europe. She didn't seem in the slightest bit interested in finding out about me. Soon our conversation lapsed and we disappeared into our own little worlds, she with her iPod and furious texting, me with my book and aimless gazing out at the lovely Fall colors.

As our train glided south through Washington State we passed such towns as Olympia and Kelso. In contrast to Seattle and Tacoma they seemed tiny and provincial despite the fact that Olympia is the State capital. However, the most striking aspects of the journey were the wonderful views of Puget Sound, the large stretches of forest and the great rivers. The mightiest of these was the Columbia River that carves its way through gorges and valleys all the way from Montana. By the time it reaches Portland, Oregon, it is a truly vast body of water and our train appeared to cross it three times. The Washington forests are almost entirely re-growth forests, since the region was systematically logged in the 19th and 20th centuries. Although by European standards the scale is impressive, locals make a point of saying how impoverished these forests are compared to the small tracts of ancient woodland that exist in State Parks. The high rainfall and rich volcanic soils of the Pacific Northwest coast makes for some of the best conditions for timber growth in the world. Occasionally, you encounter a truly vast Sitka Spruce, Cedar or Pine and I confess that despite my New Age-skepticism, I had hugged a massive spruce when hiking in the Cascade Mountains. How else can one express the delight at encountering such a vast living being?

Battling with BART

The Bay Area Rapid Transit is one of the highlights of San Francisco's public transport system: a light railway that links the key conurbations quickly and cheaply, and zooms from SF to Oakland through a sub-Bay tunnel. However BART has one vicious quirk: buying a ticket.

Realizing that life is too short to master every ticket machine in the universe I always head for a human being if at all possible. In Japan this had been a 100 percent successful strategy, especially as the machine kanji usually defeated me before I even got to choose the language. On the BART, however, there was no escape from the Machine, a friendly black woman in a booth just directed me to the wall of buttons, slots and screens. "It don't wanna know where you're going". she called out as I retreated disconsolately at the thought of having to face up to a digital vendor. A ticket machine that doesn't want to know your destination: how strange! So I managed to do the conversion from the paper chart stuck to the wall and realize that I needed to pay $7.30 for a return to North Berkley: that was the easy part. I inserted my $1 bills, but on the third one BART seemed to chew it over for rather a long time before spitting it back out with a "Rejected". I tried smoothing it out and uncurling the corners but there was no placating this recalcitrant vendor. "Okay, okay I'll feed you a clean $20". But now I discovered that my digital doppelganger was trying to sell me a $20 ticket. "I don't want a $20 ticket, I want a return to North Berkley" I said rather exasperated. "Calm down, Rijumati, just hit the *Minus-$* button", I said to myself. I managed to subtract four dollars until the virtual button disappeared off the screen to be replaced with a red text saying that $16 was the minimum payment allowed. "I just want a bloody ticket to North Berkley" I cursed under my breath, and considered how I might get my own back on this recalcitrant over-blown metallic excuse for a sales person.

Next to me a young couple were also battling with BART who had eaten their money but not come up with a ticket. The friendly black woman had now come over, unlocked BART's stomach and was digging around in his bowels to remove their lost dollars. In a gesture of compassion she called over to me "You got it worked out now?" "No" I said with some desperation, feeling that being unable to buy a ticket from a simple vending machine must qualify me as the dumbest guy on the street. "Okay, I'll come over when I get this sorted". I heaved a sigh of relief and waited several minutes while she continued to disembowel BART and discuss exactly how much money the young couple had fed him. It all seemed to depend on the exact point at which they had hit BART's *Cancel* button. BART can be very fussy.

Finally she came over surveyed my predicament and said nonchalantly "Oh, I thought you had a $10 bill" a rather gratuitous assumption on her part since I hadn't even opened my wallet in her presence. "You have to change that in the change machine over there" and she waved her hand to a primitive machine called *CHANGE*. I guess he was BART's Neanderthal cousin since all he could do was eat $10 and $20 bills and spew $5 dollar bills in return, not really a very satisfying level of evolution for a machine. I now fed $5 bills into BART and my human helper ran her fingers quickly over BART's screen, subtracting $1s and adding the 10c's until the magic number of $7.30 appeared on BART's wry visage. I pressed the magic button *BUY $7.30 ticket* and BART burped loudly as a card ticket and lots of coins plummeted from his guts. The whole procedure had taken nearly 10 minutes. "Why can't you just type in the amount $7.30?" I muttered sub-vocally to no one in particular and I contemplated the excruciating revenge I would take on BART's logic designer, like being forced to help Homer Simpson to buy a ticket. Surely the home of Berkley University and the Summer of Love can do better than to be tyrannized by such a juvenile BART-tender.

Leaving the West Coast

After two blissful weeks living on a little houseboat belonging to a friend in Oakland Harbor, the relentless rootlessness of the traveler caught up with me again. I felt sad as I packed my bag and was once more propelled into the world of cheap hotels and guesthouses. For many months I had been feeling a lack in my

carefree traveler's life, so I had gone to California to seek out Love and the Goddess. She had indeed manifested for me but in a rather unexpected form. On the very day that I was nursing my bruised self-esteem after abortive overtures to a vivacious woman in Santa Cruz, I was approached via email by my friend Siddhisvari who I had met in Bodhgaya. I didn't need much convincing, since I had admired her for a long time, and over the next few weeks a passionate love-mail exchange brought us intensely and closely together. As I lived alone on the boat I went through the upheavals and madness of falling in love. The free Wi-Fi drifting over the waves meant that I cascaded through the lover's heaven and hell without meeting a single person: I was just alone with the ducks. Siddhisvari and I had arranged to meet later on my journey, but for now I was practicing patience.

Amtrak trains from San Francisco to Los Angeles were decidedly spare. In order to make my onward connection to Flagstaff the only way to avoid an 18-hour wait in LA was to take the branch line that terminates in Bakersfield and catch a connecting bus. In any other country these two international cities would be connected by multiple, if not hourly services. Leaving behind the delights of the coastal hills and bays we headed into the vast plain of central California: endless miles of prime farming land as far as the eye could see. The neat rows of almond and fruit trees or mile-long irrigation pipes on wheels testify to the immense effort of Californian farmers and the power of large-scale planning. It is astonishing to see the scale on which farming succeeds in a land that without a huge irrigation network would be largely desert scrub.

Mr. S. our guard was a tall black man in the habit of wearing his jumper under his shirt: eccentric, but not without a certain style. At each station he made an ostentatious string of announce-ments, such as he must have made thousands of times before, yet in a charmingly upbeat manner. Whether it was extolling the dangers of getting left behind at a bland conurbation called Corcoran or offering all and sundry, himself included, the option of getting off for a "Cancer-stick" break he resembled a stand up comedian who had somehow missed the stage. His antics for Amtrak were appreciated well enough, several of my fellow passengers joining in the chuckles as he came up with yet another corker: "And if you missed that last announcement, even though I bowled it to you under-arm then look out for your bus at Bakersfield".

My bus seat companion to LA was a handsome crop-haired Marine called Isaac Gonzales. Isaac was 19 and when I asked why he had joined the Marines he said it was so that he could get away from home. His elder brother was smoking marijuana and his younger sister busting a gut for college. Isaac and his sweetheart were intending to get married a few months later and had plans for a family of three or four kids. He had never left the USA or even travelled much beyond his hometown of Fresno, though had been to Utah once when he was seventeen. He told me that he didn't remember that trip much since it was a long time ago. I rather suspect he was intoxicated at the time. He struck me as a simple, decent and naïve young man, not yet having had the opportunity to taste the possibilities of what he might become. He had joined the Marines as a career and to escape from the confines of his family, without thinking much about the possibility that it might call on him to kill, be maimed or die for his country. He seemed fascinated by the idea of London, wanting to know what the culture was like. Yet the life choices he was making meant that his chances of ever getting there were slim: what with Marine tours to Afghanistan and Iraq awaiting him at the end of his training and a new family awaiting him at the start of his marriage. Time in the Middle East would almost certainly shatter some of the boyish naivety, hopefully without replacing it by trauma.

On the Road

A week or two earlier I'd had the good fortune to undertake a genuine American *Road Trip* and taste the spirit of Kerouac and the Beats. The myth is deeply embedded in my psyche: driving to the vanishing point, passing through vast wildernesses and one horse towns, hair blowing in the wind, dust swirling in clouds as one passes, not a care in the world, abandoned to the utter freedom of this moment. The intense appeal of the freedom of the highway was also a symbol of where the inner journey had brought me. After my struggles in Central Asia, I now felt direction and movement, yet without any clear destination in view. In fact, it was apparent to me that the attempt to grasp a definite goal would betray the pilgrimage.

Anatoly, the Russian-American friend who I'd met on the way to Kathmandu, was the ideal road trip companion: a voracious driver with a love of adventure, a delight in talking Dharma and

the owner of a lovely electric blue Toyota pickup. We covered 1,000 miles in three days travelling from Fresno through the wonders of Yosemite National Park into the Sierra Nevada, camping in Death Valley National Park, and then entering Nevada for a descent into Las Vegas.

Despite their familiarity the vast ice-sculpted granites of the Yosemite valley, including the iconic Half Dome and the breath-taking sheer cliff of El Capitan (nearly a kilometer high), inspired us. Anatoly and I alternated between gazing on in admiration and frantic photography, a

hopeless attempt to capture the uncapturable, grasp the ungraspable. "You should go and stand over there" Anatoly pointed to a precipitous overhanging slab of granite, improbably balanced over a deathly abyss. I looked on in amazement, wondering if the thrill of it was worth the risk. Suddenly, something daring moved in my soul. "Okay", I said as I jumped over the railing and the signs warning "Danger Keep Out". The fear tingled on my skin, the tiny hairs rising in anticipation of a deadly threat as I clambered slowly on all fours over the rough granite surfaces, testing each handhold and foothold with utmost care. On three sides of this narrow ledge, two meters wide, four meters long was certain death. Gingerly crouching, edging forwards until the sheer drop became fully visible. The tiny specs of humanity in the valley below seemed like microscopic life forms, as though glimpsed through a lens. My breath was fast and shallow, my heart was beating hard. I composed myself, drinking deeply of the clear mountain air, before rising onto two legs, gazing into the void, utterly alive to the fragility of human existence.

We snaked our way out of Yosemite's monoliths and lakes,

picking up Highway 395 at the volcanic crater of Mono Lake, famed for its abundance of extremophile microbes, and headed south for Death Valley National Park. Highway 395, passing between the ranges of the Sierras, resembles my ideal image of the Open Road. As the perspective of the faultlessly straight carriageway leads the eye to a distant vanishing point between deserted mountains, the road ahead seems to aim for infinity. What better symbol for the way to freedom than these lonely stretches of desert asphalt?

It was already dark when we arrived in Death Valley National Park looking for somewhere to camp. Everything was Panamint: we crossed over the Panamint mountains, dropped into Panamint Valley and went through the tiny town of Panamint Springs, eschewing the mild lure of its dim motel lights for a desert

encampment. Finally we found a small road off the main highway and searched for a track to take us into the sands. By the time we had constructed the tent, Anatoly had cooked us a delicious noodle soup and we were drinking an evening mug of tea, the night sky had completely enveloped us. The constellations glittered brilliantly overhead: Cygnus, Cassiopeia, the Great Bear. I felt the joy of being touched by yet another infinity, the unfathomable vastness of the universe without mirroring the unfathomable vastness of the universe within. Anatoly and I talked about consciousness, myth and imagination with the joy of friends sharing the preciousness of this fleeting human life. Suddenly, I noticed that the stars' clarity stars had dimmed, at almost the same moment Anatoly asked, "What is that light on the mountains?" Sure enough the peaks of the western Panamints were radiating an unearthly silver-white glow. "Of course, it's the Moon rising". Soon the white desert sands began to awake, glistening mysteriously, our bodies casting long, occult shadows as the gibbous Moon rose in the east. She bathed us in

Her blessed, otherworldly radiance.

I awoke early, prompted by the inexorably slow deflation of my camping mat which left me musing indecisively on whether to emerge from my seductive sleeping cocoon into the cold desert morning. The rich midnight blue was just giving way to the dawn hues of yellow and orange over the eastern peaks as I poked my head out of the sleeping bag. Anatoly was breathing heavily, still soundly asleep. Over the next hour the mystic light of the moonshine gave way to the clarity of the dawn. The contours and gullies in the far mountains were highlighted by long shadows bestowing on them a powerful extra dimension. The bushes and grasses anchored in the sand began to seem small and familiar in place of the nighttime tangle of mysterious forms. Soon the red light of the rising sun turned the Sierras a rich pink, and the white sand of the valley floor began to dazzle. The silence was deafening ... there was nothing to compete with the buzzing of your thoughts.

Death Valley is one of the strangest places in the world. Created by spectacular tectonic shifts, in places it is nearly 100m below sea level, and sinking. Leaving the immense granites of Yosemite, one is suddenly in a land of endlessly-shifting sands and a profusion of rocks: crumbling sedimentary, rough volcanic, powerful green, jagged black, rich red, which finally metamorphose into far-flung limestone as one crosses the Spring Mountains into Nevada. Each rock type defines the landscape in a unique way, shaping the contours, fractures and landslides in a telltale pattern. The granites create smooth surfaces fractured by straight traceable cracks. The softer sandstones and conglomerates tumble in a chaotic mash of breaks and faults, leaving jagged edges and a myriad of tiny grooves. Mildly acidic rain sculpts the limestone into grey rivulet channels with sharp spires and turrets. At the very lowest point of Death Valley is Badwater Basin, where the slow trickle of mountain water finally emerges along a fault line, its labyrinthine journey through the rocks having laden it with saline solutions so that Badwater has become a natural salt flat, a white plane of crystals endlessly renewed by the water and sun.

As you travel to Death Valley there are periodic references to the satanic origins of the landscape. On the way there are the tall spires of the Devil's Postpile. In Death Valley itself you'll find the Devil's Cornfield as well as the rather more recent satanic addition of the Devil's Golf Course. Anatoly and I named one particular rock formation the Devil's Organ Pipes. Why is the Devil so often credited with striking natural phenomena around the world? Perhaps the reason is that the immense epochs of transformation that have shaped Death Valley with such intricacy seem so un-Godlike, that people come to think only his nemesis could have created them.

"Shall we check it out", said Anatoly, "Sure!" I consented as we passed the sign for Golden Canyon. A host of SUVs and pickups at the trailhead parking seemed to indicate a place of significant interest. Strange that in the vast silent emptiness of Death Valley we had alighted on the most peopled place. Golden Canyon is just that: a narrow gorge flanked by sandy golden-yellow cliffs that open into a labyrinth of ancient eroded gullies and streambeds. In a moment of spontaneous adventurousness I suggested to Anatoly that we scramble up one of the easier looking peaks to get the view and be closer to the angels. Anatoly always responds to a call of the spirit. Being an experienced rock climber he said that it would take about forty minutes. The problem was that we were scrambling up very soft conglomerate rock. So, though none too steep, it was liable to crumble beneath one's feet if one applied too much weight, or to come off in one's hand if one pulled too strongly. Anatoly led us up a sort of chimney, hugging the rising ridge from below as we slowly hauled our bodies up, leaving behind us a small avalanche of dislodged pebbles and sand. At Base Camp One, a relatively flat saddleback ledge about 50cm wide, we stopped to appreciate the view. Ahead the buttress of red organ pipe rocks that mark the head of Golden Canyon, to the sides the steeply rising jagged cliffs, behind the vast plain of Death Valley, shimmering in the rising heat, framed by the western range of Sierras. "You realize that we are climbing illegally", Anatoly said suddenly. "Well that didn't stop us before", I joked. "I mean that we are climbing without safety backup", he said. "Oh", I replied, uncomfortable at the implication that we were putting our lives at risk. "I'm more concerned about going down", I added after a moment's thought. Anatoly led the way up to the summit, managing to avoid a hairy crumbling ledge through a judicious traverse of a scree slope. "Good news from up here Riju!" he shouted down as footholds of sand and rock sped away from under my boots on the scree. "I'm on my way", I shouted, not even daring to look up for fear that I might lose my balance at a critical moment.

At the summit the views were even more spectacular, the intense blue of the sky offsetting every hue of rock one could think of from red to yellow to green to black to brown as one surveyed the cardinal points. And what is more there was a well-worn footpath leading away from the summit in the opposite direction: an unexpected gift from the angels.

Lost in Las Vegas

After two days in the deserts and mountains of California Anatoly and I descended into a rather different archetypal realm: Las Vegas. No sooner had we crossed the State line from Shoshone to Pahrump (famous for its brothel ranches) than the seduction of Vegas began to work its magic. Anatoly told me stories of people who had won millions of dollars at the casino slot machines and I began to wonder what I would do if I won the $10m jackpot. Suddenly, I was jolted into a sober awareness that the lure of Vegas was already playing upon my soul, as if the Sorcerer of Vegas had sprung his entrapment spells as soon as we hit Nevada.

As Anatoly and I dwelt on this magical pull exerted by Vegas, I realized just how badly the rest of the USA needs Nevada and Las Vegas in particular. Vegas is the City of the Dream, or the Nightmare, depending on which way you look at it. In Vegas every dream, every fantasy, every possibility can be played out. The greatest of all American Dreams is that by luck or skill you can make it big, reach the top, be whatever you want to be, and the casinos of Vegas are the very crystallization of that Dream, offering hope of its realization. Vegas bears the archetype of the America's National Dream.

And there is another reason, perhaps even more urgent. Vegas, in holding all the desires and fantasies bears the shadow of America. Here the safe, middle-class family man can come and be a secret one-night Eros, the bored housewife can feel like a Queen, the young prodigy can gamble his soul for fame and fortune. Without Vegas those fantasies would remain suppressed, festering and decaying until, becoming demons, they erupt in a torrent of madness. "What goes in Vegas stays in Vegas" says the official city slogan; a city that markets itself as a safe haven where you can live out the irrepressible in the psyche. Naturally, Las Vegas is abhorred by God-fearing Christians, yet perhaps the city guarantees the nation's sanity by letting those fantasies be played out in a contained environment.

Of course, this is also a city of the most adept and self-conscious manipulations. "If you have a loaded gun in your psyche, Vegas will pull the trigger" Anatoly informed me with a degree of self-revelation. He had lived in Vegas for seven years and experienced both the Dream and the Nightmare. The man who mistakes himself for a big-shot will find his self-image flattered until the shirt is stripped from his back. The woman who longs to be the object of desire will find herself the centre of the universe until her maxed-out credit card shatters the illusion.

At the heart of Vegas is The Strip, the colloquial name for Las Vegas Boulevard, and a synonymic reminder of the sexual and financial taboos that are waiting to be transgressed. Here are some of the greatest hotels in the world for opulence and service; the Bellagio, the Wynn, the Paris, Caesar's Palace, Treasure Island, Luxor ... each selling its own version of the same paradigm: immense success, luck, anonymous pleasure. For example, the Bellagio, which opened in 1998, cost a staggering $1.6 billion. At the time it was the most expensive hotel ever built. Every detail of the Bellagio is lavishly executed. The reception hall sports a dazzling chandelier installation of giant glass blooms; the lake and fountain displays are so intricate that they require 31 staff to maintain; there are two 5-Star restaurants, *Picasso* and *Le Cirque*.

But the amazing fact about the Bellagio and all the venues in Vegas is their complete open-minded hospitality to each and every guest. There is none of your Old World prejudice about family or aristocratic ties, or the New World prejudice about looking like the perfect man or woman. Vegas will welcome each and every person with open arms, as long as they are prepared to enter her dream and have the money to do so. The hospitality is staggering, free car-parking all over the city centre, fast food courts where a hostess comes up to offer you napkins as you dine. The staff at the world's most expensive hotels greet even a dusty Dharma Bum fresh out of Death Valley as if he were a big spender. Vegas gives everyone a sense that they are special. That is part of the seduction.

I felt that I needed to propitiate the gods of Las Vegas by making a sacrifice, a sign that I had come to visit their realm in good faith. Evaluating my budget traveler finances I made a decision. "I want to blow $20 in a casino" I said to Anatoly. "Okay", he said. If he was underwhelmed he did a good job of hiding it. "Do you want to play cards or slot machine?" "Oh, I don't want to think about it, something that is pure luck". So we went to the Wynn and wandered about the bewildering array of bright lights, alluring sounds and expectant slot machines, card tables and roulette wheels. As we walked about, I started to feel rather agitated, the choice was paralyzing. Jackpots ranging from $1000s to $1,000,000s were advertised with flashing LEDs and announced by electronic jingles. I started to feel lost, unable to decide on any option. We passed the Megabucks slot offering a $1.6m jackpot. "Let's try here", I said desperately trying to come to some decision, any decision. So I fed in $6, which entitled me to two spins of the cylinders. It was all over in about 30 seconds, I'd lost my Vegas virginity, and predictably it was a bit of an anti-climax. "Well the high jackpot means you get fewer chances to play for your money" Anatoly explained rather gently. "Oh, okay, let's try something else then". So we wandered around a bit more and finally settled on a row that called themselves 25c slots. This turned out to be something of a con since although each unit only cost 25c, it cost 3 units to spin the cylinders. I fed in the remaining $14, my electronic host struggling somewhat with the rather ragged $1 bills that I'd offered him, and sat down to spin the wheels. Spin after spin came so close to pay out, at one point three different bars even lined up and my credit rose slightly, but it seemed like the inevitable was just being delayed. On my final spin there was just a sliver of hope that I would be redeemed, and then it was all over. I had come to the Wynn and

Lost. Yet, in another sense I had won, having experienced, albeit cheaply, the hope and despair of the gambler's mind. I noticed a subtle voice that said, "If only you'd been a bit more daring, say $100, you'd have given yourself the chance of winning". Where did that thought come from? Was it hypnotically implanted or did it come in the air conditioning? Vegas is scary when it comes to psychic suggestion.

This is a city that is permanently recreating itself. Here, as perhaps nowhere else in the world, developers will think nothing of tearing down a perfectly serviceable multi-million dollar building for no better reason than that the investor needs some new energy to come into his business. So the inhabitants of Vegas are continually being delayed and diverted by colossal constructions in the very heart of the city. The latest of these, a sort of city within a city, is a $9.8 billion complex of glass and steel that boasts its own monorail and will no doubt break all sorts of financial records for being the most expensive of its kind ever built.

You don't see the homeless on The Strip. Naturally, even Las Vegas has a homeless population, but they are somehow smuggled away from the heart of the Dream, since they represent everything that Vegas wants to deny – the Nightmare of poverty, addiction and failure. But, in reality to play for the Dream, is to play for the Nightmare. By the same logic that every visitor to Vegas can leave a winner, he can also leave a loser, and of course most do. The other noticeable omission is newspapers. News from the world is not really welcome in Vegas, unless it is news of success, good fortune, the individual winning out against all odds – which most news is not. So it took several hours of walking the Strip and malls before Anatoly and I saw even a self-dispensing newsstand. When you enter Vegas you are meant to leave the rest of the world behind; that too is part of the seduction. And so we spent 24 hours tasting the delights of Las Vegas, really a very brief introduction, but enough to feel the power of the repository of Dreams that keeps the Myth of America from going bankrupt.

Canyons and Cowboys

My final adventure in the USA was to take me on one more pilgrimage: to the deserts of the South West. The Four Corners, colloquial name of the region where Arizona, Utah, Colorado and New Mexico meet, contains geological, archaeological and anthropological wonders and boasts some of the most stunning landscapes on our Earth.

Amtrak's *Southern Chief* deposited me in Flagstaff early on a frosty November morning. A classic cowboy-cum-tourist town, Flagstaff hosts a profusion of diners, gift shops and stores all cashing in on its rugged wild west past. However, at 6.00 a.m. the only place offering any hospitality was the Downtown Diner, whose patron lavished upon me a huge breakfast, large mugs of tea and news about the locality. As I explained my intention to visit canyons and deserts, one of the other clients piped up that I could enter the Grand Canyon National Park on an unmade back road without having to pay a fee. In the USA it is amazing how a complete stranger will help you to evade paying official fees, as if freedom from taxes were enshrined in the Constitution. In the end, like a good citizen, I took the main highway not wanting to risk any off-road adventures with my sporty little Pontiac rental.

How do you describe your first sight of the Grand Canyon? This geological masterpiece defies the imagination's ability to grasp it, let alone the power of words to capture it. None of the pictures or statistics really prepare you for the sense of immensity, timelessness and sublimity. At the visitor centre Ranger Jess was young, ebullient and exhaustingly upbeat as she drilled us, a small party of adults many years her senior, in the science of the Canyon and the geologic mnemonic "DUDE": deposition, upthrust, down-cutting and erosion. Though the geology is fascinating and the statistics impressive (a mile deep, 18 million years in the making, exposing rocks up to 1.3 billion years old) perhaps the best evocation is the Native American Paiute name for the Canyon, *Kaibab*, which means "mountain lying down". I spent two days descending into Kaibab, walking the rim, reading about the geology and viewing it from different vantage points like Yavapai, Bright Angel, Grandview and Desert View. At last, however, it seemed that to begin to comprehend Kaibab I needed to enter into his cradle and sit, looking, contemplating and reflecting for a long time. Gazing out over the extraordinary plateaus, gullies and mesas, ranging from jade green to sand yellow to rust red, the rocks started to soak into my soul, calling up resonances with a primordial Dreamtime. Time and timelessness, space and infinity swirled about me in the presence of Kaibab, occasionally evoking a somber existential mood, as if the brevity of my life were called into question by the vastness of his vision.

This is "Indian Territory", the Navajo, Hopi and Hovenweep all have reservations in the Four Corners and traversing these vast desert plains is like entering another country. In fact the Navajo have their own President and a time zone that differs from the rest of the state by roughly 15 minutes, depending on who you ask. In Tuba City I realized that vegetarianism was alien to Navajo culture when a waitress in Hogan's Diner simply blanked me as I requested food without meat. I ended up with a cheap burrito at Taco Bell, listening to a group of Navajo teens playing jingles on their cellphones. Time and again, in Indian country the towns I visited seemed to have a slightly depressing atmosphere, the homes of a once proud people who had lost their sense of purpose. Nowhere was this more evident than at Walpi, the Hopi village on First Mesa. The peace-loving Hopi had built a village on this yellow sandstone table with high views across the plains and offering a natural fortification from marauders. I drove to the top hoping to explore, but the tourist office, little more than a roughly-made house with a sign above the door, was closed. After walking around for a while I was eventually directed to Loretta, who was busy tending to her granddaughter and seemed reluctant to be bothered by a stranger, even for a fee. Explaining that I was from England and wouldn't get another chance to visit a Hopi village for a long time she kindly took me

on a short tour. Taking pictures in the village was strictly prohibited. The traditional houses on the mesa were mostly empty, built right to the edge of the cliff, and often connected to a ritual space entered from above and without windows. Looking over the cliff edge I could see large quantities of refuse strewn down the slopes. Loretta explained a little about Hopi culture, saying that most people only came back here for special festivals. This dramatic cliff-top village had an air of desolation and decay.

In a land of supreme geological wonders, the Grand Canyon is the king, yet there are many queens, princes and princesses. Canyon de Chelly is on a far more human scale and home to the

astounding habitations of the Ancestral Puebloans who built gravity defying villages in the cliffs and thrived for nearly a thousand years until they suddenly and mysteriously vanished in the early 14th century. The flat canyon floor meanders between towering pink sandstone walls, smoothed by eons of erosive waters. In a huge cleft part-way up one cliff is an ancient village improbably clutching the rock. The most remarkable fact is that no one really knows who these people were or why they left. Their dwellings are found all over the region, especially at Mesa Verde.

Travelling alone on the endless desert highways, staying in cheap motels, meeting few people and visiting spectacular natural wonders, I drifted into a strange twilight existence. I lived just for the road, the desert, the rocks and the phone calls to my new darling, snatched from every available landline and dodging the eight time zones between us. All the road movies I'd ever seen crowded into my psyche: the *High Plains Drifter* meting out vigilante justice, *Thelma and Louise* fighting prejudice and conventionality, *Easy Rider* looking for kicks, Natasha Kinski running from herself in *Paris, Texas*, and the anonymous aggression of the dusty road in *Duel*. Once again the familiar "Who am I?" echoed from my inner peaks and canyons, as these archetypal landscapes impressed themselves upon me. Like a scion of one of the great mesas, I felt my life was shaped and sculpted by unimaginable and timeless forces far beyond my control. The choice seemed to be between surrender and oblivion: an uncomfortable realization for the small bundle of ego that I call Rijumati.

Monument Valley is absolutely worthy of the fame bestowed upon it by John Huston's iconic Westerns. Rising from the plain like great sentinels guarding the wilderness, these immense, rust-red mesas mesmerize and arrest your gaze. Needles, pillars and tables stand improbably and beautifully silhouetted against a bolt-blue sky. Transported by the light, colors and forms, I longed to create a tribute to these ancient monoliths in paint, music or words, yet knew that I would never manage to capture their sublimity. It was the same in the Valley of the Gods, Goosenecks Canyon and Mesa Verde, and then there were the great wonders I didn't have time to visit such as the famed National Parks in Utah like Arches and Bryce. How did this land become so endowed with geological wonders? Surely the sublime has erupted into the world in this corner of the American South West.

My final initiation of this desert highway pilgrimage was the cheap motel where I landed up in the tiny town of Cuba, New Mexico. The tired carpet, minimal restroom, crass Artex swirls on the ceiling, jumbled cables hanging from the TV, air conditioner and fridge, and the omnipresent smell of cheap Chinese cleaning fluids let me know that I had finally arrived in the world of anonymous accommodation: proof that I had managed to become no one in particular. The next day I was heading for Texas, famed for its redneck, meat-hungry, oil-rich culture: an unsettling prospect for a pacifist, vegetarian, budget-travelling eco-Buddhist.

A Tale of Two Buses

With a sense of muted excitement I rose early to depart the USA, the country which had fed and sheltered me for two months. I was about to head into the confusion and complexity of an alien culture whose language I barely grasped, whose customs I didn't know and whose people were a mystery to me: I was heading for Mexico.

I checked out of my cheap, soulless motel soon after the dawn. The Red Roof Lodge, which did indeed have a red roof, was El Paso's cheapest motel chain. The staff were friendly but couldn't offer any help with my travelers questions, I just gave up after a series of "Don't knows" and "Can't help you-s" and made my way to Avis to return my sleek little Pontiac. With classic American efficiency this was easy and over in a few minutes. I asked the Avis man for help finding out where I should go for the US immigration control, having completely failed to discover this from El Paso tourist information or my hotel. He obliged by phoning the Customs who assured me that it was straight-forward to do on *The Bridge,* the border control at the Rio Grande. He was friendly and helpful, though he couldn't tell me anything about buses back into town apart from the fact that there was a bus stop on the nearby main street.

I felt sad to be giving up the joy and freedom of the car. We had spent many happy hours together plying our way along the lost desert roads of the American Southwest. We had driven over mountains, through canyons, across unmade dusty red tracks, through forests and even made it up into the snows. And lastly there was the long haul on Interstate 25 where together we crossed the whole of New Mexico in a day. I loved driving the vast open spaces of the USA and even wondered what it would be like to become a long distance truck driver. But contemplating the trucker's mind-numbing hours at the wheel, the endless progression of local music stations, the huge greasy meals and rough truck stops it seemed likely to be an effective means of spiritual suicide.

It was a busy workday morning in El Paso. Interstate 10 had long tailbacks into the city and the accommodation district on Exit 11 was buzzing with cars. Yet on this beautifully clear winter's day there was not a person on the streets as I walked in search of a bus stop. The only humans I saw not in a vehicle were some road workers putting out warning signs on the central reservation of the six lane main street. Nobody in El Paso, it seems, would ever think of walking somewhere. Once again, I felt adrift in the world of the lowlife budget traveler, suddenly severed from my wheels, the essential prosthetic extension of the American way of life. I felt how a completely simple wish – to go from the accommodation district to downtown with my luggage – was now a major logistical challenge. Of course the sensible traveler would have just booked a taxi, borrowing someone else's prosthetic extension for the job, but somehow I relished the challenge of trying to work out how to get a bus to where I needed to go, and saving myself twenty dollars.

In El Paso the bus stops are not a major feature of street life. It is a city whose abundance of road signs eclipses the plant life, as if they have crossbred. Every stretch of highway and street has multiple messages for the passing vehicles, some great, some small, some bright, some dull. The bus stop signs are small, dull, white placards on the top of a short, single pole. At first I thought the friendly Avis man had misled me, since there was nothing remotely resembling my conception of a bus stop. But as I wandered around, clambering over the woodchips that line the sidewalk I noticed an unassuming little placard with a single bus graphic. There was no schedule, no route number, no infor- mation of any kind, just a black graphic about 25cm high stuck on a pole. As the huge pickups and SUVs growled past I felt like a lost alien in a new world and that perhaps I was being a total schmuck standing hopefully in this asphalt and concrete desert.

Miraculously within ten minutes I spied in the far distance something that looked like a bus coming towards me. It must have seemed rather strange to the driver to see this backpacking foreigner waving vigorously with the enthusiasm of a man escaping from the wilderness. And when his orange indicator signified that he had seen me and was actually going to stop I could hardly contain my joy. He was faultlessly polite, "Well sir, to get to downtown you need to be on the *other* side of the street at that bus stop". He was pointing vaguely to a direction in which I couldn't make out anything that might be a bus stop "you want the 15 or 18 bus, there will be one coming in 5 or 10 minutes". The relief I felt at getting some seemingly reliable information was immense. "Do you mean by that bench over there?" I asked, pointing at the only distinguishable object in this urban jungle. "That's right sir" as promptly the door closed and off he went.

With a little skip in my heel I headed for the pedestrian crossing. It seemed like an age as I waited for a green crosswalk sign, a lone homo sapiens trying to traverse six lanes of mean looking automobilus grossus. "Oh there's my bus!" At last the grinding traffic light logic boards gave me a green light and I dashed across the highway, dragging my wheelie backpack at an illegally dangerous speed. But too late, though the bus stop was only 30m away, the no. 15 was passing it and I hadn't been seen. He stopped at the lights directly in front of me. I motioned vigorously that I wanted to embark, but the driver, though stationary, just shook his head with complete resolve showing me that my plight was hopeless. He made that utterly useless gesture that American bus drivers always make when you know they're not going to help you: he pointed another mile up the street as if to say "you get to that stop before me and I'll let you on". For all I knew there might be only a single bus in the whole morning in El Paso and, somewhat forlorn, I plodded the 30m down the street to the putative official stop and parked myself there. "Well I guess $20 for a taxi is better than standing here all morning" I consoled myself as a Plan B. However I need not have worried. Within ten minutes the 18 bus had rolled up. Though the driver let me on he was talking on a wireless device and mostly ignored me as I tried to ask how much to pay, where to alight for the Rio Grande immigration point and stuff my coins into the ticket machine. Embarrassingly these jammed and he had to use some force to push them through, whilst still talking on his wireless ... Some things in the USA don't work as well as you might imagine.

Eventually, I arrived at the "chasm" of the Rio Grande. The river itself is nothing like a chasm; at this time of year the concrete water channel that directs the river is mostly dried up. The chasm is between the two worlds that collide along the boundary: El Paso and Ciudad Juarez. The Rio Grande bridge symbolizes this collision perfectly, spanning merely 150m, its broad bulk is permanently choked with vehicles queuing in one direction: leaving Mexico to enter the USA. On either side of the carriageway are two walkways, cloistered with metal roofs and barriers. To the West is a free flowing channel of pedestrians leaving the USA, to the East a slow moving queue of Hispanics attempting to enter the USA. This sociological tide never ebbs, it always flows in the same direction. You can't help feeling that the implication is that one day Mexico will be completely empty of people and the USA will be very crowded. But for the time being the zeal of US immigration officers has stemmed the tide.

You would think that leaving the USA is a relatively easy thing to do, but the ordeal at the Rio Grande immigration point, was reminiscent of bureaucratic nightmares in Russia and Kazakhstan. I could have walked out of the country with absolutely no immigration control, but common sense told me that unless my green visa waiver was processed I would most likely face an impenetrable wall of red tape when I next tried to visit: it would seem as if I had never left the country. When I got into the no man's land on the bridge itself I asked a woman immigration officer how to get my exit properly processed. "Oh, you have to pay your 35c" – the toll for pedestrians on the bridge – "and exit through that metal gate, go over to the other side and get processed there. That gentleman will open the gate for you" she said pointing to a well-armed Texan immigration officer who seemed to embody the frontier swagger of the Big State. "And watch out for the cars when you cross the carriageway", she added in a sort of uselessly helpful way since the stationery lines of bored drivers seemed in no danger of running down a snail, let alone mowing down a lone pedestrian.

I duly paid and ended up joining the interminable queue of friendly Hispanics trying to get into the USA. I was greatly moved that an elderly gentleman, seeing my plight, let me join the queue in front of him rather than walk back another few hundred meters to the end. I asked two more US immigration officers how to get my visa waiver processed and in an utterly bored voice one of them said "queue here and then go to gate no. 6". To their credit, in efficient American fashion the long queue did actually move quite fast. But when I got to the gates, the door to no. 6 was the only one which was well and truly shut with a sign announcing it as *Permits* and a large group of Mexicans sitting around rather forlornly. It was already 10.00 a.m. and I asked if anyone knew when it would open, one man answered "We don't know, they say it open 8 o'clock". It was one of those moments of bureaucratic frustration that takes you to your limits. I said under my breath, "But I'm just trying to leave the bloody country!" On an intuitive whim I tried the door handle anyway and, lo and behold, it opened to reveal a small office in which a standing elderly Mexican gentleman was conversing in rapid Spanish with a seated woman US immigration officer. The air was of deference on his part and professional distance on hers. I stood in the doorway looking for an opening in their dialogue and at last I caught her gaze. I explained that I wanted to quit the USA in a legal fashion. With a momentary glance at my passport she extracted the green visa waiver and she deposited it in a rather less than reassuring way on her desk saying, "`We'll process it later" sending me on my way back into no man's land.

If US departing immigration was casual, then Mexican incoming immigration was non-existent. At the other side of the bridge was a smartly-uniformed Mexican official who was talking vigorously to someone, and two soldiers sporting automatic weapons. I tried to ask how to get my arrival into Mexico authenticated but the officer just pointed me to a metal button in the barrier saying nothing else. I was bemused. What did it mean? He carried on talking, so I pushed this metal button and wondered what to do. Nothing happened. The pedestrian corridor is very narrow at this point and with my wheelie rucksack I was causing a considerable blockage. Suddenly one of the soldiers motioned to me to move on with a degree of intensity that left me certain I shouldn't argue with him. So I passed through the barrier and into Mexico, confused, uncertain, and no one had even looked at my passport. I had in fact crossed the bridge the previous day to collect a Mexican immigration form which had been stamped with a date, so given the lack of any discernable customs and immigration control I just had to assume that the stamped form would be sufficient, but was I going to fall foul of some minor official somewhere and have to pay my way out of bureaucratic hell?

Though I had only travelled 150m, I was suddenly back in a real city whose streets were crowded with people wanting to make a buck and tightly-packed ramshackle buildings. I immediately loved the dynamism of these peopled streets compared to the lifeless Texan boulevards. At the same time I felt uneasy, Juarez is well-known as a violent city with regular drug-related killings between rival gangs or the police, and muggings and thefts are common. Here I was a lone tourist who had just walked into the middle of the stage, without a clue whether or not I was in the right place. I suppose a little reflection would tell you that the district right next to the border would be so heavily patrolled that it would not be a natural place for gangland violence to take place.

I made for the smart-looking office *Transportes Chihauhenses* at which I had inquired the previous day and discovered that their tickets to Mexico City were thirty percent cheaper than those bought in the USA. Here I made my first Mexican friend. Francisco spoke pretty good English and translated for me as I tried to buy the bus ticket to *Mexico* as the city is ubiquitously and confusingly called. Problem number one: the ticket office did not accept credit cards, and having just entered the country I had no Mexican cash. Problem number two: the bus left in 30 minutes from the *Central Camionera* (bus station), which was way across town. Francisco took me on a walking tour of Ciudad Juarez to find an ATM, which he explained were rather rare. I was in that classic position of foreigner confusion – not knowing if this was some sort of elaborate scam or if Francisco really was just trying to help me out. I was less than reassured by our first encounter, when we took a short cut through the car park of a very official looking building and were stopped by a uniformed woman with a gun in holster and Francisco proceeded to explain to her in rapid Spanish that I was a tourist needing to find an ATM to get cash to buy a ticket. "Now why are we in this car park explaining my circumstances to a uniformed woman with a gun?" I wondered, and at the same time all the Hollywood movies featuring Mexican police corruption erupted into my mind. After a while she seemed satisfied enough and Francisco explained to me that because of the drug-gang problems in Juarez the police were very suspicious. I wondered if I looked like an American cocaine courier, but quickly rejected this ridiculous hypothesis, for the alternative hypothesis that I was just a rather eccentric budget traveler who had a habit of doing things the hard way. Most sensible travelers would have bought a bus ticket by credit card in the USA and let the bus company deal with all the hassles of crossing the border.

The entrance to the large official building, which turned out to house several banks and financial offices, was complete chaos. A high-tech security system was sprawled across the foyer with wires hanging everywhere, soldiers sporting yet more automatic weapons and people squeezing through the gaps in the security gates. The atmosphere felt more like that of a fiesta celebration than a financial hub. Lo and behold, hidden in one corner was an ATM of the HSBC bank. I literally had to squeeze through a gap, brushing with my backpack the machine gun of one of the soldiers who gave me a warm smile and waved me on, as Francisco once again explained my plight. Ah, the hope and the disappointment. I tried three times to withdraw cash but on each occasion at the very end a plaintive message came up in Spanish saying the poor machine was unable to dispense any cash on this occasion. On the third try I asked Francisco to confirm that I had understood the message correctly, though in a moment of travel wise caution I turned my body to block his gaze as I typed in my pin: I still wasn't sure if this was an elaborate scam or not.

Francisco looked rather downcast at our failure. "There are not so many ATM in Juarez", he said with a degree of finality. Instead of the dismay and doom this might once have caused in me, I felt a strange sense of excitement. "Well, how is this going to work out then? I'm stuck in Juarez and can't buy a bus ticket!" I guess some of the disasters of my year-long travel made this problem seem rather minor. Then Francisco's eyes lit up as he dialogued with an elegant woman in a half-constructed booth. "There is another ATM", he said, as if he were referring to a rare species in danger of going extinct. So we headed back to the main street and just a few meters away from the bus ticket office where we had started was a small convenience store, the sort you might find anywhere the USA, selling all the usual mix of groceries, booze and snacks. There, snug in the corner was a shining HSBC ATM. I did the business in a couple of minutes. "Better you get

2,000 pesos" said Francisco helpfully as I decided to withdraw enough to cover the bus ticket and several days in Mexico City. I couldn't help feeling that the supposed dearth of ATMs in Juarez was much more an aspect of Francisco's awareness than of the reality.

Back at the ticket office it was too late for the 10.00 o'clock bus, so I took the next option for 12.00 o'clock. But problem number two remained. Francisco and the two salesmen debated vigorously about how I should get to the Central Camionera which was 40 minutes by bus or 20 minutes by taxi. I was very surprised by this statistic, Juarez being a much bigger city than I had imagined. "Taxi is $10, bus is 4 pesos (30c)" they informed me. "Well I've got two hours to get there, I may as well try the bus" I said, Francisco looked very uncomfortable "Is okay for you?" he asked with touching concern. "Well, if I don't make it I will come back here and get a taxi". He seemed to concur. So they duly drew me a map of downtown Juarez, pointed out where I should get the bus and, shaking hands, we parted. I waited a moment to see if Francisco was expecting a tip or payment, but he just turned away as if going on to his next job. I thanked him politely, "Muchas gracias", and my sense of the basic honesty of most people that you meet was once more confirmed.

A slight sense of foreboding entered into my mind as I wandered off down the street. Catching a bus in a new country where one doesn't speak the language is always an adventure – recollections of the infinitely confusing choice of micro-buses in Siberia came to mind – but at the same time, learning the bus basics of any culture is a satisfying achievement. No two cultures do their buses the same way. After a few misdirections I eventually found the right spot at which to wait. Though there was no structure at all to indicate that this was a bus stop the long lines of people waiting and the continuous stream of vehicles arriving and departing made it obvious. Problem number three: I had no idea which bus to take. I just got on the first one that came and asked in my best Spanish. "Por favor, señor, Central Camionera?" The driver shook his head gravely and directed me to a man on the street who was carrying a clipboard and had a hands-free earpiece stuck to his head. I tried out my Spanish again on him, and he laughed "I speak English, you need a bus with this name". He handed me a piece of paper with some writing on it "And wait on that corner", he said, pointing vaguely to somewhere on the next two blocks. "Is there a bus number?" I asked rather dubiously as I tried to decipher the long title in Spanish that began with a "P". "No", he said curtly, and that was that. I wandered down to the next block and stood there hopefully as bus after bus rolled by with large numbers painted onto their chasses.

Mexican buses are a rather different species from their American cousins. In place of smooth machine-tooled surfaces, glass expanses and LED displays, are rough hand beaten panels, variously-fitting windows and hand painted signs. They stop anywhere at any time for anyone. A little old lady puts out her stick from the shattered remains of a dusty concrete sidewalk and you literally shriek to a halt, brakes screaming. And it is best not to look too closely at the tread on the tires either. In fact, through a miraculous pseudo-Darwinian process, they have evolved to be very like South Asian buses.

After about fifteen minutes I was getting a little restless, the unceasing tide of buses had produced none whose name began with a "P". Since my ticket to Mexico City was for a fixed time I couldn't risk being late, so I began to wander past the throngs of waiting people looking for some reassurance that I was on the right track. My eyes picked out Jesse, a short guy in his thirties who had something bright and friendly about him. I tried out my Spanish again, handing him my paper, and was relieved that he spoke perfect English. "Oh that's the bus I'm taking, just wait here" and no sooner than that our bus arrived. Jesse made sure with the driver that he was going to my stop and then we sat on the long wooden benches and started talking. His story was rather tragic, though he had no air of despair about him. He had worked in San Francisco as a builder for nearly fifteen years, was married to an American and had two daughters. However he was an illegal immigrant and the US officers eventually caught up with him and expelled him. He had been trying to get back to be with his family for five years. That was how he came to be in Juarez, though he confessed to disliking the city greatly. Somehow his demeanor didn't quite carry the intense sadness that a story like this warranted, and though I was confident of his honesty I wondered if there was more to the story than he was telling me. We agreed how heartless the US immigration bureaucracy was. Jesse wanted to know all about me, where I had been, what I thought of Mexico and what I thought of El Paso and Ciudad Juarez. He seemed untiringly interested in people. We got on famously and for the first time since I had left South Asia I felt myself in a world where meeting with strangers was just a natural way of life. I knew I was going to love being in Mexico. When Jesse got off the bus he took me up to the very front seat and once again made sure that the driver would drop me at the Central Camionera. I was greatly touched by this small yet essential kindness: travelling solo is a continuous lesson in receiving human kindness. The driver deposited me with little more than a grunt and a wave from his six year-old daughter who seemed to be permanently glued to the gear box.

The Central Camionera was an incongruously well-appointed building. Leaving the dusty, broken roads and sidewalks you entered a smart world of polished marble floors, long airport style counters and lots of bored-looking staff. You could be anywhere in the world of international travel, apart from one small but exceedingly important detail. The huge clock that dominated the fascia inside the terminal was giving the wrong time by 20 minutes. At first I became alarmed that my watch was 20 minutes out (a recipe for travel disaster) but then it became clear that it was the bus station's grand clock that was wrong and just wrong enough so that the unsuspecting passenger would think it was right.

I wandered about taking the measure of the place, rather reassured from the façade of smartness that I wasn't going to be mugged at knifepoint here. I cursed as I tried to squeeze myself and my baggage through the 2m high paying metal turnstiles that protected the toilets. And I rejoiced that there was a Customs point: perhaps someone here could help me with proper passport control. I hoped in vain, my passport was given a cursory glance and I was waved on. Two soldiers sporting automatic weapons babbled at me in Spanish until it became clear that they wanted to inspect the contents of my pack. The inspection was even more cursory than the passport control, but perhaps my air of indifference told them that hunting through my pack wasn't likely to produce a haul of drugs or weapons.

Finally I took my place on the Transportes Chihauhenses coach: the most elegant and sleek coach I had ever encountered. With gender-dedicated toilets, three video screens and seats that almost reclined to horizontal, it left all the American and Canadian long-distance buses standing. Unfortunately in the twenty-five hours it took us to arrive in Mexico City, we were subjected to no less than ten hours of Hollywood movies. Most were eminently missable, but the loud speakers blared unbearably and when I eventually asked the driver to make the sound quieter with an ambiguous, "Muy tranquilo por favor" he actually turned the sound up. This was Mexico and I was loving it.

Clash of Cultures

I spent several weeks living with friends in Mexico City, one of the most populous concentrations of humanity on the planet. The relentless energy of *Mexico* is both enticing and exhausting, and the city, laid out with long boulevards and parks, has some amazing cultural highlights. I did my best to acquaint myself with its wonders, and of course to master its bus network.

Museo Antropologia

Visiting the *Museo Antropologia* in Mexico City must rank as one of the most exciting and unsettling of all museum visits a European can make. Educated in a Eurocentric view of history, which only grudgingly acknowledges the heights of Asian culture, and barely even mentions pre-Colombian America, my discovery of the breadth, depth, diversity and antiquity of Meso-American cultures came as a huge shock. I wandered around the *Antropologia* for several hours in a sort of stunned daze, drifting from room to room, through a 4,000 year sequence of staggering cultural efflorescences. I learned that while Northern Europeans were living a barbarous tribal life and before the flowering of ancient Greece, the Olmecs were laying the foundations of a culture that produced colossal and iconic statuary around 2,000 BCE. At the height of the Roman Empire, around the start of the Common Era, the formidable city of Teotihuacan was already established. When Europe was just beginning to grow out of the dark ages the people of Teotihuacan were already gone and forgotten, though the huge pyramids of the Sun and Moon and their 200,000 strong city with its elaborate temples, dwellings and boulevards remained. For the Aztecs, Teotihuacan (an Aztec name meaning "The place where men became gods") was an ancient, sacred and mysterious place. They stayed there on their 200 year tribal migration before founding Tenochtitlan, now

Mexico City, in the middle of Lake Texcoco. The Aztecs learnt much about architecture, religion and culture from Teotihuacan and emulated its majesty in their own great city floating on the lake: a city that utterly astonished Hernan Cortes, *Conquistador* of Mexico. I realized that the threads of cultural development stretched far back into the past.

The diversity was also mind-boggling. Between the Mayan civilization that thrived in Mexico's Yucatan and the cliff cities of the Ancestral Puebloans of Mesa Verde in Colorado, was as great a difference as between Greeks and Scots. Suddenly it dawned upon me that in pre-Colombian America there were whole episodes or even chapters of the human story of which we Europeans were ignorant. If Teotihuacan's pyramids have an Egyptian majesty, then Tenochtitlan, floating on Lake Texcoco evokes Venice; Monte Alban, the Zapotec cliff top city in Oaxaca, rivals the Acropolis of Athens; Mayan Palenque and Uxmal lost in the jungles are as impressive as the Hindu and Buddhist temples of ancient India. And so the story continues...

The feeling of being overwhelmed by culture shock was not pleasant, but there seemed to be no other way to let the forms and histories into my European soul. I kept stopping to breathe more deeply as I saw yet another stunning image or read another amazing historical reconstruction. I found myself fascinated by the figure of *Quetzalcoatl*, the feathered serpent god of the Aztecs and Toltecs, a fusion of snake and eagle. Both these animals are powerful archetypes in the iconography of the Green Buddha on whom I have meditated for many years. Despite my repugnance to Aztec and Toltec sacrificial practices, I could not deny that *Quetzalcoatl* had a powerful attraction for me.

Much of the Meso-American art remains highly stylized, but there are some striking exceptions. The celebrated Mayan boxing man has all the dynamics of a Praxiteles sculpture, and the Aztec god of Love, Flowers and Music, Xochipilli, holds much grace and pathos, his face carrying a tragic expression, even as his body shows the marks of festivity. I emerged from the *Antropologia* rather shell-shocked in a positive way, much more open and raw to the story of our species than I had been before.

The Virgin of Guadalupe

The Basilica of the Virgin of Guadalupe is the second most visited Catholic pilgrimage site in the world after the shrine at Lourdes. This fact alone tells you just how powerfully Guadalupe features in the soul of Mexico. Although her cult originates in a statue discovered in 13th century in the eponymous Spanish town in Extremadura, it is in Mexico that the Virgin of Guadalupe has reached her zenith. It is said that Mexicans don't trust the government or the police or even their football team (and who can blame them), they only trust two things: the Land and the Virgin of Guadalupe. So I knew that on my visit to Mexico I must meet Her, and I wasn't disappointed.

Jose Luis was an old friend. We had lived together in a Buddhist community in the UK some years previously. He had offered to accompany me as I explored Mexico City and in particular to visit the Virgin. We picked our way slowly through the avenue of stalls leading up to the Basilica. Here every possible religious artifact was available, from utterly gory cruci-fixes, with blood pouring from the open wounds on Jesus Christ's tortured body, to large T-shirts sporting the Virgin's dark synthe-sized form. The big square in front of the two Basilicas, old and new, was thronging with people, processions, bands, costumes: a thriving fiesta atmosphere. We stopped for a while to enjoy the spectacle of people taking the trouble to express their beliefs in a colorful and exciting way.

The Virgin of Guadalupe is a very powerful symbol, a dark skinned woman, clothed in a shawl of stars, standing on a black moon. I felt the universality of her form, even though she appears in a Catholic context. She spoke to me of the infinite, the shadow world, the hidden depths and of acceptance and kindness. A

 possible source for her form is *Revelation Chapter 12,* which describes a woman clothed in the Sun, standing on the moon, with a crown of stars being persecuted by the dragon. The same passage also mentions the snake and the eagle, the emblems of *Quetzalcoatl,* evoking deep resonances for Mexico. Coincidently one of William Blake's most impressive paintings *The Woman clothed in the Sun* is inspired by this same passage.

As Jose Luis and I sat watching the thronging masses I took in the atmosphere of the new Basilica, a modern circular building from the 1970s. It was heavy, respectful and a little oppressive, I didn't really like it much, especially the centrality of the huge and bloody crucifix. We took the moving walkway to go past the apron of San Diego (on which in 1531 the image of his original vision miraculously appeared) along with hundreds of the faithful, all trying to get the ideal photo. The old Basilica, which is sinking heavily into the mud of the now non-existent Lake Texcoco, was almost entirely taken up with internal scaffolding and building works. Though noisy and dusty the devotions of the faithful still reverberated through its vaults.

The site of Guadalupe abounds with all manner of chapels, churches and gardens apart from the main Basilicas. My favorite was the Capuchin chapel, which was a much brighter and joyous place. The crucifix was very small, as if it were obliged to be displayed but that such gore was not really wanted here. The main feature was a large joyful mural of the *Sagrada Familia* and the ceiling frescos of a smiling San Diego. We climbed *Tepeyac*

Hill through the beautifully laid out water gardens. Flowing around a graceful statue of the Virgin was water gushing from the mouths large stone Aztec snake heads: the Catholic Fathers have always been good at incorporating pagan power into their traditions. When we arrived at the exact spot where San Diego had his vision there was an arresting pastiche of indigenous and colonial figures all engaged in adoration of the Virgin. At the hill's summit we visited another chapel with sickly sweet paintings of submissive natives converting to Catholicism that left me feeling rather nauseous.

Most striking was the atmosphere of adulation, faith and devotion from the thousands of people visiting on this ordinary workday. Particularly notable was the prevalence of pregnant women and young mothers to whom the Virgin gives especial blessing. Around the time of Guadalupe's festival, in early December, it is said that millions visit the shrines and that it is impossible to move around the precincts. The cult of the Virgin of Guadalupe is vitally alive in Mexico, and I can honestly say that I believe this is a good thing for the people of this deeply religious country. For She comes from them, an eruption into Catholicism of something deeply archetypal in the Mexican soul.

Museo Carillo Gil

At the suggestion of a friend I went to see the paintings of the *Carillo Gil* gallery. On the first floor is Señor Gil's amazing collection of works by the three greats of 20th century Mexican painting: Rivera, Orozco and Siqueiros. The Rivera collection is rather small, his works being scattered around various museums all over the city, though there was a lovely nude of his wife, Frida Kahlo. Rather it was the paintings of Orozco and Siqueiros which were to touch me deeply.

Almost the first painting that you meet is Orozco's *Christ cuts down his Cross*. I was utterly arrested by this image, its ramifications resounding through my heart and mind, and leaving me

reflecting on how powerful and shocking this must have been when it was first seen in the 1940s. Even today it is a wonderfully shocking and liberating image: the martyr rejecting the implement of his martyrdom. The middle-aged curator was watching me closely as I stopped, dumbstruck by Orozco's painting. Since there was no one else in the museum I guess he had little else to occupy him. I asked if I could take a photo and he explained in Spanish that I was supposed to buy an additional ticket for that, but then in true Mexican style he added generously that one or two photos would be okay. He seemed to want to express something to me and as I listened intently somehow my understanding of his Spanish rose to the occasion. For the next 30 minutes I was given an impromptu tour of the great works in the collection by a man who obviously loved them and had studied them for many years.

Interestingly our first painting, the *Christ cuts down his Cross*, was the context for a dispute between us. He explained that Orozco was a communist and that this was a purely political painting, pointing out the symbols of burning books and fallen columns that represented aspects of the Mexican organs of government. I had to agree that there was a strong political intention, but disagreed with him that it was a purely political painting. The image of Christ, axe in his stigmatized hands, was affecting me in a profoundly religious and even transcendent way. He was insistent that there was no religious meaning, I knew in my heart that there was. But no matter, we moved onto the next paintings and he kindly expounded the meanings and images as he understood them. Orozco created a series of four paintings of the Spanish Conquest. Though only three are in the Gil collection, the tragedy and brutality of the images is stunning. Courage, sadness and even anger leap out of these paintings. Orozco captures the ambivalence or even resentment in the Mexican psyche to the Conquest. It is significant that nowhere in the city will you find statues or streets honoring Hernan Cortes who is generally regarded as a greedy and brutal man.

There was one more painting that was to arrest me strongly, this time by Siqueiros, a painting of *Zapata on his Horse*. The yellows of the canvas and the abstract almost Franz Machian form of the horse were intensely pleasing to look at, evoking feelings of vitality and beauty. Though solely suggested by the hint of his broad sombrero, Zapata's name conspired to give the painting a powerful emotional impact. He is one of the great heroes of Mexican history, an honest and lifelong revolutionary who, unlike so many Mexican strong men past and present, didn't use the power he gained for selfish ends. His motto "Tierra y Libertad" echoes through the revolutionary movements of the 20th century and still holds power today for instance in the peasant uprisings in Chiapas. And like a truly iconic figure he died for his cause. So add Siqueiros' beautiful forms to the story of Zapata and one has an inspiring and emotive masterpiece. I left the Carillo Gil with a deep respect for the modern Mexican artistic tradition and a little more understanding of the sadness and inspiration that have shaped the Mexican character.

All three of these visits had touched me deeply, and I felt myself opening up to a broader, bigger story of our species. Once again the outer journey extended inwards and I felt an opening, another layer of resistance falling away as I contemplated how marvelous and strange it is to be a human being. I was left with deep feelings of gratitude and a desire to give.

Mayan Musings

I was back on the *Mexican Bus*. This legendary mode of transport has certainly evolved since budget pioneers sent back dispatches of chickens, goats, insane drivers and travelling on the roof. The plush Intercity from Mexico to Oaxaca was extremely comfortable. I was heading to Mexico's most easterly city, Cancun, a journey of nearly 2,000km, and on the way planned to see some of the amazing archaeological sites about which I had heard so much. As we left the haze and smog I was finally able to catch a glimpse of the volcano *Popocatepetl* capped in snow, sleeping guardian of Mexico City. Much as I had loved my three-week sojourn in the capital there was a definite sense of relief and spaciousness at quitting this vast metropolis of twenty million souls. As the bus climbed into the Sierra Madre we entered a spectacularly alien landscape, the mountains were carpeted in a forest of saguaro cacti. Instead of the spreading habit of conifers or broadleaves, the undulating contours were populated by millions of tall needles, like pale green slashes on a canvas.

Oaxaca is famous for its *mole*, a thick brown chocolaty sauce, and for the ancient Zapotec citadel of Monte Alban which sits astride a decapitated mountain above the city. In the absence of historical documents archaeologists have pieced together a story spanning a thousand years. It is estimated that with the tools available it took the Zapotecs over one hundred years just to flatten the mountaintop so that the citadel could be built. Here they created a heavenly acropolis of spectacular views comprising pyramids, palaces and courts for the mysterious *ball-game*. By the time the *Conquistadores* arrived the Zapotecs were long gone, no one even knows what their city was called: Monte Alban refers to the beautiful white flowers of the Morning Glory tree that the Spanish discovered when they arrived. Oaxaca itself is a delightful city on a very human scale. Amongst its many

jewels are the state museum, the artistic archaeological displays in the Museo Tamayo and the stunning stucco tree of the Dominican lineage in the Iglesia Santo Domingo which covers the whole ceiling. Most of all though, I loved hanging out in the *zocalo*, the central square, where of an evening the whole town would congregate in a festive mood.

High in the hills of Chiapas lies the village of San Juan de

Chamul. Amid the swirling mists and rough gusts chaffing the market place, the tall white church was decorated in vibrant greens and adorned with long strands of flags. These were flapping incessantly in the strong cold December wind calling up images of Tibetan temples. It was the day of the Virgin of Guadalupe and beneath her banner crowds of people thronged around the entrance, dressed in traditional thick woolen skirts and trousers, broad-brimmed woven hats and colorful costumes.

This was an indigenous population and barely a Spanish-looking face could be seen. A band was playing loudly and I had to pay to enter the church through the mêlée. Inside was an altogether otherworldly scene. The floor was carpeted with sheaths of cut grass, hundreds of candles were burning amid shrines to dozens of brilliantly-colored saints. Devotees were prostrating, praying and chanting in an atmosphere of intense devotion. Thankfully, the few tourists present had been banned from taking photographs. This was Catholicism as I had never experienced it before. Raw, powerful, visceral and connected to the land; the mood was primal, almost pagan. Though the devotion flowed to the Virgin and the Saints, you could just as well have been in some chthonic vault in South India. I was left speechless at the religious power emanating from this tiny town, so alien to my own beliefs, yet in some way so compelling.

Palenque on the edge of the great Yucatan plain is a jewel of Mayan civilization and perhaps more than any other ancient city calls forth the mystery and magic of the Maya. The pyramids and palaces tumble from the jungle hillside, so woven with nature's fecundity that it almost seems they are still growing. At any moment you expect to see Indiana Jones darting from a deep

vault pursued by a posse of blowpipe warriors. Skull-like friezes add a threatening air to this primeval scene. The steep-vaulted chambers, cartoon-like script and tall observatory tower evoke a highly sophisticated yet utterly alien culture. The Maya never discovered the engineering properties of the arch, yet they had invented the zero a thousand years before Arab philosophers introduced it into Western arithmetic. As I wandered around the ruins and archaeological museum at Palenque I was once again struck by the remarkable flowering of human creativity and ingenuity that had happened here.

The Yucatan

The Yucatan is a unique and strange landscape. Almost entirely flat, it is covered with dense and impenetrable dwarf forest, and pockmarked with *cenotes*. In the absence of any significant rivers these huge natural waterholes irrigate this hot, dry land. There are said to be over 3,000 cenotes on the Yucatan. They are connected by subterranean rivers that eventually flow out into the Caribbean and some are as much as fifty meters deep. Human history on the Yucatan is also truly remarkable and hundreds of Mayan temples are scattered throughout the forest, many of them unexcavated. It is said that every hill you see on the Yucatan is a Mayan temple awaiting discovery. It had long been a dream of

mine to visit this mysterious world.

From Valladolid I hired a taxi to visit the little known Mayan temple of *Ek Bal'am*. My taxi driver was called Gonzalo, and he had a big round face and a portly belly to go with it. In the front seat sat his two-year-old son with no baby harness, seatbelt or restraints. Though our communication was limited to my meager Spanish we exchanged pleasantries and, as I found so commonly wherever I travelled, he immediately asked about my marital status and why I didn't have any children. Gonzalo suggested we take an alternative route, though I didn't quite get his meaning, but following my usual practice of taking interesting diversions I assented. Suddenly we abandoned the road signs to *Ek Bal'am* and were off the metalled road and driving along dirt tracks through the dense vegetation. For a moment I felt some fear: was he taking me to some sort of ambush? But then I saw the absurdity of this scenario in the presence of his two-year-old son. Gonzalo finally came to a halt just as the dirt road seemed to peter out. "Where on earth has he brought me?" I wondered. He got out of the car and proudly showed me a small gap in the trees through which there was a metal structure. As I got closer I realized it was the hand rail to a spiral staircase that disappeared into a hole in the ground, and looking down I could see it was strung precariously over a large circular cenote, perhaps thirty meters across and twenty meters from the rim to the water's surface. Gonzalo beamed contentedly as I expressed amazement.

His son seemed rather unimpressed and just looked at me blankly with his deep brown eyes. I descended the spiral staircase, hung with nothing more than rusting steel rope, down to a platform that dangled just above the water's surface. The water was perfectly still, sprinkled with fallen leaves, and teeming with small black catfish. The roots of trees, matted into solid trunks, dropped down into this subterranean oasis. Given the great depth of this cenote they were clearly just hanging in the water, anchored to nothing. Yet in the mirror stillness of the surface these mighty trunks gave the impression of pillars resting on water, on whose capitals the limestone roof was raised. The eerie silence and hidden depths impressed me deeply: an abode of magical spirits and creatures.

Ek Bal'am means the Black Jaguar and archaeologists tell us

that the temple complex is named after the king who had raised it from the monotony of the forest flatness in the Late Classic Mayan period (600-900 CE). With hundreds of steps it rises thirty meters and towers above the trees. It seems a stupendous achievement for an ancient culture to have raised this pyramid in such a flat landscape. Where did they get all the stone? The reward for an arduous sweat-drenched climb is a stunning panoramic view of the jungle. Vaguely in the distance you can make out the great pyramid of *Chichen Itza*, perhaps the most famous of the Yucatan pyramids. By contrast, at *Ek Bal'am* you can still contemplate the magnificence of Mayan architecture in relative solitude. The statuary is exquisitely preserved: human figures, some almost angelic, adorn a gateway into the inner sanctum surrounded by giant curved teeth – as if leading to the very belly of the Beast. The mood is of a primeval place. I don't know if blood rituals were practiced here, but it must have seemed an abode of the gods to those who lived here 1,300 years ago. Next to the main temple is a large forested hill, and from the hint of ruins amongst the trees it is clear that this too is another pyramid, still dressed in a dark green cloak of vegetation. Several tourists came and went in silence as if rendered speechless: a striking contrast to the loud throng of visitors at Uxmal, Palenque and Chichen Itza.

Like visiting the *Museo Antropologia*, meandering through the Mayan heartlands moved me greatly. The daring of these people rivaled the Pharaohs, and the decay and destruction of once-great cities filled me with pathos and the sense of mankind's fate in the hands of eternity. I had glimpsed an opening into another world, and now that the veil was drawn it would forever be part of me. Something staggering and wonderful had happened in these jungles thousands of years ago, and the story has yet to be fully told.

Finally, I reached the very different world of Cancun. Hub of the Mexican tourist industry on the Caribbean coast, it is a sprawling, over-developed and hard-edged city. Though parts have been landscaped with some care, the overall impact is of ugliness. It isn't so much the architecture, which is as indifferent as any high-rise beach resort, but rather the frenetic flow of people and the money-grabbing malls, such a contrast after the sedate provincial towns of Oaxaca, San Christobal de las Casas, Palenque, Merida and Valladolid. Evading a scam by a very charming woman at the tourist information desk to stay at the budget accommodation of *her* choice, I made my way to the Hotel Tropicale Caribe. I was back in the world of cheap city hotels, so familiar and so soulless. It was my last night in Mexico and I felt the urge for one more miniature adventure: to feel the caress of the Caribbean waters before departing this great country. From the centre of town it was several kilometers to the beachfronts, most of which were privately owned by the high-rise hotels; but I managed to squeeze my way onto a packed bus and get off at the first visible sight of public sands. I strolled barefoot along the shore, gazed out towards the East, contemplating this last phase

of my journey home and was blessed with the sight of a double rainbow above the waves. Tomorrow I was flying to Cuba, land of the eternal revolutionary (the US embargo precludes a ferry link), and meeting Siddhisvari for a long-awaited romantic rendezvous. The rainbows seemed to herald an auspicious reunion and return journey.

Cuban Cameos

"Hey, we're in the same building xxx" chirped a text message as I made my way though immigration at José Marti airport. "Sir, excuse me! May I see your passport!" repeated someone insistently. In a haze of loved-up anticipation I was about to walk straight past a young man standing in the corridor and dressed informally in jeans and a short-sleeved shirt. Checking his ID card I realized that he was some sort of immigration officer. Cubans obviously don't go in for uniforms. "And what is the purpose of your visit…?" That was indeed the question. I was in Cuba because I was once again heading east, because it was the land of legendary revolutionaries, and most of all because I was in love.

Siddhisvari was standing calmly behind the throng of excitable relatives and bored taxi drivers, leaning against a pillar with her battered old green backpack. She looked sleepy after her long-haul flight, but a beautiful spark flashed in her blue eyes as she saw me emerging from baggage reclaim. The longed for embrace, the racing heartbeat, the momentary shyness, holding hands tenderly as we sat in the taxi: we were like teen lovers on their first date. After being apart for so long I was suddenly speechless, euphoric, turned upside down, turned inside out. In the preceding weeks and months, separated by continents, I had been through the insanity of falling in love. The amorous emails became long, desirous epistles; the passionate texts became besotted late-night phone calls until my credit ran out. Soon I was toppling over the edge into lover's madness: "I haven't heard from her; does she still love me?" "What if something has happened to her?" I plunged into the maelstrom of euphoria and anxiety, abundance and loss, exhilaration and exhaustion, adoration and blindness. "Why go through this all over again?" I asked myself. I couldn't really answer other than saying, as with all beloveds, she really is special, and that I was saying "Yes" to life on a deep level. Our days in Cuba were like a dream: timeless, stunning, wonderful, delicious and delirious.

Despite our honeymoon reveries, having eschewed a package holiday we still had to negotiate the country's idiosyncrasies and, even for a seasoned traveler, arriving in Cuba is a shock. I constantly felt a jaw-dropping sense of "How on earth does this country work?" At the airport none of the ATMs would accept any of my cards, and though Siddhisvari and I had a stash of dollars and Euros, this wouldn't be enough to cover our whole our stay. In a phlegmatic mood I just put the problem aside assuming that somehow we would find a solution. In fact, money was universally confusing and troublesome in Cuba. The financial infrastructure felt more like the 1970s than the 21st century. Long queues emanated from the banks managed by major-domos who billeted you to young Cuban beauties: at least that aspect of the banking system was appealing. There was only one place in the whole of Cuba that accepted my Cirrus/Maestro debit card: Guantanamo Bay. Since visiting the USA's expatriate torture camp didn't seem like the ideal activity for a romantic holiday I decided that I would have to bite the bullet and make a cash advance on my credit card. This not only incurred Cuba's crushing 11% tax on dollars (they only accept credit card payments in dollars) but stung me with the interest and exchange rate charges from my own bank. The whole deal was a killer, leaving me wishing we'd read the guidebook more carefully and brought a large bundle of Euros. I consoled myself by reflecting that in this country desperately strapped for foreign cash we were certainly doing our bit to support the regime, in a country where, whatever your political persuasion, the high literacy and world beating healthcare seem more honest and worthy than in many developing countries.

The other utterly bizarre aspect of Cuban money is that there are two currencies, the *peso nacional* (peso), used by the majority of the populace, and the *Cuban Convertible peso* (CUC), used primarily by the tourists. Despite a long explanation from a highly-placed Cuban professional I never really understood how this worked or why it was even necessary. The definitions are clear enough: 24 peso nacional = 1 CUC. But when is one currency used rather than the other? Do you pay the equivalent price in either currency? Why are some shops purely in CUC and others in peso? How can you tell which currency is being quoted? These and other arcane details of the dual currency system led to the classic tourist cock-up of paying 24 times too much for our first taxi trip. I gave the young black Cuban driving an old heap of a 1950 Chrysler 10 CUC, instead of 10 peso for a short hop up Avenida Rampa. His eyes rolled a little as he accepted the windfall, and I felt very stupid later on. But isn't it nice to feel that you really made someone's day! From croissants to pizza, from bus tickets to Cuban beer, I never really knew in which currency or how much I should pay. And, of course, add to this the opportunistic pricing that all Latin American countries practice for the unsuspecting (or even the suspecting) tourist and you have a recipe for confusion and large infusions of your hard won cash into public and private Cuban coffers. It is just part of the deal: however you play it, a visit to Cuba is going to be expensive.

No vista is quite as evocative of Havana as a walk along the *Malecon*. The Atlantic breakers spraying over the paving stones make for an exciting if perilous stroll as you gaze at the gentle curve of the bay along Vieja Habana to the harbour entrance and castle. This boulevard is utterly emblematic of modern Cuba, and here you see the wonderful contradictions of a country living in a time warp. Alongside grand, crumbling colonial buildings from the fin de siècle are quite passable Communist-era high rises. Rolling along the broad rutted carriageway are iconic Chryslers and Chevrolets still going after nearly fifty years, belching out clouds of unburned petrol fumes, being overtaken by sleek new Peugeots and even the odd Toyota and

Mercedes. A gap between richer and poorer is opening up even here in Communist Cuba. Generously scattered along the sea defenses are the *jiniteros*, or touts, each with a story and wanting to make a buck out of the rich tourists walking their streets. Miguel approached Siddhisvari and me as we were sitting on the massive concrete seawall reading about Che Guevara and the Cuban Revolution. He was racially negro, handsome with bright eyes, wore a smart little cap and addressed me as "Friend". We started talking about Cuba and what it was like for a young man living in Havana. "We are in a prison", he said unprompted. And it isn't hard to see why he felt that way since the prospects of travelling outside Cuba were very remote for Miguel and his contemporaries. Owning a camera or mobile phone was largely out of his reach as he explained that he could only earn 12 peso per hour, equivalent of fifty US cents. We talked for a while about the changes taking place in Cuba and I asked the big question that everyone thinks about here "What will happen when Fidel dies?" Miguel had no real answer to this, any more than others I asked, but it was clear that he was desperate for an opportunity to break out of the limits of a world in which he felt trapped. In a way, he was really just facing the challenge that every young man faces in his life: how to go out into the world and prove himself. Had he lived fifty years earlier perhaps he would have been part of the heroic band of eighty-two revolutionaries who set sail from Venezuela for Cuba in 1956 to liberate the country from its oppressors. As it was, Miguel was a grandchild of the *Revolucion* and looking for a way out. After twenty minutes of seemingly innocent and friendly exchange of ideas and experiences the invitation that I had been expecting finally arrived. "I can take you to the Buena Vista Social Club very near to here, just two blocks". The warmth and rapport were by this time so strong that I almost accepted his offer, which no doubt would have included an expectation of some sort of payment. But instead we just thanked Miguel and continued with our walk along the *Malecon*.

He seemed quite unperturbed and just started chatting up two pretty girls sitting a few meters away from us, clearly Miguel was an incorrigible opportunist.

Like money, shopping in Cuba is not easy. Trying to find somewhere to buy a few rolls or croissants for breakfast can take hours of looking into the front windows of seemingly residential buildings hoping to spy goods for sale in a dark and dingy room. While this can be rather frustrating, there is something wonderfully refreshing about the absence of the globalised shopping mall. Most striking is the complete lack of advertising hoardings. What billboards there are all dedicated to lauding some aspect of the *Revolucion*. Here you will find no Gap, no Starbucks and no McDonalds, but rather a hotchpotch of private and state-owned establishments, most of them devoid of consumer hype and with hand-written price tags on a limited collection of wares displayed in fading cabinets. And that's if you're lucky. The sense of relief at actually finding a bread shop is palpable, as if one had finally achieved the source of the Nile, or discovered a lost city in the jungle. As I waited to buy a few rolls and cakes in a windowless corner shop – little more than a room opening onto the street – a stream of women came in and presented their little ration books. A tick was duly made therein and they left hurriedly clutching their rolls and loaves. The baker kept putting up his palm, asking me to wait as he served these rapid little Cuban women. But finally my turn came and he accepted my CUCs in payment with a questioning look as to whether I wanted any peso change. As usual I had no idea whether I was paying the right amount, so I just gave him two CUCs and left gratefully clutching my purchase.

Accommodation, too, is riddled with idiosyncrasies and confusions. Broadly, one has two choices, grand tourist hotels with English speaking staff, slick service and a price tag to match or *casas particulares*: living en famille in a rented room. These vary from the plush grand colonial suite with bathroom to the rough and ready concrete floor with peeling paint, reminiscent of an Indian budget hotel. Amazingly, they all seem to charge roughly the same price. Perhaps this is just communist indifference to the capitalist ideology of supply and demand.

Arriving in Havana we stayed in *Verdado*, the delightful colonial district east of the old city with its broad tree-lined avenues. Siddhisvari had found Esteban and Barbara's elegant marbled penthouse apartment on the Internet. Off to the side of a grandly-furnished hall we had our own room, replete with elegant wooden cabinets, marble-topped dressing tables and a beautiful bathroom. On either side of the large hall were balconies overlooking the tree-lined promenade. It seemed like the perfect find for two lovers in the Caribbean. However, true to Cuban form things were not entirely what they appeared to be. Firstly, Esteban was very pushy about money, which he wanted upfront. And secondly, in a Kafkaesque drama the apartment started to dissolve. One day we returned from exploring the byways of Havana to find that some of the pictures had disappeared. I didn't think much of this at first, and even wondered whether I had misremembered the décor. But the next time we came back a ceramic laughing Buddha who greeted you in the vestibule had seemingly evaporated, and the time after that the table on which he sat had gone. Slowly more and more furniture disappeared followed by the other guests and finally the cleaning staff. I wondered if one day we would come back to find our bed had disappeared and that there was just a pile of our things on the floor, or if part of the building would have ceased to exist and I would open the door to our room and find an empty gateway into the Void. At last all that remained were Siddhisvari, Barbara and me with a few tables and chairs that inexplicably moved about the apartment at different times of day as if doing their best to make it feel lived in. Barbara and Esteban were having a tragic and rather messy divorce, while their guests were still on hand. Fortunately I had reduced our booking to only seven days so we were able to extricate ourselves from the matrimonial trauma rather sooner than we might have. Esteban only seemed to turn up when money or officialdom were called for, usually when Siddhisvari and I were passionately engaged. Barbara, on the other hand, never seemed to leave the premises and spent the evenings bemoaning the tragedy to an ever-changing circle of friends. We offered our sympathy, but kept our heads down as much as possible. On our final night I said farewell to Barbara and in a touching moment of self-transcendence she apologized profusely for the inconvenience that her tragedy had caused us. Naturally, not wanting to add to her pains, Siddhisvari and I didn't complain but just offered her our sympathy.

Sea, Sun and Salsa

No tale about Cuba can be complete without some mention of beaches and music. In Trinidad we found both. The town, founded in 1514, is most famous as the place from which Hernan Cortez gathered his army of Conquistadores and set off on his greedy, lucrative and brutal conquest of Mexico. Apparently, he took with him so many of the young men from Trinidad that the town virtually disbanded for the next hundred years. However, Trinidad has more than recovered and is blessed with the fabulous beaches of the nearby Ancon peninsula and endless evenings of Cuban music tumbling out of every casa.

And what beaches! With hundreds of islands in the archipelago, an abundance of low-lying *cayos* (Keys) and long stretches of both Caribbean and Atlantic sands, Cuba must have thousands of kilometers of perfect beaches. Many of them are taken from a Bacardi advert: thatched huts surrounded by palm trees looking out over perfect blue-green waters and offering rum cocktails served by beautiful young Cuban bartenders. Is it any wonder that many wealthy widows flock here? Global tourism has a habit of tainting whatever it touches and there are many tourist-only resorts, with sprawling monolithic hotels from which Cubans themselves are barred. Siddhisvari and I studiously avoided these and made our way to the long golden sands of the sweeping Ancon peninsula as it curls into the Caribbean Sea. We spent happy days soaking up the sun, swimming in aquamarine waters, snorkeling with vibrantly colored fish, walking along the mangroves or just gazing out across the Caribbean and dreaming of pirate adventures à la Johnny Depp.

Halfway up the broad steps rising from Trinidad's main square and adjacent to the church is the patio of the *Casa de la Musica*, the salsa centre of town. Every night another band would have pride of place and the tourists and locals would take to their feet for what the major-domo invariably announced as an evening of "wakey-wakey, shakey-shakey!" The standard of dance was quite daunting, and we suspected that many of the tourists were salsa teachers coming for some fun and to brush up on their steps. As for the locals, salsa was in the blood. There was something wonderful about seeing a couple in their seventies gracing the cobbles. Like us, many of the visitors just sat on the steps gazing in amazement at this wonderful free fiesta. Occasionally, an elderly Cuban gentleman, often with a toothless smile, would drag a protesting young or not so young tourist onto the cobbles and swing her with great aplomb and a huge grin on his face. As well as the salsa on the steps there were many bars, each with their own offering of music and dance, usually for little more than one dollar entrance. The most startling show we saw was a Yoruba dance troupe of tall and very beautiful negro men and women accompanied solely by drums and chanting. The sheer power and energy of the male dancers was breathtaking, jittering their arms so hard that I thought they might erupt from their shoulder sockets. Their prowess as they wielded machetes to the pounding rhythms left me very glad that we weren't in the front row in the direct line of fire. The women danced in a sexual but unaffected and natural way. The forebears of these dancers were taken from West Africa as slaves, but there was no hint of despair or oppression. The dance was alive, vital, visceral and indomitable. There is something very remarkable about the spirit of these people who were stolen from their homes and endured so much at the hands of the Europeans. In Cuba music seems to penetrate every aspect of life, whether it is in a bar, a *casa de la musica* or just blaring from a taxi.

Siddhisvari and I were obviously very much smitten and the response from most of those we met was one of knowing smiles and sympathetic delight. "How are the lovebirds this morning?" asked another of the guests in Havana. At a lovely casa in the Vinales valley our presence seemed to evoke sadness from our hostess, whose husband was rarely present. We, however, fell into that charmed moment of the first flush of romance in which selfishness seems to abate for a little while. "What would she like to do, what would make her happy?" gave me more joy than following my own desires. Every choice and decision seemed to be made effortlessly, each of us easily deferring to the wishes of the other. The tiny grating moments of experience seemed to have all but dissolved, at least temporarily, and even Cuban bureaucratic hassles barely touched us. It was close to a heavenly existence. "Can this happiness last?" I would wonder occasionally. But deeming it best to leave such reflections alone I just gave myself fully to loving Siddhisvari in the present moment. In the wisdom of William Blake:

He who binds to himself a joy
Does the winged life destroy
He who kisses the joy as it flies
Lives in Eternity's sunrise.

Songs in Santa Clara

The decisive moment of the Cuban Revolutionary War was the Battle of Santa Clara which took place from 28th to 31st December 1958. A daring Revolutionary Brigade led by Commandante Che Guevara attacked and captured this strategically crucial town at which point Government resistance crumbled, Fidel Castro commenced his victorious march from Santiago de Cuba to Havana and Batista, the American-backed dictator, fled the country. Having traveled here to pay our respects at the Che Guevara memorial, by chance we arrived in Santa Clara on the 29th December 2008, amidst grand celebrations for the 50th anniversary of the Battle.

The Santa Clarans are clearly proud of their Revolutionary moment and they were thronging in the spacious Plaza Vidal where a thousand seats had been arranged in front of a temporary stage and large video screen. As the band arrived, performers hung about in the wings and the Plaza filled, veterans of the war with their uniforms and medals took pride of place in the front row. Many were the warm embraces and handshakes, the greetings of old friends from a heroic time. When the band started to play the Cuban national anthem immediately the entire crowd rose to their feet and an air of respect descended on the Plaza. There followed a rich program of readings, singing and dancing by the young and beautiful or old and venerable. One artiste sang a haunting melody for *Commandante Che Guevara* whilst she accompanied herself on guitar. A young man and woman read inspiring excerpts from the revolutionary speeches. As the performances proceeded original footage from the victories of 1958 was played on the video screen, and occasionally in between the musical offerings one would hear the voice of Fidel or Che declaiming passionately thus lending a historic and triumphant air to the evening. The piece de resistance was the arrival of the formidable grey-haired Cuban diva, Sara Gonzalez, the sort of woman who you feel you recognize immediately, even when you have never seen her before. She came onto the stage amidst rapturous applause. With a swinging backing band she sang three celebratory songs, the last finishing on a powerfully-held note with her fist in the air as the crowd burst into cheers and the firework display exploded into life. By this time the mood of the crowd was palpable: celebration, victory, joy and mutual congratulation. I felt privileged to witness the people of Santa Clara celebrating a defining moment in their history. The strange irony of our chance festivities in Santa Clara was that it was the only event we managed to attend celebrating fifty years of the Revolution in Cuba. In Havana we searched in vain. Apparently, the three hurricanes of 2008 and the struggling economy meant that there was no money for big public events of that kind. I felt it was sad that the country wasn't able to celebrate its defining moment in style.

As our honeymoon drew to a close I reflected that falling in love with Siddhisvari was deeply part of the journey I had undertaken. Perhaps this seems too trite or glib, as if I am too

easily grafting my romantic and sexual longings on to a spiritual journey. But I knew in my bones that falling in love again was what I now needed to do. It wasn't that falling in love was the culmination or final aim of the pilgrimage, but rather that something essential in the emerging transformation was incomplete without it. I had been travelling under my own steam, following inspiration as it arose, but almost always on my own terms. Wonderful as the journey had been, within it there was still a lack of turning away from myself, and turning towards others. It would be naïve to suggest that romantic love is the end of self-transcendence, but it would be cynical to maintain that it can't be a beginning.

The Return Journey

A Conflict of Principles

Some weeks before I arrived in Cuba I received an urgent email from my agent in London: my transatlantic crossing by freight ship had been cancelled. The US embargo of Cuba meant there was no possibility of entering or leaving by boat. So I had arranged to take a short flight from Cancun to Havana to get into Cuba, and another short flight from Havana to Nassau, Bahamas, from where I would pick up a freight ship bound for Barcelona. The email said that *Maersk* (the biggest shipping line in the world) had rerouted the ship on which I was bound. From her reference to other reroutings I got the impression that the 2008 credit crunch was hitting *Maersk* hard and they were being forced to consolidate their activities. She offered me three other options, though only one of these was remotely viable and meant leaving Cuba a week earlier than I had planned. I was thrown into a quandary as my time with Siddhisvari would be curtailed by the new departure date. I seemed to face an irreconcilable collision of principles: to abandon my no-fly rule and get a passenger jet from Cuba to Europe or to abandon Siddhisvari in Havana for a week. I tried hard to make it all fit: neither rearranging Siddhisvari's flight nor inviting her to join me on the freighter worked out. After a couple of weeks of trying this or that option reality was still obstinately refusing to budge. And for the first time in a year or more I felt trapped by schedules and deadlines beyond my control. Were I travelling alone I would have just adapted in some way to the conditions; but now I had somebody else to take into account, and someone at that who was very special to me.

I had only compromised my no-fly rule when faced with political roadblocks or mortal dangers such as getting out of civil war-torn Sri Lanka or crossing from India to Central Asia without risking life and limb in the Taliban badlands. In these cases I had taken the shortest possible flight to get me back on my journey. As a principle it had served me magnificently, keeping my eco-conscience light and taking me to some wonderfully unexpected destinations. Also I had set my heart on crossing both of the great oceans, Pacific and Atlantic, by ship. But, as I considered the alternatives, I began to realize that I had become rather attached to the no-fly principle and the kudos it would give to say that I had circumnavigated the globe without a single long-haul flight. And then I reflected on what kind of person would leave their new lover stranded in a foreign city for a week? The answer was patently obvious: only a heartless bastard would do such a thing. So my decision became clear: I should sacrifice the transatlantic ship, spend my time with Siddhisvari and catch a long-haul flight back to Europe. This all turned out to be very time-consuming and expensive, January being the height of the tourist season in Cuba. Yet I couldn't help feeling that underneath all the hassle, frustration and expense something important or even essential was working itself out. For a year or more I had done things my own way, in my own time, when I wanted, how I wanted. This sense of freedom had been wonderfully exhila-rating, but I had missed a deeper connection with others. A major theme of the Return Journey was re-connecting with people and in remaking these connections I had to give up something of the footloose freedom of the open road. As a lesson in over-coming selfishness it seemed timely, and as a heartfelt statement of intent at the start of a relationship it seemed essential: "I am prepared to sacrifice something that I really want to do to be with you". And naturally our holiday in Cuba was wonderful, I wouldn't have missed a moment of it. Thus it was that in January 2009 I arrived in a Spain so blanketed in snow that my Iberia flight was diverted from Madrid to Barcelona.

Europe by the backdoor

Arriving in France via Cerbère was like entering Europe by the backdoor. After a grindingly slow local train that seemed to stop at every barn between Barcelona and Port Bou, we finally pulled in to its dimly-lit sidings. Cerbère was like a Paleolithic terminus, a throwback to an earlier dark age of international travel, a no-mans land between the different rail gauges of RENFE and SNCF. As I wandered about looking for somewhere to await the night train, the only passengers in evidence were a few hardy backpackers and a Japanese couple desperately trying to make their connection to Narbonne. Even the sign to the station toilets merely led to a darkened dead-end. I followed signs for *Sortie* pleased to be in a country in whose language I spoke fluently after three months of blundering in Spanish. However, the main exit to the station seemed to be nothing more than an entrance to a railway siding and a tunnel for motor vehicles with no pedestrian walkway. A balding Frenchman was having a smoke as I muttered mostly to myself, "Ce n'est pas beaucoup!" "Beaucoup de quoi?" he inquired promptly with a tone of mild pique. "De bars et restaurants" I added quickly to cover my tracks. He explained hurriedly that in the winter the town was more or less shut down, that I might find something in the town centre, but even that was small. I thanked him warmly and decided to walk down the hill in search of sustenance. Cerbère nestled around a tiny bay, the road clinging to the cliffs as it dropped down to a small harbour and before climbing over the hills into Spain. The town hall, fire and police stations were all efficiently combined in one building on the promenade: this "International Terminus" was the most parochial of destinations. There was only one bar open. With a long wooden counter, Formica tables and polystyrene tiles hanging from a suspended ceiling it had a down at heel charm, I took to it immediately. There was a momentary stutter in the atmosphere as an unshaven, unwashed, unkempt Englishman trailed his backpack into this quintessential small town French bar. Two men at the counter looked up from their conversation, a young woman held onto her child tightly. Was this strange apparition a threat? The bartender warily made his way towards me but everyone seemed to relax as I asked for "Un café au lait, s'il vous plait". After all the thrills and adventures it felt strangely appropriate to steal into Europe by the backdoor, a solitary incognito tramping northwards.

The Return is in fact one of the hardest parts of a long journey: whether it is finding yourself shoehorned into agendas and schedules beyond your control, adjusting to ordinary life with all its conventions and demands, or navigating the assumptions that others make about you. On many occasions I found myself wincing at the attitudes elicited by my return. For instance, "You've been enjoying yourself, now it's time you got on with something serious in life", or finding it impossible to meet with a friend who I hadn't seen for a year because his diary was so full. Purpose and time are so utterly different when traveling compared to living at home that it is hard to even begin to reconcile them. For the traveler time is one of life's great abundances. When you meet someone with whom a connection develops it is quite natural to give your time and energy freely. Not so with modern householder existence, where everything is tightly scheduled so you can make the most of each hour of the day: phone dates, appointments, personal time, quality time, work time. All of it compartmentalized into maximally efficient units, with but one problem: there is no room for the unexpected, the spontaneous or even the apparently useless.

Then there are the practical difficulties: finding somewhere to live, an income, rebuilding a social network, and so on. I was aware of the immense pressure on myself and other travelers with whom I kept in touch to *get a life together*. But amid the scramble to get back into the world of accommodation, work and social life some of the most precious insights from the journey were often abandoned, lost or subtly eroded. Usually underpinning the compromise was anxiety about money and security. Although money is important, it pays not to rush into the business of getting it.

The great myths of the Return Journey are all beset with trials and tribulations. In the Western canon the prime example is Odysseus and his decade-long homecoming to Ithaca. When he eventually succeeds in returning he finds his place supplanted by greedy suitors and he must use all his strength, guile and cunning to regain his rightful place. Both Jason and Agamemnon fall foul of female ire after their heroic return and are murdered by their wives. The Buddha's homecoming is also dramatic and difficult. He waited for two years after his Awakening before returning to Kapilavastu, city of his birth, and in their first meeting his father sorely berated him for appearing as a lowly beggar. The Buddha was eventually able to convert his entire family to the truth that he had discovered, but it would seem that initially the old adage runs true: no man is a prophet in his own country.

Thus the Return is both mythically and practically marked with difficulty. Why should this be so? A long journey changes you, especially one undertaken with the pilgrim's purpose. But the people you left don't see this, most of them relate to you as if you were the same as before. This can feel unbearably constricting and limiting after the openness of life on the road. Often it feels as if you have simply dropped into the world from another universe. And of course the converse is true, the traveler returns to people and places that have also changed. Add to this the deep shifts of heart and re-evaluations affected by a pilgrimage and then misunderstanding and frustration seem inevitable. It is as well to be prepared and to have some reserves of patience, kindness and cash for the final challenge.

The very last irony of my voyage occurred when I least expected it. "And what exactly were you doing in Kazakhstan?" insinuated an English policeman at St. Pancras International rail terminal, as though I had a visa from *Waziristan*. He grilled me for a few minutes as if I were a potential terrorist. Thus the one and only time on my entire journey when I felt myself come under suspicion of being a public enemy, was on return to my home country by Eurostar from Paris. Perhaps it was my new grown beard, my long absence from this fertile island on the edge of a continent or just that in my soul I felt less English than ever before. Yes, England and I had changed and there was no going back.

Lessons from the Road

Shortly after returning to the house in Cambridge from which I had left fifteen months earlier, I woke at 4.00 a.m. with a feeling of panic and confusion. "Who am I?" "What am I doing here? "Where is my life going?" The familiar questions reverberated in my mind at that uncharitable hour. Once I recognized the taste I relaxed. "Oh, you're just falling apart again Rijumati", I chuckled to myself, and I drifted off to sleep once more.

Falling apart – the uncomfortable sense felt in the core of my being that I no longer knew who I was or where I was going – reached its apogee in the Ala Archa, Kyrgyzstan. But though this was the most intense visitation, it was by no means the only time that it knocked on my door. The experience of falling apart was present throughout the journey, whether I was lost in bureaucratic labyrinths, adrift in cultural incomprehension or freefalling into love.

Falling apart is emblematic of true pilgrimage, an indication that the story we tell ourselves about who we are is out of kilter with reality, starting to break up and no longer fits. The fact that returning home precipitated this experience in me is telling. After more than a year on the road I had built up a new story in which I was a globetrotting traveler, and returning home left me momentarily bereft. We build up stories about who we are all the time. In fact, without some sort of story it seems almost impossible to function in the world in a normal way. It is not just that over the years we get into the habit of imagining ourselves in a particular form, sometimes it happens in a matter of hours or minutes: "I'm this sort of person, I do these sorts of things, I have these kinds of possessions and these sorts of friends" ... Without this background reassurance we collapse into a directionless heap, unable to come to any conclusions, which is presumably why we fear 'losing the plot' – the story of what we are about.

But the story is *always* false at some level. Any story, however good, is too literal to encompass all that is potential in a human being. I may gloss myself as a Buddhist, lover, son, friend, disciple, teacher, student, writer, traveler, businessman, mystic, mathematician or scientist, but none is fully true. On my travels I learned more clearly than ever before that if I start to mistake my story for the reality that confronts me then sooner or later a shock will follow, exposing the mismatch between life and my image of it. And the more I'm attached to a particular story the more traumatic the shock will be. I believe that the only way to live a free and authentic life is, from time to time, to lose the plot completely and let all the stories go – even the good ones.

By its very nature, falling apart meant risking everything, just as truly honest communication meant risking everything. The alternative was that the slyness of the concealing mind would make me dishonest. This was a communication with reality in which I was stripped naked, the veils rent asunder. Once I had accepted the inevitability of falling apart I discovered the possibility of diving into it like a huge breaker crashing onto the shore of my self view. I knew that such a wave could not be stopped, but perhaps I could roll with it, feel its power, and in time even learn to surf the energy it unleashed. From my episode in the Ala Archa I learned that falling apart was an extremely uncomfortable yet necessary stage in growth. The alternative was that my calculating mind would desperately try to keep control of life in the face of change and declining power. I learned that to embrace falling apart was to embrace life. And sharing my life with friends who held similar values was perhaps the greatest safety net I could have.

The experience of falling apart sometimes triggers panic, as it had for me in my cabin crossing the Indian Ocean. The only way I know to face this is to stay rooted and firm in this present moment of experience, returning to bodily sensations, the experience of breathing, the feeling of gravity, the touch of the skin and turning the mind away from the proliferation of panicky or depressive scenarios with which it is becoming obsessed. Panic is a consequence of letting go of an old story. Like leaping from an airplane for the first time, you need faith that the parachute will catch your fall. If you attend patiently, the panic always subsides, replaced by an uplifting touch of confidence in something greater than your old self.

Every journey into the Unknown involves fear, and pilgrimage demands courage. Fear was often my companion and it came in many guises: baffled by cultural incomprehension in Russia and Japan; lost in the Tian Shan mountains as night drew in; rattled by the undertow of aggression in Mexico's drug war ganglands. The important question was not how I could avoid fear, this was impossible, but how to live with the fear. Without cultivating this courage I would have been paralyzed at the idea of casting myself adrift on an ocean of experiences so utterly beyond my control. Why are we so afraid of fear? The most primal fears arise when we feel deeply threatened. The Buddha suggested that fear has a purchase because we are attached to a fixed idea of self. Just as the stories we tell ourselves inevitably fall apart, so the sense of our self is destined to dissolve, often in an unpredictable or unexpected moment and this provokes fear, dread, panic and terror. We fear that we will lose what is dear to us, get what we don't want, and ultimately we fear death. Paradoxically fear sometimes heralds a new beginning as the rigid self cracks open. Facing fear is also an unpleasant but essential stage in becoming free and independent. The intensity of fear can be overwhelming, so it is as well to have made some preparations.

Since I first encountered Buddhism and meditation in my early twenties I have deeply believed that *awareness is the way to freedom*. In fact it seemed to be something that I had always believed but never articulated clearly until I found the Dharma (the Buddha's teaching). By awareness I mean a rich, broad and inclusive awareness imbued with warmth that can cradle both the intensity of fear and the realization that there is a larger space within which fear plays itself out. Here fear becomes just another powerful emotion evolving in this larger awareness that holds it lightly. For those prepared to undertake meditative training reciting a mantra in a challenging situation is also a powerful tool against being overwhelmed by fear, as I discovered on the night I faced desperate soldiers in the Sri Lankan jungle.

The decision to leave behind my nice, settled life in Cambridge was the hardest decision of the whole journey. That first step demanded boldness, the remaining steps unfolded naturally as a consequence. Mysteriously, as if the universe were somehow responding to my boldness, I often felt unforeseen resources springing to my aid: a chance meeting with a kindred spirit; a book, the right book, turning up; support appearing from an unexpected quarter. Or perhaps it was simply that I knew this was the right step, the best step, the time to begin. To take that first faltering step was to cherish my life, and no one else could do that for me.

Deep communication can sometimes arise between complete strangers: a fellow passenger, a chance encounter in a café, someone in a budget hotel. Like the character in Tolstoy's *Kreutzer Sonata* who unfurls the untold tragedy of his life to a stranger on a train, many times I unexpectedly shared the outpourings of the deepest heart in such circumstances. The anonymity of these encounters allowed us to take risks that would seem reckless in more settled conditions. Knowing that we, most likely, would never meet again temporarily created a hallowed space in which the heart's burden could be revealed. As a traveler, my need to reach out and connect often overcame my superficial resistances and the veils lifted so that the true person could be seen; a selfless exchange took place and I felt truly alive. These precious moments of transcendence in communication seem to prefigure a communion with life itself, in which energy flows unobstructed and I am transparent to the universe. Since this spiritual communion calls out from the depths of every soul, it is no wonder that, time and again, human beings find ways to overcome their fears and prejudices and truly meet one another.

Paradoxically, while living out of a single backpack and consigned to the cheapest accommodation, the abundance of life flourished for me at every turn. I felt that time had become child-like again, each day seeming immensely long and filled with fascinating and unfamiliar riches, like going to a supermarket in Siberia to look for washing powder. This shifting relationship with time also provided a foundation of patience when I faced hours of bureaucratic tedium. Being able to give and share time felt so liberating after years living a busy life of neatly packaged time. The sense of impoverishment that I felt when I had more money and more security seemed to leave me as I voyaged further into the Unknown.

Travelling unfamiliar pathways on a budget requires help and luck. When I arrived somewhere completely ignorant of how to find even the basic needs of food and shelter, strangers repeatedly helped me, often going out of their way to do so. Though there were some cheats and touts they were few, instead ninety percent of the people I met were happy to help me. I feel immense gratitude to all these people, many of whose names I don't even know. Experiencing so much generosity has had a profoundly heartening effect, creating a web of common humanity across the globe. All of us are recipients of such deeds from the moment of conception through to our deaths. Surely then, the most basic human emotion should be one of gratitude, for without such help and support none of us would be here.

It also really helped to keep a sense of humor. Why on earth did I spend sixteen hours queuing for ferry ticket to Sakhalin Island, or several hours locked in a bureaucratic farce in Kazakhstan? Only a sense of humor can come to terms with such a reckless waste of energy. Even more vital was not taking myself too seriously. Rather than thinking "Why doesn't this idiot give me a key that opens my hotel room?" I laughed and saw the parallels between second-rate hotels in South Asia and the British hotels so timelessly epitomized in the John Cleese's *Fawlty Towers*.

Other insights continue to reverberate: the importance of *walking* a pilgrimage; how things often work out in the most unforeseen ways; the seeming madness of ordinary life from the pilgrim's point of view; the proximity of death and renewal at every step along the way; the repeated culture shock at each major transition. Perhaps the most significant insight of all was the impossibility of going back. The old cage was shattered, and lay uselessly mangled in the dust. There had been a change of heart that could not be undone. The outer journey eventually comes to an end, but the inner and secret journeys continue: the road stretches onwards, beckoning the next step towards freedom, love and truth.

BOOKS

O is a symbol of the world, of oneness and unity. In different cultures it also means the "eye," symbolizing knowledge and insight. We aim to publish books that are accessible, constructive and that challenge accepted opinion, both that of academia and the "moral majority."

Our books are available in all good English language bookstores worldwide. If you don't see the book on the shelves ask the bookstore to order it for you, quoting the ISBN number and title. Alternatively you can order online (all major online retail sites carry our titles) or contact the distributor in the relevant country, listed on the copyright page.

See our website **www.o-books.net** for a full list of over 500 titles, growing by 100 a year.

And tune in to myspiritradio.com for our book review radio show, hosted by June-Elleni Laine, where you can listen to the authors discussing their books.

MySpiritRadio